Dedicated to the memory of Skipper Gordon,
who died while giving the best and *only* scenic tour on the island.

A NOTE ABOUT THE PHOTOS IN THIS BOOK:
The images in this book have been sourced from a variety of places.
Many were dug out of closets and shoeboxes while others digitally scanned in
from slides and negatives. Some images were downloaded by archeologists from
old flip phones that surely pre-date the dinosaurs. Every effort has been
made to present these pictures in their best possible quality for the book.

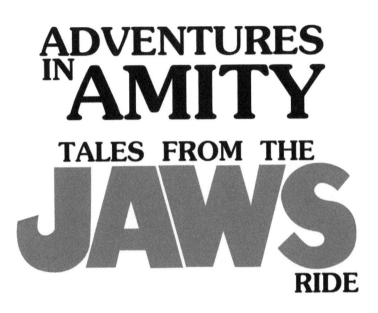

# ADVENTURES IN AMITY

## TALES FROM THE JAWS RIDE

By Dustin McNeill

Introduction by
J. Michael Roddy

# TABLE OF CONTENTS

# TALES FROM THE JAWS RIDE

# Introduction by J. Michael Roddy

## 1975

JAWS. A simple word that evokes not only terror but for many… inspiration. I was six-years-old the summer of '75 and had already been exposed to the classic Universal monsters and disaster films such as The Towering Inferno. I remember seeing the movie theater marquee with the word Jaws boldly advertised in red, and asking my father, who was a fisherman, what it was about. I assumed it had something to do with the human mouth. He told me it was about a shark. As a kid, there are two types of really cool animals – dinosaurs and sharks. I begged and begged that weekend until we went to see it. I loved it. Jaws crashed into my little imagination like a freight train. The most remarkable aspect I recall was the collective sound of the audience as they gasped, laughed, screamed, and cheered. I spent every waking hour that summer reliving the movie. My backyard swing set became the Orca. I set up a pool under the slide and died over and over as I imitated my best Quint sliding down into the gaping mouth of the shark, only to be magically reborn as Brody with my toy rifle. My Mego action figures of Captain Kirk and Dr. McCoy became waterlogged as they fell prey to a rubber replica of the twenty-five-footer.

Then one day at the local supermarket I found myself drawn to a book with that familiar blood red lettering. The Jaws Log by Carl Gottlieb. I had to have it. It was more adult than my six years, but it was about Jaws! I begged for it until my mom finally relented and allowed me to have it. On the ride home, I skimmed every page for photos. Then I saw a black and white image of that familiar shark. The photo had been taken underwater during the brutal attack against Matt Hooper. As I studied it, I came to realize that there were other people underwater. I didn't remember that, so I looked closer. One of them had a camera. And then my six-year-old brain truly clicked. Someone made this movie. I knew that I wanted to be a part of that somehow. Since that time, the film has always served as an inspiration and a reminder that the medium of storytelling, when done right, can transport you and immerse you. If only that sense of make-believe and play could continue…

# 1990

When Universal Studios Florida opened on June 7, 1990, I was there. So were a few of my friends including my fellow Shark Is Still Working co-producer Erik Hollander. We drove up from our hometown of Jacksonville where we were recognized among the community as "those kids who make the movies." We loved movies and moved heaven and earth to be there that opening day. What a blast. Lots of people were complaining because of the inoperable attractions, but to us, we were among Hollywood royalty. Everywhere you looked were legends like Anthony Perkins, Janet Leigh, and Jimmy Stewart. Our sights were on the man that had created so many cinematic memories for us. We met Spielberg that day. I proudly showed him a photo from All That Jaws, our forty-minute homemade parody of our favorite film shot in and around Jacksonville Beach, including a full day of filming on the Atlantic Ocean. Laughing, he looked up and said, "*Oh my God... that's funny.*"

Then we made our way to the Amity section of the park. After years of loving Jaws, there now existed a whole land and attraction dedicated to it. Here you could buy merchandise and stroll under a banner proclaiming that today was the town's 4th of July celebration. We didn't realize it at the time, but we were so lucky being among the few who saw the original version of the attraction. As an added bonus, actress Lorraine Gary was on our boat. The most surreal aspect for me was that it felt absolutely real. It was an assault on all the senses. You heard John Williams' score, you smelled the ocean spray, and you felt the shark attack. For those few minutes, I was in the movie. We went back later that day, but Jaws was closed due to technical difficulties. Cue the ominous music.

# 1993

A few years later, I was hired as an actor at the park. Unfortunately, Jaws had shut down by this point for a complete re-design. Then one day a beautiful billboard appeared outside the ride stating that Jaws would resurface in the summer of 1993. Adam Bezark had been tasked with implementing the new version, which would prove to be anything but easy. I was so excited to hear that the man who brought the Ghostbusters to Universal Studios Florida would be tackling Jaws. I *had* to be a part of it, so I auditioned to be a boat skipper. I remember doing the Quint monologue for him. Unfortunately, my status as an actor in the live show entertainment division would not allow me to be cross-trained as a skipper, which fell under ride operations.

# 1994

I was there again when the park re-opened Captain Jake's Amity Boat Tours. It was so rewarding, both as a fan and as a team member for Universal Studios. The original attraction was far more serious in tone, whereas the new execution was notably more lighthearted. The storyline moved away from transporting you to 1975, instead placing you in the town today and positioning the original film as work of fiction based loosely on real events. The ride had added so many new elements, including a shocking finale that recreated a key scene from Jaws 2. It once again allowed guests a real opportunity to be part of that classic story. The original elements were there... the water, the feel of the spray, the music, along with the newly added feature of fire, and of course a remodeled, giant, killer shark hell-bent on destroying you.

# THE SHARK IS STILL WORKING

The documentary producer with Richard Dreyfuss, Roy Scheider, and Bruce the shark.

One highlight was the ability to experience the attraction at night. In the early years of Universal, guest demand allowed for the park to stay open much later and Jaws was a perfect attraction for the dark Florida skies. The ride, while fun and thrilling by day, became so much more intense and terrifying at night. I would take in a trip to Amity many times a week during my time at Universal. I never had the opportunity to be a Jaws skipper, although I could have easily jumped aboard Amity Six and recited the dialogue verbatim. The ride became a way to stay connected to the movies.

## 2005

I had left Universal and was now a freelance writer and director. Early in 2005, I was hired to be a creative director for an event celebrating the upcoming 25th anniversary of Jaws on the real-life island of Amity – Martha's Vineyard, Massachusetts. That work provided me access to the original filming locations and it was wonderful to see how well the ride's art director had captured the flavor of the town. I became friends with some of the actors and artists that had brought the original film to life, which was how our documentary, The Shark Is Still Working, was born. One of the elements that we wanted to cover was the enduring legacy of Jaws. We approached Universal Studios Florida to help tell how important the attraction was to that legacy, but were turned down. We were told that Jaws as a brand was not a priority. So, we moved our sights to Universal Studios Hollywood where we were given a tour and interview with creative director John Murdy on the backlot. I reached out to my old friend Adam Bezark who gave us a candid interview and inside look at how he had brought the ride back to guests complete with a roaring shark. We also interviewed a few Jaws skippers, all of whom we later had to cut due to Universal Florida's absence of participation.

One of the most surprising discoveries for us in making the documentary was learning how the Jaws ride was also an inspiration for so many. The skipper community was and continues to be a remarkable group of people who all share a love for that experience. They took their duties seriously and entertained millions of guests throughout the years.

## 2011

The Jaws ride faced many challenges during its run. Effects would be missing or in some cases completely removed. Costly repairs and maintenance would contribute to Universal's decision to close the ride. The attraction's last day was announced as being January 2, 2012. Fans, skippers, and patrons alike visited the park to bid farewell and adieu. I did not choose to ride that day. I instead decided to keep the memory of my last ride when Jaws was fully functioning.

My thoughts on the closing of the attraction are bittersweet. When asked how I felt about its closure, I quoted one of the film's original stars, Roy Scheider. "*There is no culture on Earth that doesn't have Jaws ingrained into it.*" Despite its demise, which came not at the hands of an aquaphobic police chief but at the hands of park menu planners, the Jaws ride won't soon be forgotten.

## 2018

It's been over five years since the permanent closure of Captain Jake's and the area has been completely redesigned into a breathtaking experience based on the Harry Potter films. Every so often, I will hear someone talking about Jaws and how it remains a key moment in film history. The film will go on. But for those who never experienced the attraction, how do you explain the fascination? If I could convey one thing to someone who never got to ride it, I'd say it truly gave you the opportunity to find yourself in the middle of a classic movie.

For those that visited Universal Studios Florida from 1994 to 2012, the Jaws ride was an anchor to the park, and without it, Universal is completely different. It's like leaving high school only to come back and realize how much things have changed. It will never be the same again.

But for those of you who never had a chance to experience the attraction except through YouTube videos, our good friend Dustin McNeill has written the all-encompassing history of the ride. His enthusiasm and attention to detail are obsessive in the best possible way. Not only is this book a testament to the many artists who toiled to create the attraction, it is also a great testimony of the skippers that put their heart and soul into making you believe you were braving the menace of Jaws five minutes at a time, each and every day.

My hope is that you take this book, put on John Williams' score, and celebrate the stories contained within. The Jaws ride, while gone, is still working.

J. Michael Roddy

Top Left: J. Michael Roddy and Erik Hollander telling Steven Spielberg about "All That Jaws" at the opening of Universal Studios Florida.

Middle Right: J. Michael Roddy meeting actress Lorraine Gary just before boarding the Jaws ride.

Left: Posing with the hanging shark

Opposite top: On location in Martha's Vineyard for "The Shark Is Still Working" documentary.

Opposite bottom: Erik Hollander, J. Michael Roddy, and Chuck Gramling in "All That Jaws."

ALL THAT JAWS

# A Note From the Author

Parents: *"Dustin, are you excited to ride Jaws tomorrow?"*
Me: *"No. I'm not riding it."*
Parents: *"What? But you love that movie!"*
(I glance down at a brochure depicting a shark big enough to eat the boat whole.)
Me: *"Definitely not riding it."*

I vividly recall the above exchange with my parents over dinner the night before we visited the park in 1994. I can still remember the electric excitement of flipping through that glorious fold-out brochure that Universal Studios Florida used to have. Nickelodeon Studios looked like fun. The Ghostbusters Spooktacular Show? Sign me up! Kongfrontation? Uh, *maybe*. Getting on a boat with Jaws in the water? No sir. It looked terrifying to this kid. Yes, Jaws was my favorite film, but I still had a lot of life to live. I wasn't ready to die!

I did wind up getting on that boat the next day. Not surprisingly, my parents literally bribed me with cash, which I immediately blew on the merchandise cart near the ride exit. It turns out my bravery can be bought for the low price of fifty bucks. As for the ride itself, it was so thrilling and fun. Whether as a child or an adult, it remains an unparalleled delight to have the opportunity to physically step into the world of your favorite movie, which in this case was Amity Island. When you crossed over into that section of the park, Jaws came to life all around you. For this fan, it was nothing short of *amazing*. Not everyone gets that chance, but I did.

My family returned often to Universal Studios Florida in the years that followed. Jaws was a must-ride on every visit. Some attractions grow old and need replacing. Others remain timeless. Jaws was in that latter category - a true classic. Honestly, I was quite sad in December 2011 to learn it would be closing for good. My family was fortunate enough to visit the attraction one final time during its last week of operation. It was still so much fun. There's nothing else like it at Universal Orlando or anywhere outside of Osaka, Japan.

Here I am years later publishing a nearly three-hundred page book on the Jaws ride and I still can't put into words what was so bloody magical about it. All I can tell you is that it was. I guess I'll save that enigma for the sequel if I ever figure it out. That aside, it has been so incredibly gratifying to learn just how many other people look back on the attraction as fondly as I do. That's really the main point I'd like to make with this project. If you're still crazy about the Jaws ride all these years later, know that you're not alone!

In closing, I want to take a moment to thank everyone who ever worked at Captain Jake's. Whether you were a skipper for Amity Boat Tours or a ride technician, thank you. If you contributed in any way toward the creation of Universal Studios Florida, the Amity section, or the Jaws ride - thank you. Thank you for allowing us to "ride the movies." And if you contributed stories, photos, or artwork to this book... *thank you most sincerely*.

Dustin McNeill

My family at the ride in 2010.

The brochure I was looking at.

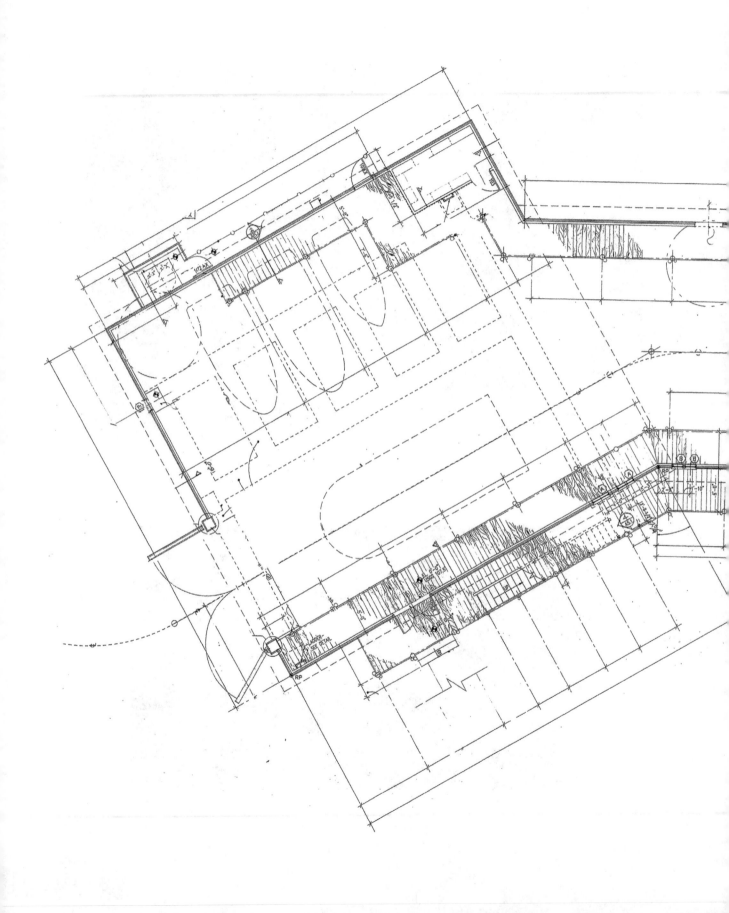

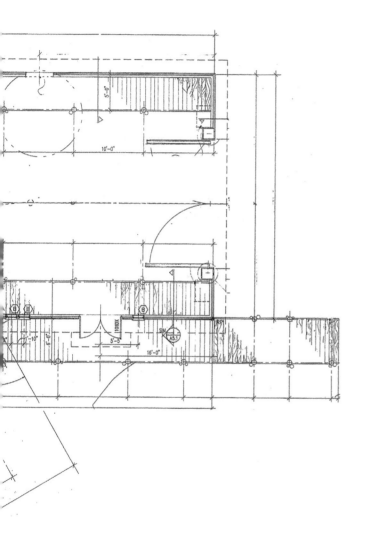

# ATTRACTION
# GUIDE

# A Brief History

Before we dive into the murky waters of the Jaws ride, it's important that you have at least a cursory awareness of the attraction's history. Maybe you rode it, maybe you didn't. Maybe you've been on the Universal Studio Tour in Hollywood, maybe you didn't even know that tour existed. Many of the interviews in this book are going to assume you already have some knowledge of Captain Jake's Amity Boat Tours, so here is a brief history of the Jaws ride in the event that you're unfamiliar with this world. We are going to run through the ride's creation, destruction, re-creation, and re-destruction. Diehard Jaws fin-atics are welcome to skip ahead.

Universal Pictures first released Steven Spielberg's Jaws in June 1975, forever redefining the summer movie-going experience. The nation quickly found itself in the grips of "Jaws Fever," which the New York Times likened to an epidemic. The film was so immensely popular that Universal sought to add a Jaws experience to their backlot tour in California less than a year after the film opened. More of a scene than a full ride, the backlot attraction took guests through a re-creation of Amity Harbor on the tour trams. As the scene begins, a menacingly large dorsal fin stalks an unsuspecting fisherman in a rowboat. The fisherman is dragged underwater and devoured after which the shark vanishes. (The victim became a diver in later years.) Water cannons explode a moment later as the creature resurfaces alongside the trams to chomp at guests. This attraction, while somewhat cartoony, has remained a signature part of the backlot tour for over forty years. It would become a crucial part of the Jaws ride's DNA.

Although Universal regularly updated its studio tour with new scenes and attractions, none were bigger or more complex than the addition of King Kong in June 1986. Kong's enormous success gave studio executives the confidence needed to create a full-fledged theme park in Orlando based on Universal's most popular properties, many of which were already represented in some form on the backlot. In Hollywood, Jaws and Kong were but brief moments on Universal Studio Tour. In Orlando, they would be expanded into their own blockbuster rides situated within areas themed to their respective cinematic geographies.

Florida's original Jaws ride was widely seen as the most advanced attraction of its kind at the time of its creation. Guests would set sail with Amity Boat Tours on a scenic cruise around the island. Shortly into their trip they would happen upon the sinking wreckage of a fellow tour boat. This is quickly revealed to be the work of a great white shark who then launches an attack on the ride vehicle. The boat skipper attempts to kill the shark with a grenade launcher, though the beast dodges these explosions. At one point, the shark bites down onto the boat's front pontoon - deflating it - before violently dragging the craft through the water. The brave skipper manages to land his final grenade in the shark's mouth, which detonates seconds later as the creature descends. Guests witness a powerful underwater explosion of bloody shark guts. With this, the menace of Jaws is conquered!

Universal Studios Florida officially opened its doors to the public on June 7, 1990. Nationwide advertising promised guests one-of-a-kind ride experiences like Kongfrontation, Earthquake: The Big One, E.T. Adventure, and, of course, the Jaws ride. Less advertised were the many show offerings which included Alfred Hitchcock: The Art of

Making Movies, the Animal Actors Stage, Murder She Wrote: Post-Production, and Phantom of the Opera Horror Make-Up Show. Guests were bitterly disappointed to learn that Universal's most anticipated attractions were simply not ready for opening day. Both Kong and Earthquake closed within hours of opening while Jaws hardly opened at all. As a result, excessive lines formed for the smaller capacity shows and attractions. Furious park-goers flooded guest services who issued free admission vouchers en masse so that patrons could return when the park was fully functional. To make a long and painful story short, Universal's opening day was a fiasco they would rather forget.

When Jaws did finally open three days later on June 10, it did so intermittently due to various problems mostly involving the mechanical sharks. While park engineers were able to improve reliability on both Kong and Earthquake in the months that followed, they were unable to achieve the same on Jaws, which continued to experience technical issues on a daily basis. Universal's frustration would peak in late August with the ride's permanent closure and the filing of a lawsuit against manufacturer Ride & Show Engineering citing poor workmanship, defective design, and missed deadlines. According to the park's complaint, Ride & Show used non-waterproof parts on the attraction which had contributed enormously to its ongoing issues. The suit would be settled out of court the following April. Universal's initial hope was that a new team of engineers might be able to fix the Jaws ride's design flaws as on Earthquake, which was now reliably operational. A thorough assessment by an outside party in 1991 deemed this economically unfeasible. The Jaws ride's issues were so severe that the best course of action was to completely gut the attraction and start over. Keeping only the most basic structural framework and theming, the park ripped out millions of dollars worth of sharks, boats, and related equipment.

Universal gave the monumental task of rebuilding Jaws to multiple world-class companies rather than to just one. For the sharks, they hired advanced robotic systems manufacturer Eastport International, who were soon acquired by subsea engineering outfit Oceaneering International. For the underwater track, they hired renowned coaster manufacturer Intamin Amusement Rides. For the boats, they hired Regal Marine Industries. For the ride system, they contracted ITEC Entertainment with whom they had already worked well with on several other projects. This impressive lineup would help ensure the attraction's eventual success upon re-opening. The new ride would be under construction by late 1992 poised for an opening sometime in 1993. Universal declined to publicly set a firm re-opening date in the interest of ensuring ride reliability.

Hoping to avoid the pitfalls of the 1990 version, the redesigned Jaws ride would include several new scenes. In place of the shark biting the boat, the skipper would now accidentally fire a grenade at a gas dock attempting to hit the shark. This would result in a massive explosion and subsequent wall of fire blocking the boat's path forward. The new version would also drop the exploding shark finale for one in which the creature bites down onto a floating power cable, fatally electrocuting it. That the new version was less technically ambitious than the first was an attempt by ride makers to guarantee its smooth operation for many years to come.

The second Jaws began technical rehearsals in August 1993 to rave reviews from guests. More than half-a-million park-goers experienced the attraction during this soft opening period. The Orlando-Sentinel reported that Steven Spielberg returned to the revamped Jaws in September, this time with his children who "went crazy for it." The ride officially re-opened to the public on Friday, October 1, 1993 with a ceremony that included Spielberg and the original film's stars. With this, Universal Studios Florida had officially conquered the last of its opening day demons. The Jaws ride would go onto thrill millions of guests across the next nineteen years with a respectable track record of reliability. When most people think back on the ride, it is almost always this second version they remember.

As a theme park attraction, the Jaws ride had a lot going for it. For one, it enjoyed a sustained popularity right up until its closure. A November 2011 assessment by ThemeParkInsider.com noted that only Hollywood Rip Ride Rockit, Revenge of the Mummy, and The Simpsons Ride bested Jaws in average wait time. Also beneficial was the fact that Jaws was widely known to be a "people eater," meaning it could cycle through a lot of guests very quickly. According to Universal's own internal numbers, Jaws could theoretically handle over 2,700 guests per hour. That number assumed the attraction was running roughly fifty-four dispatches per hour with six boats in rotation.

Unfortunately, Jaws also had a lot working against it, most of which had to do with operating costs. Amity Boat Tours required a large staff to run, all of whom were paid above the usual rate earned by Universal ride operators due to the spieling component. The ride's boat fleet ran on costly diesel up until 2008 when the entire resort switched to a more environmentally-friendly biodiesel that was even more expensive. Jaws also burned through a great deal of natural gas every other minute with Scene Four's exploding gas dock. Then there was the attraction's constant need for hydraulic fluid to run the sharks, who themselves required frequent maintenance that often involved custom-made parts. In late 2005, the ride's operating costs soared due to runaway fuel prices caused by Hurricane Katrina. Universal elected to close the ride during this time resulting in a firestorm of guest complaints. They subsequently re-opened the attraction in January 2006.

There was also the fact that Universal Studios Florida was increasingly appealing to a younger and hipper demographic. As of 2012, the Jaws ride had the unfortunate distinction of being the oldest film in Universal's library to have a ride based upon it still operating in the park. It didn't help any that the last Jaws sequel came out in 1987 to crushingly bad reviews. The Spielberg film may have been a landmark cinematic achievement, but hip it wasn't.

In retrospect, June 2010 marked the beginning of the end for the Jaws ride. This is when Islands of Adventure officially opened The Wizarding World of Harry Potter, the park's first new island since its debut in 1999. The Wizarding World was at once a phenomenal success and an enormous jolt to the entire resort. By year's end, Universal Orlando had broken a slew of internal records including both net and operating profit. Attendance soared seventeen percent from January to December. Merchandise sales more than doubled. In just seven short months, the Wizarding World had managed to serve up more than a million mugs of its signature Butterbeer brew.

Universal Orlando officially announced the Jaws ride's closure on the morning of December 2, 2011 with its final day of operation slated for January 2, 2012. That an expansion of the Wizarding World was announced on December 6 made it clear that Amity would soon become Diagon Alley. The Jaws ride may be long gone, but its legacy lives on in small tributes scattered throughout the park, this very book you now hold, and in the hearts of theme park lovers everywhere.

# Developing the Story

Development on the Jaws ride first began in early 1987, more than three years before Universal Studios Florida would open its doors to the public. The ride was originally called "Jaws: The Adventure" and featured Amity Bay Tours rather than Amity Boat Tours. Although the project underwent numerous changes leading up to and beyond its grand opening, the basic storyline has always remained the same. Guests set sail on a local scenic cruise of Amity Island. Rounding Lighthouse Cove, they discover a fellow tour boat sinking with no sign of survivors anywhere. A massive great white shark surfaces nearby and begins to attack the tour boat. The skipper seeks refuge in a nearby boathouse only to have the shark force its way inside. The frenzied attack continues as the tour heads out of the boathouse until the intrepid skipper manages to slay the angry shark. There are essentially two versions of the attraction, each with its own distinct tones and nuances. The 1990 version placed guests within the titular film's continuity while the 1993 version unfolded in present day long after the events that transpired in the motion picture.

The 1990 ride saw Amity recovering from a recent "shark problem" that Mayor Vaughn believes has been solved, hence the great white shark hanging up in Amity Circle for guests to take photos with. Scene One of the original ride began just as the later 1993 version did with the skipper welcoming guests on board before setting sail for Lighthouse Cove. In 1990, the main ride vehicle was Tours One and the sinking boat Tours Three. These later became Amity Six and Amity Three respectively for the 1993 revamp. Another change involved the name of the sinking boat's ill-fated captain. In 1993, he was known as Skipper Gordon, but in 1990 he was Skipper Herb. Both versions of Scene One have the tour guide showing off their company-issued grenade launcher to safeguard against shark attacks. Unlike the 1993 iteration's 40mm launcher, the original ride's APC-14 grenades explode after a short delay rather than on impact. As explained by the skipper in a 1987 spiel draft, "The grenades take a few seconds to go off, but if a shark eats one, he'll know it." The skipper was also originally going to have a second weapon at his or her disposal – a bang stick, though this idea was dropped prior to the attraction's opening. Another important detail revealed in the 1990 spiel's opening lines involved the ride vehicles. The skipper refers to the boats as being part of Captain Jake's "newest line of inflatable pontoon cruisers," which are built for safety and comfort rather than speed. The pontoons were exclusive to the 1990 ride vehicles and would feature prominently into Scene Four.

While Scene One of the 1993 ride drew attention port toward Chief Brody's house, the 1990 version directed guests to look starboard toward Quint's shack outside of which the iconic Orca was docked. Guests would overhear a heated disagreement between Quint and Brody reminiscent of their film dialogue. "It's not the shark, Chief. I'm tellin' ya, the shark hanging out there ain't big enough to be our shark. Our shark swallow ya whole. A little shakin', a little tenderizin', down ya go." The skipper was to dismiss Quint's claims about the hanging shark as drunken ramblings. "On a sober day he's the best fishing guide around, especially if you're after the big ones. Today is obviously not one of his sober days."

UNIVERSAL STUDIOS *Florida*
AN MCA CINEPLEX ODEON JOINT VENTURE

**TIMED SCRIPT / STORYLINE**

**REVISED 12-16-87**

*R & R*
*CREATIVE AMUSEMENT DESIGNS, INC.*
*2413 E. Lincoln Ave. Anaheim, Calif. 92806*

"JAWS" : THE ADVENTURE

The adventure of "Jaws" begins as our guests enter the sleepy coastal town of Amity.  As they board the Amity Tour Boat and pull away from the dock, they are assured that the bay is safe and the reported shark attacks are exaggerated.

But lurking in the murky waters off Amity is a monster 25 foot Great White Shark waiting to attack and devour anything venturing into his territory.  As the Tour Boat narrowly misses disaster at every turn, the adventure and terror builds to the ultimate deadly confrontation between the shark and our guests!

In both versions, Scene Two began as the tour rounded Lighthouse Cove to find the sinking tour boat. Early script drafts saw bloodied clothing floating amongst the debris, though this was later omitted. Another detail axed from Scene Two involved an awkward dig at Walt Disney World. After encouraging guests to scan the water for survivors, the skipper was to have pointed toward a floating Mickey Mouse hat and quipped, "Humm, mouse ears! That's what happens when you go to the other park first. Did any of you go to that other park?" Wise was the decision to cut this as it would have arguably destroyed what was otherwise a harrowing moment in the ride story. The gargantuan shark then appears on the portside before swimming underneath Tours One/Amity Six and surfacing starboard. The skipper fires two grenades at the beast, missing both times.

In the more familiar 1993 ride, the skipper alerts Amity Base that they plan to hide out in Quint's boathouse in an effort to evade the shark. This moment played out differently in 1990. For starters, Chief Brody himself radio's in to advise the skipper to unload his passengers in the boathouse. In the later '93 ride, Brody only chimes in during the final moments after the shark has been killed. Furthermore, the boathouse originally belonged not to Quint but to Jay in further tribute to then Universal Studios Florida President Jay Stein. The massive "Jay's Boathouse" sign was removed from the show building following the 1993 re-design and relocated to the queue.

## 1987 Script

```
1:22
        CAPTAIN: (over the top of the above line):  It looks like they
        didn't make it. Everybody look for survivors.

1:26
The Captain points towards a Mickey Mouse hat floating in the water
past the sunken boat.

        CAPTAIN: (Light)  Humm Mouse Ears!  That's what happens
        when you go to the other park first. Did any of you go to that
        other  park?
```

## 1989 Script

```
        CAPTAIN: It looks like they didn't make it.

The Captain points towards a Mickey Mouse hat floating in the water
next to the sunken boat.

        CAPTAIN: Look at those Mouse Ears!  I'll bet they never
        got a thrill like this at Disney World!
```

Scene Three played out much the same in both the '90 and '93 versions. The terrified skipper enters the boathouse only to find it dark and abandoned. A moment later, the shark is heard trying to force its way inside by repeatedly slamming into an exterior wall. The beast is eventually successful, surfacing starboard with chomping jaws. Jolted by this, the skipper floors the throttle thus exiting the dark ride portion of the attraction. While the boathouse scene changed little from 1990 to 1993 (save for some engine trouble in '93), it changed dramatically throughout the ride's early development. As first pitched, the shark's presence was to have only been suggested rather than outright shown. This scaled-down approach was jettisoned upon the hiring of show designer Tom Reidenbach to redevelop the scene into what we now remember.

There existed circa 1987 an alternate script for the dark ride sequence. This iteration saw the boathouse belonging not to Jay or Quint but to the Coast Guard. The skipper would have cruised inside to find the half-sunken wreckage of a Coast Guard Cutter. "Looks like someone or something got here before us. Only a great white could do this much damage." The shark would then bump into the downed ship, tilting it to reveal a massive hole in its hull. This nudge would have also caused the dead body of a sailor to fall out of said hole, startling the skipper and guests. As the downed Cutter continued rolling back, it would have hit the boathouse wall causing its engine compartment to "erupt into flames." The shark would then proceed to tear the boathouse apart causing support beams, boat engines, and equipment hoists to crash into the water. Tours Three was to have narrowly escaped the boathouse's destruction. "This shark is really starting to burn me up!"

Scene Four has long contained one of the more infamous discrepancies between the 1990 and 1993 versions. Per the original ride, the shark was to have chomped down onto the boat's front pontoon, audibly popping it. The shark would then drag the boat through the water several yards before letting go. The deflated pontoon was meant to heighten the perceived danger of the situation. Guests would be made to feel as though the boat might sink in the event of another attack. The skipper: "I hope he's given up! I don't think she'll hold together through another attack like that!" In the 1990 ride, the shark drags the boat until it simply stops and swims away. An earlier version of Scene Four had the skipper using a bang stick to force the shark's jaws off the front pontoon, though this idea was cut prior to the ride's construction. The revamped Scene Four that debuted in 1993 went in a different direction with the shark surfacing portside. This startles the skipper enough to make them accidentally fire the grenade launcher at Bridewell's Gas Dock, resulting in a massive explosion. Although the path forward is blocked by a wall of fire on the water, the skipper insists, "We gotta go for it!" Fortunately, the flames dissipate just before the boat travels over them.

The climactic Scene Five also differed greatly between the two versions. The 1990 ride echoed the ending of Spielberg's original whereas the 1993 revamp appeared to take inspiration from the ending of Jaws 2. In the original ride, the skipper fires a grenade into the shark's mouth, which a moment later detonates into a bloody underwater explosion. The revamped ride saw the shark accidentally bite down onto an electrical cable in its attempt to eat the passengers of Amity Six, electrocuting itself in the process. The skipper's triumphant "Call off the marines!" and request for guests to be discreet about "this little fish episode" were exclusive to the 1993 version. The 1990 Jaws ride ended a slightly more tongue-in-cheek note: "Well, I hope your tour of Amity Bay has been an interesting one - and just when I thought it was safe to go back in the water again!"

# About the Area

For nearly three decades, Universal Studios Florida has allowed guests to visit striking re-creations of well known cities both real and fictional. Within the boundaries of the park, fantastic locales such as London, New York, and Hollywood are suddenly within walking distance from one another. The area that contained the Jaws ride was Universal Orlando's original island of adventure - Amity Island. Modeled after the filming location from the original films, the Amity section of the park offered guests a thematically rich environment. Up until Diagon Alley, it remained the only area within Universal that had a unique storyline beyond the star attraction it housed.

Curiously, the Amity of Universal Studios Florida was not the Amity of Steven Spielberg's Jaws. Universal's Amity was purported to be the real Amity upon which the motion picture was loosely based. As such, there existed several discrepancies between the theme park locale and the movie. For starters, Captain Quint was never eaten by the shark - only partially chewed and spat out. Also, Mayor Vaughn vehemently denies Amity ever had a shark problem to begin with. (In the film, he personally witnesses an attack on the beach.) According to official theming literature by attraction lead David Gasior, Amity was founded in 1693 and named for Amity Hopewell, a suspected witch who took refuge with a family on Long Island. She was discovered, however, and taken to Salem where she was executed by hanging. Frustrated by this turn of events, residents moved to settle new parts of Massachusetts and named one of the uncharted islands in honor of Amity Hopewell.

Gasior's theming guide tells that the island fell into an economic slump following the theatrical release of Jaws in 1975. Swimmers shunned Amity in favor of the beaches at Cape Cod, the Hampton's, and Long Island. According to Mayor Vaughn, "The damn shark was more dangerous dead than it was alive." Many local businesses shuttered during this period including the Maine Lobster Co-Op, which would later become one of the ride's queue buildings. Amity's fortunes changed in 1987 when short order cook Jake Grundy offered to give a family of rich Canadian tourists a tour of where the shark attacks happened. Grundy borrowed a friend's motorboat and spun a wholly fictional account of the attacks for which he was paid handsomely. Recognizing a lucrative opportunity, he dubbed himself Captain Jake and started Amity Boat Tours with a fleet of Army surplus boats. Shark-related tourism to the area soared which led Amity's other residents to get in on the action.

Mayor Vaughn humorously lamented Amity's shark fever in Gasior's guide: "Since the shark attacks supposedly took place during the Fourth of July holiday, which has always brought in a large influx of tourists and thus the greatest income of the year, I declared that we celebrate this holiday year-round with games and activities that reflect our country's independence and our citizens' patriotism. Now the town has been transformed into a hustling, tacky tourist trap... the Orlando of the Northeastern seaboard."

The hanging shark under construction in May 1990. (Photo courtesy Thomas Meyer)

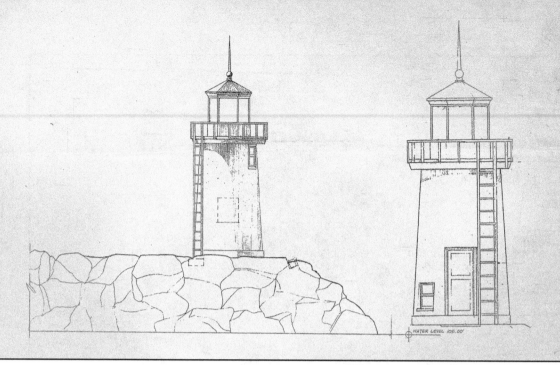

As the area's main attraction, the Jaws ride occupied eight acres of land and featured a six-million-gallon lagoon. The ride also contained ten thousand cubic yards of concrete, which were reinforced by seven thousand tons of steel. Jaws featured three interior queue buildings that could house up to 2,127 people at a time with additional outdoor queues available during peak season. Shopping-wise, the area contained the Jaws merchandise cart by unload, Quint's Surf shack opposite the hanging shark, and Oakley's beside Amity Circle. Numerous carnival midway games lined the streets hoping to prey on gullible tourists.

The architecture of both Amity and the Jaws ride contained numerous references to members of the attraction's original creative team. Norm's Boat Repair was a nod to executive art director Norm Newberry. Jay's Bait & Tackle across from the load platform was named for Universal Studios executive Jay Stein, though this facade was changed to Glenn's Bait & Tackle upon the '93 revamp. This revamp also saw Quint's shack changed to Stevens Cannery in honor of team member Greg Stevens. The Tommy-Jim's facade near the unload dock was named in tribute to architect Tom Reidenbach.

The various business facades seen throughout the ride were home to equipment essential to its operation. The lagoon's filtration system was contained within the Amity Holy Ghost Church. The ambient light sensors that adjusted the ride's effects during evening hours were located upstairs in Mayor Vaughn's home. Vaughn's basement contained the hydraulic pumps that propelled the sharks through the water. Not surprisingly, Bridewell's Gas Dock contained the fire controls for Scene Four's explosive effects.

Many of the nautically themed props seen throughout the Jaws ride were authentic décor rather than Hollywood replicas. In designing the attraction, Universal sent an art team to scour Northeastern fishing communities for such scenic elements. A handful of items came from Gloucester, Massachusetts, which would later serve as the backdrop for Universal's A Perfect Storm. To decorate Quint's shack, art director Diane Stapleton traveled to Oviedo, Florida to visit a real-life Quint who specialized in shark hunting. She returned to Orlando with a truck bed full of shark jaws which were used throughout the attraction.

# Welcome
## Amity 4th of July
### Celebration

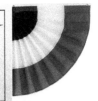

Prizes

Games

Each area within Universal Orlando has its own carefully selected soundtrack. The Amity playlist was compiled by former skipper Justin Stone, who chose songs that were released on or before July 1976 per area theming. The full playlist appears here courtesy Skipper Justin.

"Two Tickets to Paradise" by Eddie Money
"Tears of a Clown" by Smokey Robinson
"Good to See you Again" by England Dan/John Ford Coley
"Good Vibrations" by The Beach Boys
"Maggie May" by Rod Stewart
"Crystal Blue Persuasion" by Tommy James & Shondelies
"Don't Go Breaking My Heart" by Elton John & Kiki Dee
"One of Those Nights" by The Eagles
"Nothin' from Nothin'" by Billy Preston
"Sittin (On the Dock of the Bay)" by Otis Redding
"Old Black Water" by The Doobie Brothers
"Summer in the City" by Lovin' Spoonful
"Will It Go Round in Circles" by Billy Preston
"Down on the Corner" by Creedence Clearwater Revival
"Crazy Little Thing Called Love" by Queen
"Still The One" by Orleans
"Rockin' Me" by Steve Miller Band
"Funk #49" by Joe Walsh
"Baby, I Love Your Way" by Peter Frampton
"Summer Breeze" by Seal & Crofts
"I Want You Back" by The Jackson 5
"Dancing in the Street" by Martha & The Vandelias
"Listen to the Music" by The Doobie Brothers
"Ramblin' Man" by The Allman Brothers
"Fallin' in Love" by Hamilton, Joe Frank, Reynolds
"Saturday in the Park" by Chicago
"Show Me The Way" by Peter Frampton
"Joy to the World" by Three Dog Night
"Magic" by Pilot
"Already Gone" by The Eagles
"Free Ride" by Jefferson Airplane
"I'd Really Love to See You Toinght" by Dan Fogelberg

# About the Queue Video

One unforgettable aspect of the ride was its fifty-minute queue video, which Universal added to the attraction for its 1993 re-opening. The queue video depicted the bizarre and often comedic broadcasts of WJWS - Channel 13, whose main program was a talk show called "Hey There Amity!" The show featured quirky hosts Jack Balone and Melody Klarn interviewing Amity's unhinged locals who are quick to deny having another shark problem but equally quick to cash in on shark mania. At one point, Balone asks, "Sure, it was a really awful, truly gruesome tragedy... but was it really such a bad thing for the town?" The video's tone is a terrific blend of '90s Nickelodeon and Twin Peaks.

"Hey There Amity" featured several interview segments with local residents most displeased with their depiction in the 1975 Steven Spielberg film. These include the *actual* Chief Brody, Martin Hooper, and Captain Quint - all of whom claim to have single-handedly killed the shark. Hooper claims to have slain Jaws using the spear while Quint insists he was spat back out after giving the shark food poisoning. Brody is simply unhappy his film counterpart missed so many times while trying to shoot the oxygen tank in the shark's mouth. As for why Hooper, the only non-local, is still residing in Amity... he claims the Spielberg film's negative depiction of him has ruined his life. "I was in line for a Nobel Prize! Now I'm stuck in this crummy two-bit town teaching fifth-graders how to breed guppies! It's an outrage! An outrage!!!"

The queue video also contained numerous advertisements for local Amity businesses every bit as strange as its residents. These included Helen's House of Huge Helpings, Wacky Wally Stereo, and Mom's Restaurant. In one ad, Chester Pattengill, "Taxidermist Extraordinaire," boasts of having stuffed the hanging shark in Amity circle, which took him "2,391 work hours and more super glue than I'd care to admit." Commercials promoting Captain Jake's Amity Boat Tours reveal its owner to be an unabashed shyster with tour prices increasing between commercial breaks. These ads boast of Captain Jake's having such "comforts" as seats ("Seats not available on all boats."), shade from the sun ("Canopies not available on all boats.") and skippers ("Some boats are guest operated.") One spot concludes, "Mention this ad and get an *actual* life jacket - subject to availability." The only non-fictional business featured in the queue video was Oceanspray, who sponsored the Jaws ride for much of the '90s.

As first envisioned in 1987, the Jaws queue was to have featured a radio broadcast as part of its preshow presentation rather than television. Dubbed WKGO, there would have been frequent music breaks to report local Amity news as well as to advertise local businesses such as Amity Bay Tours. While every bit as cheesy as the WJWS video, the originally planned WKGO radio show would have referenced the events of Jaws in real-time including the recent disappearance of fisherman Ben Gardner, the suspicious destruction of Morgan's Pier, and the the catching of a "large predator that supposedly injured some bathers."

## Original 1987 Queue Show Pitch:

The Queue Line Show consists of a radio program being played over
a sound system in the waiting line area.  The radio station is WKGO,
a local broadcasting business.  The staff consists of Rick Martin,
the DJ, and Shiela Brant, the field reporter.  The program consists
of music and local reports and news items by Martin and Brant.

The music format of the station is light middle of the road
instrumental music from "Jaws" including "Promenade", "Out to Sea"
and similiar none conflict scores.  Rick Martin is the local DJ who
has spent some time at larger, more urban stations and while interested
in the community, finds humor in the local characters and businesses.
Shiela Brant is a young, enthusiastic local female working for the
station.

The atmosphere generated in the Queue area is that of the Seaside
town of Amity during the initial time when accidents and disappearances
were occuring in the area, but the local officials would not admit
that these problems were due to any shark activity.  The radio show
is approximately 25 to 30 minutes long to accomodate the longest wait
experienced in the Queue line structure.

# About the Sharks

Not unlike its namesake film, the Jaws ride utilized multiple mechanical sharks to simulate the attack of one massive ocean predator. Both the 1990 and 1993 versions of the attraction featured seven sharks in total strategically placed throughout the lagoon. These may have somewhat resembled their big screen cousins in appearance but were otherwise quite different. The movie sharks were pneumatically-powered using pressurized air while the ride sharks ran on hydraulics. One possible reason for the switch to hydraulic power may have been the unavoidably loud hiss of air passing through the pneumatic tubing on the movie sharks. Not that the ride's approach was without complication. Park engineers regularly encountered the very problem shark maker Bob Mattey hoped to avoid on the film - rampant hydraulic fluid leaks. So environmentally unfriendly was the Jaws ride's polluted lagoon that it eventually drew negative attention from state officials in 1995 for contaminating local stormwater ponds.

The first shark encountered by guests was remarkably low-tech. In fact, there was nothing technical about it at all. This was the iconic "hanging shark" strung up in Amity Circle for patrons to snap pictures with. Orlando's hanging shark was inspired by a similar photo-op previously on display at Universal Studios Hollywood. Installed outside the visitors center in 1975, this original hanging shark was created from one of the actual shark molds used in the making of the Spielberg film. This original Bruce was replaced with a generic-looking shark in 1990, which was then moved to a location near the studio tour entrance. Hollywood's hanging shark would disappear altogether in 2014 with the construction of Springfield. Its Orlando cousin, however, remains standing having been moved to the San Francisco section of the park upon the closure of Amity in 2012. While the hanging shark resembles neither its cinematic nor ride counterparts, it remains a warm relic of the bygone attraction.

Each of the ride sharks moved through the lagoon on an underwater track system contained on a submergible platform. These platforms could be lifted completely out of the water for nightly inspections, which greatly simplified their maintenance. While some tasks still required certified dive technicians, most shark repairs could be made without techs ever getting wet. While the 1993 version retained the same mechanical sharks throughout its entire run, the latex skins were replaced bi-annually due to wear and tear as well as discoloration from the contaminated lagoon water.

The Jaws ride sharks moved through the water at a maximum speed of twenty-feet-per-second or roughly fourteen-miles-per-hour. That may not seem terribly fast, but the force required to propel them through the water was equal to the lift-off of a Boeing 737 airliner. The revamp sharks were so incredibly powerful that they were unable to perform show movements at full speed while above water without breaking. While the '93 sharks were undeniably more reliable, the 1990 sharks were arguably more realistic in their movements. The original ride's undersea animatronics boasted a wider range of maneuverability and eyes that rolled over white when attacking. The 1993 team would attempt to mimic real great whites by installing tail fins that moved back and forth in the water, though this effect was later blamed for repeatedly knocking sharks off their track and ultimately disabled.

SEQUENCE · BOAT OPERATOR
PULLS TRIGGER ON GRENADE
LAUNCHER · SHARK OPENS
MOUTH AND AN IMPACT BLASTS
BLOOD FROM THE FAR SIDE OF
THE SHARK MOUTH · SHARK GOES
UNDER ·

# ATTACK SHARK
SCALE 0' 1/2" = 1' 0"

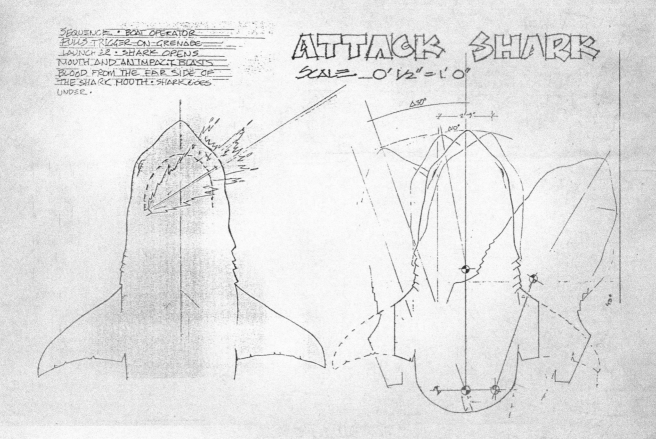

JAWS II
UNIVERSAL STUDIOS, FLORIDA

WATERLINE

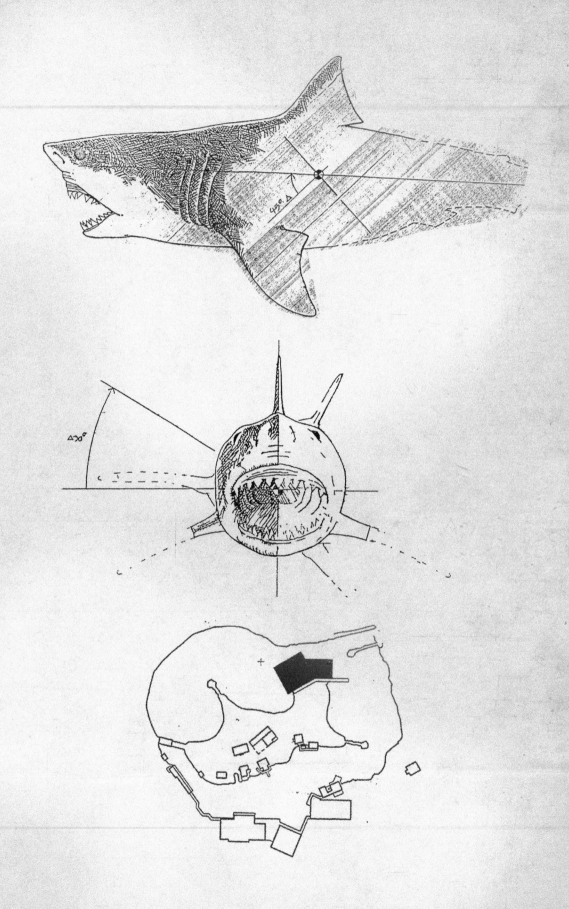

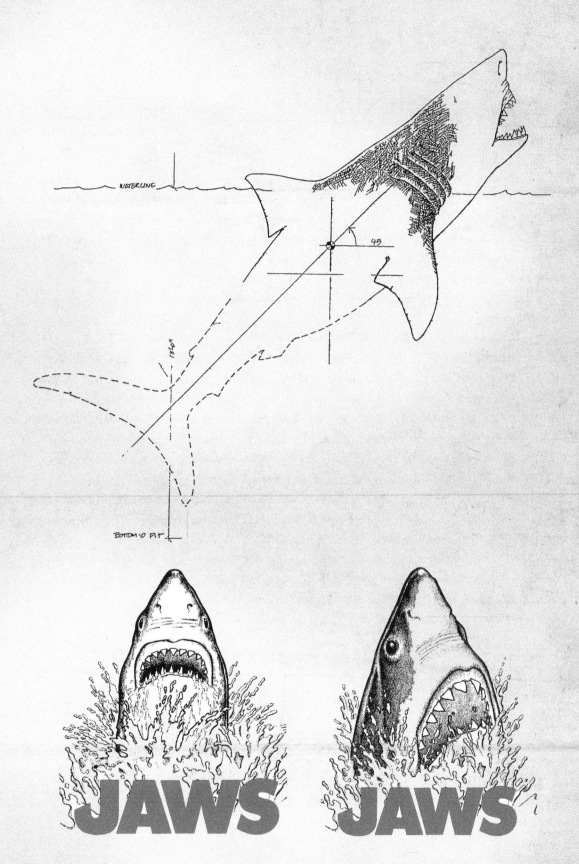

# About the Boats

To call Captain Jake's fleet of canopied cruisers "boats" is a bit of a misnomer. While the original 1990 attraction did utilize pontoon watercraft, the 1993 re-design most people remember featured ride vehicles that traveled along an underwater track. In truth, neither Tours One nor Amity Six were boats in the truest sense of the word. Unlike their 1993 counterparts, the ride's original boats were free floating in the lagoon, though they were submerged within a narrow underwater pit that ran the length of the ride. While skippers could control the speed of Tours One, they were unable to affect its direction due to said pit that guided each boat through the ride. This pit was outfitted with more than a thousand feet of underwater track for the 1993 revamping, which automated the ride vehicle's movements through the water.

Jaws had eight ride vehicles in total, all of which were referred to on deck as Tours One/Amity Six for story purposes. The attraction could handle up to six boats in rotation at a time with one boat on standby across from unload and another in the maintenance boathouse. While the pumps at Bridewell's Gas Dock were fake, the diesel pumps near the unload platform were quite real. Boats could also be re-fueled near Stevens Cannery in Scene One. Per attraction theming, the Jaws ride's eight boats were named after Mayor Vaughn's eight daughters. In actuality, these names were inside jokes for the technicians that helped relaunch the ride in 1993. Among the boat names were Joanne Scott, Lisa Marie, Paula Marie, Denise Alicia, Sara Ann, Valerie Ann, and Brittany Sarah.

Amity Six could hold up to forty-eight passengers per voyage not counting the skipper. This made it one of the most populous ride vehicles in all of Universal Orlando. The boat's six rows of seats were installed on a slope so that each successive row sat slightly higher than the last. This ensured each guest a decent view of the action without being blocked by the rows in front of them.

While the 1990 boats were sold off to another theme park after that's rides closure, the 1993 fleet was destroyed with the attraction itself. Perhaps poignantly, the closing team ended the ride's operation on the evening of January 2, 2012 with an empty boat at the load platform still waiting for guests.

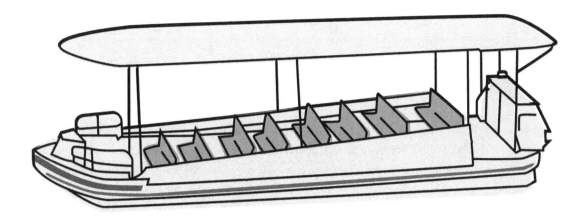

(Artwork courtesy Josh Bailey - JoshBaileyDesign.com)

Top Left: Amity Six from the shark's perspective. Top Right: The underwater boat track in '93.
Bottom Left: A ride vehicle sits idle in the dry lagoon. Bottom Right: The seldom seen wheels that guided the boat along the underwater track. (Photos courtesy Bing Futch)

# About the Skippers

There were many components to Jaws from the sharks and effects to the boats and theming, but the heart of the attraction was the skipper. Noted for being one of the most challenging jobs in the entire park, the weight of the guest experience at Jaws landed squarely on their shoulders. They were responsible for bringing together the attraction's various elements into a cohesive narrative. Without them, the ride simply would not have worked. To paraphrase skipper Michael Skipper, who spieled the final public tour: "It's not the ride but the people that made Jaws amazing."

Reciting the dynamic spiel script was but one part of a Jaws skipper's multi-layered performance. They were required to have meticulous timing and choreography with their dialogue and movements in order to synchronize with preprogrammed events. Their radio interactions and use of the grenade launcher were among these cues. Being a mere second off responding to "Amity Base" or firing their weapon would have been immediately noticeable to guests. Then there was their pantomimed operation of the boat itself. Many skippers have commented that pretending to drive a boat is far more difficult than actually doing so. In addition to this, the skipper was also responsible for ensuring guest safety and that the ride was operating as intended.

Skippers were tethered to their boats by a "kill cord," which would have instantly shut down the ride upon disconnect in the event they collapsed or fell overboard. While the boat's wheel and throttle were fake, the skipper's headset was functional and connected them to a tower operator who could advise of technical issues mid-ride. Jaws skippers worked in a rotation system that allowed them time off boat during shifts in order to keep their performances fresh and energetic. Even so, a skipper could easily perform sixty or more shows in a single shift.

The importance of the skipper cannot be overstated - they brought a crucial human element to an attraction full of mechanical sharks. They single-handedly elevated the Jaws ride to something more than a ride. The skipper's performance was akin to a show that just happened to take place on a moving ride vehicle. Sadly, we have not only lost the Jaws ride at Universal Studios Florida but this entire way of storytelling as well. Jaws and fellow spieling attractions Kongfrontation and Earthquake are now long gone. Screens, it would seem, have replaced the spieler.

## Skipper Role Description circa 1987:

> The Tour Guide/Ride Operator is referred to as "The Captain". The Captain relays an attitude of confidence in his duties and a good knowledge of the Sea and boating. He is friendly and routine in his mannerisms as the tour begins, assuring the guests that the bay is safe as the town officials and his managers have told him. He is however personally cynical about their evaluation of the danger of venturing out into the bay. This cynical attitude quickly begins to appear as the Tour Boat is attacked and takes the form of comical and snide remarks about the situation. This attitude has also prompted the Captain to bring aboard the "APC 14" grenade launcher rifle just as a little "personal insurance", even though the Tour Boat Company has not authorized its use.

Skipper Voltaire Guinigundo jumps into action! (Photos courtesy Jesse Dillon)

# JAWS

## (1990 version)

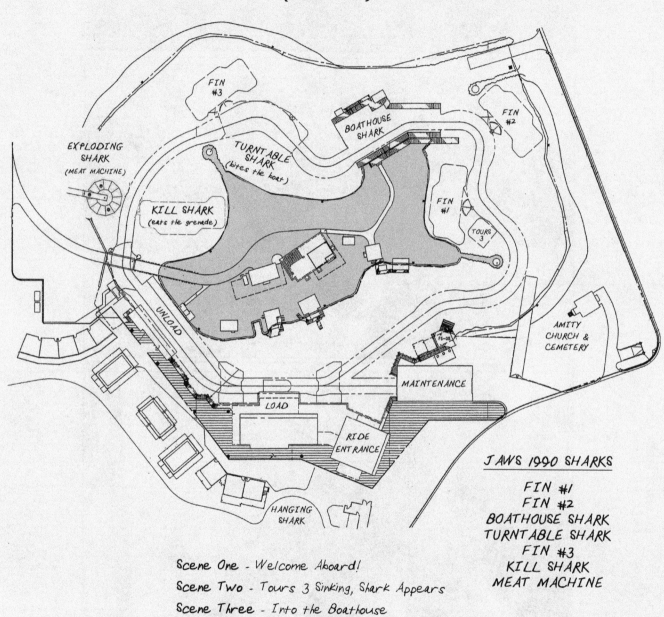

**FIN #3**

**EXPLODING SHARK** (MEAT MACHINE)

**TURNTABLE SHARK** (bites the boat)

**BOATHOUSE SHARK**

**FIN #2**

**KILL SHARK** (eats the grenade)

**FIN #1**

**TOURS 3**

**UNLOAD**

**AMITY CHURCH & CEMETERY**

FS-08

**MAINTENANCE**

**LOAD**

**RIDE ENTRANCE**

**HANGING SHARK**

### JAWS 1990 SHARKS

FIN #1
FIN #2
BOATHOUSE SHARK
TURNTABLE SHARK
FIN #3
KILL SHARK
MEAT MACHINE

Scene One - Welcome Aboard!

Scene Two - Tours 3 Sinking, Shark Appears

Scene Three - Into the Boathouse

Scene Four - Shark bites boat, pops pontoon

Scene Five - Shark eats grenade, blows up

# JAWS II
(1993 version)

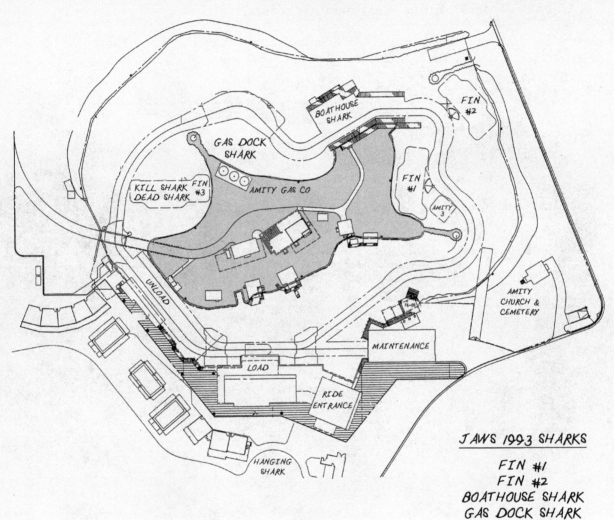

FIN #2

BOATHOUSE SHARK

GAS DOCK SHARK

KILL SHARK
DEAD SHARK   FIN #3

AMITY GAS CO

FIN #1

AMITY 3

AMITY CHURCH & CEMETERY

UNLOAD

MAINTENANCE

LOAD

RIDE ENTRANCE

HANGING SHARK

JAWS 1993 SHARKS

FIN #1
FIN #2
BOATHOUSE SHARK
GAS DOCK SHARK
FIN #3
KILL SHARK
DEAD SHARK

Scene One - Welcome Aboard!

Scene Two - Amity 3 Sinking, Shark Appears

Scene Three - Into the Boathouse

Scene Four - Bridewell's Gas Dock Explosion

Scene Five - Shark bites cable, electrocutes self

# Jaws Ride '93 Map
## by Artist Steve Brown
### http://iamstevebrown.com

Artwork by Tom Ryan (BySeaAndStorm.com)

# TALES FROM
# THE JAWS RIDE

# WE'RE GOING TO NEED RIDES.

## an interview with

# PETER ALEXANDER

**Vice President of Planning & Development**
**Executive Producer - Universal Studios Florida**

Peter Alexander's legendary work in the theme park industry
has spanned four decades and multiple continents.
(Photo courtesy The Totally Fun Company)

**You were heavily involved in the development and creation of Universal Studios Florida. Had the Jaws ride always been planned as part of the opening day lineup?**

Heck, no. Then again, we hadn't planned on there being *any* rides at Universal Studios Florida in the very beginning. It was originally going to be a bigger and better version of the studio tour they had been doing out in California. We have Disney and myself to thank for there ever being any rides at Universal. Disney had essentially copied our design for the Universal Hollywood Tour and put it into their MGM park. That drove Jay Stein positively insane. But it wasn't something we could sue them over because it wasn't a direct copyright infringement.

The original design team for Universal Studios Florida included Bob Ward, Barry Upson, Terry Winnick, and Jay Stein. I only got involved in designing the attractions once Terry left. Realizing that Disney had already stolen the golden goose and was doing their own studio tour, I went to Barry and said, '*You know, this Universal tour thing isn't going to work now. We can't compete with Disney's tour. We're going to need rides. Big ones.*' He said right away, '*That's great except that we've never built a ride before. How much are they going to cost?*' I said, '*I'm not sure but they need to be big. We'll make them cheaper than Disney but they're going to cost a fortune compared to what we usually spend on the tour.*' Right away he went and told Jay, who said, '*Okay, Pete. You go tell Sid Sheinberg.*' He was the chief executive officer of Universal at the time. I went and told Sid what we needed and he also asked how much. I figured they'd cost at least twenty-five or thirty million dollars a piece. And he said, '*Why would we ever spend that kind of money building rides? We don't have the faintest idea how to build a ride!*' I told him, '*You've got to build rides or else you're not going to be able to compete.*'

With that wild encouragement, we began figuring out ideas for the different attractions. I got Bill Martin from Disney to come in and help us out. Jaws was my least favorite concept, but it was Jay's most favorite – he liked Jaws quite a bit. So did Sid. I said to Bill, '*Okay, let's have a water ride and we'll put in a few different scenes and one of them will be Jaws.*' Bill then laid that attraction out for us. Jay came in to look it over and went, '*No, Peter! Jaws isn't part of a ride. It's the whole ride! We want Jaws to be its own thing!*' We had Spielberg involved by that point, so the park was kind of a bifurcated project. Things that involved Amblin Entertainment I took direct to Spielberg. Everything else went through Universal management. Jaws was one of the projects Universal wanted to manage themselves even though Steven had directed the film. Jay and Sid felt particularly close to the property. Sid would say things like '*You know, I've made a lot of money off of sharks in my time!*'

**So you're given the mandate to expand Jaws into its own ride. Where do you go from there?**

I immediately looked at how much Jaws would cost if Disney were to do it, which would've been about fifty or sixty million dollars. I knew we couldn't do that. Disney's approach back then was to put a ton of cool stuff all throughout a ride so that people will want to ride it again and again. The best example of that is Pirates of the Caribbean. You could ride Pirates five times in a row and not see everything. Unfortunately, that approach cost about four times as much as we had to work with. We budgeted Jaws at around twenty million and I think it came in at twenty-one.

Early concept artwork for the Jaws attraction.

We started with the idea that Jaws would have one big, unforgettable scene partway through it. That's also how we approached Kongfrontation. The big moment on that ride was when Kong picks up the tram and drops it. With Jaws, I asked myself, '*What do you fear most about Jaws?*' For me, it was having the shark attack your boat. That's what he did at the end of the original movie. Jaws smashes up the boat that Roy Scheider and Robert Shaw are on and eventually sinks it. I knew we couldn't do that on the ride, but maybe Jaws could grab the front of the boat and drag it through the water. That could be our big moment. I immediately thought of Ride & Show Engineering, which was run by two good friends of mine, Bill Watkins and Ed Fuerer. Bill had been the chief mechanical engineer at Walt Disney Imagineering when I worked there. Ed had been there with him. They had previously built a big piece of show action equipment for us, which was the sliding bridge on King Kong in California. The old King Kong Encounter, which later burned down, had a really cool moment where Kong shakes the bridge you're on. We knew enough at the time to not have Kong *do* anything. His arms actually hung loose on the bridge cables. Instead, we made a tilting bridge that would rock the trams back and forth. The effect was terrific. I figured if Ride & Show could do that, they could probably handle taking a boat and spinning it around with the shark in tow.

I knew the ride had to be more than just the boat attack, so I got Tom Reidenbach to work on the scene just prior to that, which was set inside a dark boathouse. Tom had helped us out in California with the design of Kong and the animatronic dragon in the Conan show. I always thought he was an all-around great guy, a talented architect but also a good show designer. The rest of the ride was figured out by a team of art directors under Craig Barr. We knew we needed to somehow kill the shark for the big finale, but how? The only thing we could think of was the old '*let's blow up the shark*' thing, so we had a shark explosion machine made. (laughs) We thought this was a decent approach to the attraction and that we might be able to do it on a reasonable budget. Keep in mind that twenty-million dollars was completely unreasonable by Universal's standards back then. Of course, they spend four or five times that much on an attraction now. That's about what a parking lot costs now.

**Of all the ambitious rides slated to open with the park, did you expect that Jaws would be the most challenging?**
Definitely not. I was more focused on Back to the Future than I was Jaws. We were terribly understaffed engineering wise and we knew it. I remember a meeting we had about a year prior to opening the park. Jay, in his inimitable style, said, '*You know, Peter... none of this fucking stuff is ever going to work!*' And I said, '*Yeah, we've really bitten off a lot here. I'm just afraid that if we don't at least try to go big we're going to get blown out of the water.*' Jay's main thought was that we needed better staffing to pull it all off, so I brought back my predecessor, Terry Winnick, and put him on Back to the Future. I thought that was going to be our biggest challenge. I'll admit that there was some ego involved in this decision as Back to the Future was totally my invention, if you will. I really didn't want to see that project screwed up, so I put Terry on it. He was more than capable.

I had Craig Barr handling Jaws and Kong, which I thought was the right decision because he was so technically savvy. We hired Ride & Show Engineering to work on those. I didn't think Ride & Show would fail on Jaws because they hadn't failed previously on anything they'd done for us. They'd done a great job on Earthquake out in California. Ride & Show produced a lot of that attraction including the tanker truck that slid down, the crashing train, stuff like that. So I thought they could handle Jaws. They also had the premiere engineering staff. Not only did they have Bill Watkins and Ed Fuerer, they had *the* John Zovich, who was chief engineer of Walt Disney Imagineering when I worked there. Basically, Ride & Show had the A-team. But that didn't stop the Jaws ride from being a mess and that's absolutely what it was. Jaws was a horrible mess.

Craig was out there day after day trying to make Jaws work. I eventually went out with Jay to see how it was going and said, '*Craig, let me ask you something. Has there been one boat ride around this lagoon where everything worked?*' He paused and then he looked at me. '*No.*' That's when I knew we were in trouble. We had to do something else. Jay suggested we go with a much simpler approach. I said, '*Well, the simplest thing we can do is flame. We know* we can do it because we've already done it on other attractions.' And Jay said, '*Why would there be flames on the water?*' I said back, '*I don't know. Maybe the shark bites something. How about he bites a wire and lights a fire?*' I had that drawn together and the idea eventually ended up with Adam Bezark. That's how I pitched the new Jaws ride. I even called it that, '*shark-bites-wire-catches-fire*.' I was pretty burned out by then and left shortly thereafter, so I wasn't around for the re-design of the attraction.

**I don't think anyone could blame you for feeling that way after how Universal Studios Florida debuted. Looking back on it, how would you describe the park's opening day?**

In one word? Chaotic. Only half the park was ready by opening day, which meant that half the park wasn't. We were just starting to encounter the more serious problems on Jaws with Ride & Show Engineering's... uh, engineering. All the other attractions eventually ran smoothly once we got the bugs worked out. Jaws never did. It never really operated the way it was supposed to even though they had tested it extensively. I guess whatever life cycle they had on those parts wore out during the testing!

**How big of a part did Steven Spielberg play in launching Universal Studios Florida?**

It never would have happened without him. I'm not sure if you know this, but Universal Studios Florida basically died around 1986. Lew Wasserman did not like the original version that Jay, Terry, and Barry had put together. That was the old tram tour and front lot studio idea. He didn't think it was good enough. The way he stopped it from happening was to tell Jay, '*If you can get a business partner that will invest fifty percent into this thing, we'll go forward.*' So we tried to get everybody we possibly could. That's when Jay pitched Michael Eisner and that's where Eisner got the idea for the MGM park. Learning that Disney was going to do their own studio tour effectively killed Universal Studios Florida at the time. MGM was Disney's pre-emptive strike against us. The MGM Studio Tour was their attempt at dissuading us from ever building Universal Studios Florida. They took Jay's idea and spent twice as much money doing it as Universal ever would have.

In addition to that, we ran out of people to get as partners and the project died. We cut down the staff. The whole department was whacked. By the time we did Kong on the studio tour, it was just me, Larry Lester, and Barry Upson. Barry did the construction, I did the design, and Larry did the production and supervision. We got Kong up and running for about seven million, which wasn't too bad in those days. One day Steven Spielberg comes riding into Kong while we're programming it. Steven had been my roommate in college. He walks up and asks what we were doing so Craig Barr and I showed him Kong. He then went right up to Sid Sheinberg and said, '*You guys need to do that Universal Studios Florida project. If you can do it like Kong, you can compete with Disney. You've really got something special here.*' And so Sid came to me all excited and said, '*We had no idea you were roommates with Spielberg! That might just be your most important credit, Peter! He just told us to green light the Florida project!*' We knew if Spielberg liked it then Lew would like it. Sid and Lew totally trusted Spielberg's judgement. That was monumental in getting the project started again.

Above: Steven Spielberg cuts the ceremonial film strip ribbon on June 7, 1990 to officially open Universal Studios Florida. He is flanked by actor Robert Wagner and Woody Woodpecker creator Walter Lantz on his right and Universal executives Jay Stein and Sid Sheinberg on his left.

Right: The original admission ticket which cost a scant $25.40 on opening day.

On the surface, it was a crazy idea. There was no way someone could build a studio tour ten miles away from Disney's brand new studio tour. No one in history had ever competed with Disney and no one had ever tried to build a Disney ride other than Disney. *No one*. It was impossible what we did. If it hadn't been for Jay Stein and Steven Spielberg, it never would have happened.

**Don't you think it's funny how Disney's efforts to discourage Universal Studios Florida ultimately shaped it into the park we know today? Really it seems we have them to thank.**

Exactly! If they hadn't built the MGM park, I couldn't have then said, '*We can't compete with their studio tour. We need rides!*' That never would have happened. We would've just done a tram tour if we did it at all. We had such a tiny staff at the time. Universal literally did not have a single engineer on staff when they began the Florida project. Not one! I had been a staff engineer at Hughes Aircraft, but I'd never designed anything. I just coordinated the designs of other people who knew what the heck they were doing. We began the Florida project with five guys on staff – that was it!

**How did Spielberg's involvement with the Florida park evolve from there?**

His initial mandate to me was to make a Back to the Future ride that would rival Disneyland's Star Tours. George Lucas was kind of ragging him at the time. He said, '*Steve, I want to show you what real theme park designers do,*' and he took him on Star Tours. As they got off, Lucas continued, '*Universal could never do anything like that. They're just not in Disney's league.*' Steve called me up right away and told me to go ride Star Tours immediately. He wanted Universal to come up with something that would beat that, which is where the Back to the Future ride came from. I think that was the start of what Spielberg envisioned for the Florida park.

I had gone through about three different iterations of Back to the Future without success when I finally thought back to my time working at Hughes Aircraft. I had worked on the F-14 Fighter Jets, which had the very first domed interactive flight simulator. I went to see that as part of my job and thought it was so cool. When you're in the cockpit of that thing and you've got this dome screen that goes beyond your peripheral vision, you really feel like you're flying. I thought to myself, '*What if instead of a two-person simulator, we had twelve or more people? And what if it was a giant OmniMax dome? I bet that would work!*' I brought this up to Jay Stein in a meeting and he said, '*It's too good of an idea. It'll never work. Someone else must have done it before.*' I told him no one had done it before because no one in aerospace works in the theme park industry. Jay then asked us to do a test, which we did at Ceasar's Palace using their OmniMax Dome. We didn't even have a motion base for it. We just had a mock-up of the DeLorean. Just before we started the film, Craig Barr says to me, '*This is never going to work.*' And I said, '*I'll bet you twenty bucks it does work.*' The minute the test film turned on, it felt like you were flying. Craig handed me twenty bucks right away.

Back to the Future opened about a year after the park did. Around that time I get a call from Steven who says, '*I'm going to take George Lucas on the ride and I want you to be there.*' I can still remember waiting at the ride exit with Steven's wife. We suddenly see him and Lucas coming down the walkway after having ridden it and Steven is smiling ear to ear. Lucas, however, looks *really* pissed off. I ask Steven what he thought and he goes, '*It was sensational! So much better than Star Tours!*' (laughs) That was the day he had his revenge on George Lucas.

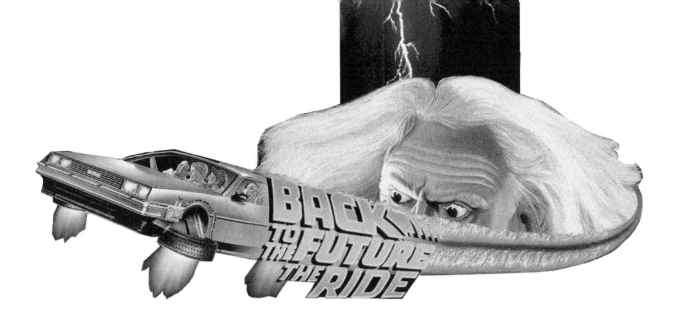

The grand opening of the Back to the Future ride on May 2, 1991 was a red letter date in history for both Steven Spielberg and Universal Studios Florida.

**As director of the film, how did Spielberg view the Jaws ride?**

I believe he was disappointed with it. He liked everything else in the park but he was disappointed with Jaws. We went out to ride it once with Sid, Lew, Jay, Steven, me, Barry and Bob. It was a boat full of management. We went around the ride and half the stuff didn't work. I said, '*I know we've got to get this up and running soon.*' And Steven said, '*You're going to have to do a lot more than that.*' I took that to mean he didn't really care for it even if it had worked. By this point pretty much all the other rides were working. E.T. was working. Earthquake was working. Kong was working. Then again, Kong worked from day one. It just wasn't safe for guests from day one. I personally escorted Spielberg's group onto Kongfrontation. I told him, '*Steven, you can get on this ride but I can't promise that Kong won't poke his hand into the tram car and hit you with it. Basically, I can't really guarantee your safety.*' The group he was with immediately all said, '*Wow, that sounds cool! Yeah! We want to go on this!*' So we did and it was a lot of fun.

**You've mentioned several times how Universal was spending more on the Florida attractions than they'd ever spent on the studio tour. Did the budget ever become a restricting factor on Jaws?**

No, not on Jaws. We did have to be budget conscious. The ride most affected by that was Earthquake. On Jaws, Kong, and E.T., you loop through the entire ride and wind up back at the start. If you'll recall, Earthquake didn't quite work that way. That attraction essentially had one big ride scene and that was it. The original idea was to have four or five scenes. I took that plan to Sid Sheinberg, who loved the movie it was based on. It was one of his movies. He liked Earthquake similar to how he liked Jaws. He looked at what I had and said, '*Peter, we just don't have this kind of money. What if you cut it in half?*' I replied, '*Why not just make it one big scene? You could start out in the station, go directly to the big scene, and then go right back to the station instead of looping through an entire ride.*' And Sid said, '*Yeah, that would be better.*' Our thought was if we've only got one ride scene, we'd better hit a home run with it.

**I know you moved onto Six Flags after your work with Universal, but did you ever go back to ride the redesigned Jaws ride and, if so, what was your impression of it?**

Yes, I think I did. I'm sure I did. I guess it was maybe 1991 that I told Jay Stein I was feeling burned out and wanted to start my own company. He said, '*You can't quit!*' But he let me quit on the condition I kept a consulting contract with the park, which I did. They would have me come back every so often and look at stuff. I remember we changed some things around with the Horror Makeup Show. I came in once to look over what Adam Bezark was doing on the Jaws re-do and that seemed to be going well. I very quickly became persona non grata at Universal once I started working for Six Flags in 1992. I was making Universal-esque attractions for Six Flags on about a tenth of the budget Universal had been spending. They didn't like that too much.

**Wasn't there quite some distance between the Six Flags parks and Universal, though? You're saying they still cared about you doing similar work for other parks despite that?**

You bet they cared. I remember around 1992 I was just finishing putting a Batman stunt show into Six Flags Magic Mountain. It wasn't a very big arena we were working with on that one. In fact, it was pretty crummy. Six Flags didn't much like the idea of a stunt show. They only wanted rides. Phil Hettema stopped by one day. Phil was a really sharp guy. He came by after the show and I asked him how he liked it. He went, '*It was okay, but that show in Texas was sensational! And the one in Jersey was great too!*' I said to him, '*Phil, you went to Six Flags in Texas and Jersey?*' He goes, '*Oh yeah. Universal insisted that I go.*' I knew at that point they were worried about me stealing their thunder. I certainly had the capability to do so because that's essentially what Universal Studios Florida was. We were a bunch of ex-Disney guys working to create something that could compete with Disney. We weren't really ripping them off, though, just as I wasn't ripping off Universal with my work for Six Flags. I eventually became an executive producer at Six Flags. We didn't take anything from the Disney or Universal family of attractions because we couldn't possibly afford those kinds of attractions. We did take bits and pieces, though. Stunt shows we could afford. Magic Mountain had an almost entirely young adult audience before the Batman stunt show. As soon as we did that, we started getting tons of families visiting the park. Universal didn't care for that at all.

**What was it like hearing that Jaws would finally be closing in early 2012?**

Someone called me and said, '*Not only is Kong gone but Jaws is going too!*' I said, '*Oh well, time marches on.*' The fact that it lasted that long to begin with was a testament to the property of Jaws and the re-engineering that was done after I left. I take a lot of credit for things like Kong, Earthquake, and Back to the Future, but Jaws was a shell of a ride when I left. The new team inherited an empty shell and turned it into something very successful, so I give credit to those guys. The re-design is what kept it going all those years.

The original offerings of Universal Studios Florida.

# THE UNIVERSAL EVOLUTION

an interview with

## BOB WARD

### Senior Vice President for Design & Planning

Bob Ward in the New York section of the park on June 7, 1990.
(Photo courtesy Bob Ward)

**Developmentally, Universal Studios Florida languished for years. What finally set it in motion?**

Jay Stein. None of it would ever have happened if it weren't for Jay Stein. It's that simple. He was a true visionary and so passionate for the project. He was not going to be denied in his efforts to create businesses for the company that would be very successful. Lew Wasserman was also a big part of it. He was truly the last living mogul of Hollywood. Lew was such a mogul that when the Pope made his first visit to the United States in 1984, he helicoptered into Universal City to have dinner with Lew in his private dining room. That's the kind of mogul he was. I still remember something he said to me when I first joined the company. Lew goes, '*You know, Bob. We're really not in the entertainment business. We're in the business of entertainment. There is a difference.*' And he was right. It was all about business on the Universal lot back in those days.

The studio tour started very modestly in '64 with only a few attractions like the Animal Show and the Stunt Show. There were also shops and a few other things. The tour relied on the trams because nothing on the backlot had been built to code. You couldn't ever get out and walk around. Universal had patched this tour experience together using guys from the metal shop, the welding shop, the special effects shop, and so on. They would add various things every so often like Battlestar Galactica or the parting of the Red Sea. They weren't rides, though. They were just scenes you rode past and they didn't always work. Movie guys tend to make things that work once or twice and that's it. After that, they walk away. They don't even always take it with them. So they had to have a whole different mentality creating things for the studio tour.

The short story as to how that evolved into Universal Studios Florida was that we all grew up in the '60's watching Walt Disney on television talk about this new park they were building in Florida. The Universal Studio Tour started up just as Disney was building this big park out in Orlando. I intersected with all of that right out of school in early '71 with a job at W.E.D. that would become Disney Imagineering. I joined nine months before Walt Disney World opened in October 1971. That's how I came into the world of destination themed entertainment. Jay was watching all of this happen and really pushing Lew and Sid to expand Universal. The problem was that Lew and Sid weren't convinced Disney was going to be successful with their Florida park. Everyone looks at what a huge industry that is in Orlando today, but that industry didn't exist back then. There was nothing. Walt Disney World became a huge success because ninety percent of people on the eastern seaboard had never been west. They'd never seen anything like this. Plus, it was an easy route to get there. Everyone wanted to put the kids in the station wagon and drive down to Disney World.

That success spawned the development of their second park, Epcot. Meanwhile, Jay is going to Lew and Sid saying, '*Look, they're already building a second one! All we've got to do is build something next door to that!*' Without his persistence and perseverance and tenacity, we wouldn't have Universal Studios Florida. He truly doesn't get the recognition he should for creating the spark that ignited Universal parks as we know them all today.

**I understand the Florida project was initially planned as being another studio tour like in California. Tell me about that original vision and how it morphed into a theme park.**

Yes, that's true. The original plan for Universal Studios Florida was really just a souped-up version of the tour out in Hollywood. There was going to be a main tour center and then a backlot with various sets and attractions scattered throughout it. We eventually came to realize how that wasn't going to work anymore. Epcot had opened by this time. Between Epcot and Magic Kingdom, it was obvious that Disney had set the bar very high. It was clear that what we had been doing with the studio tour was slowly becoming less relevant.

When I arrived at Universal, no one was challenging who we were as a company. They were only trying to build upon what was already there. If you're only doing a souped-up version of what you've already done, you're holding yourself back. Philosophically, the studio tour was not unlike taking a tour of General Motors to see how cars are made. That's not a theme park. A theme park is significantly different. Several things happened to guide us toward that conclusion. We started going, '*Rather than having thirteen attractions strung together on a tour, we need to find a specific ride system and tell three different attraction stories that way. Maybe one is a water ride and another an aerial ride.*' We figured each of those attractions could incorporate three or more movies to help tell a larger story. That was the direction we were going in.

Another thing we came to realize was that the tram part of the tour was a huge cost. Buying and maintaining those trams was not cheap at all. If you change up your idea and no longer string together attractions on a tour, you no longer need the trams. That's something big you no longer have to spend money on. Not that you won't spend a bunch of money on something else. Ideas like this slowly but surely took us further away from the core DNA of the studio tour approach.

We were trying to find a much more compelling and competitive way to engage our guests. I spent a lot of time on the Universal backlot in those days. I was divorced and single, so I practically lived there. That's when I realized what each and every guest on the tour really wanted was to get off the tram and wander the backlot like I was able to. They wanted to go inside all these soundstages to see all of the incredible things that were going on. That was the experience we needed to give them. That would have been much easier to do in Hollywood since the Universal backlot has such an incredible history to it, none of which existed in what was essentially swampland out in Florida. The Florida park would have none of Hollywood's legacy and heritage. That was an enormous challenge.

**It's sounding like the Florida park came together as a very organic progression of ideas.**

Inspired by the true genius of Jay Stein. Our ideas were also embraced by the great leadership of Barry Upson, who hired all of us. The magic component in this mixture is raw passion because when you're doing things that have never been done before, you're not going to make it unless you're passionate about it. You also have to be not afraid to fail, which we did in a number of ways. However, we eventually learned from and overcame our failures. That's how the transition from studio tour to theme park really came about. Then Peter came in as a scheduling guy and wanted to help develop attractions. We would often have these great engaging conversations. Peter, Barry and I dreamed up the first Kong attraction in Hollywood, which is what got Spielberg interested in the Florida project in the first place.

Bob Ward presenting an incredible scale model of Universal Studios Florida to the press in 1986. With Kong to his right and Earthquake to his left, the actual park would very closely mirror this conceptual vision. (Photo courtesy Bob Ward)

I remember Barry, Peter, and myself went to lunch one day at Rive Gauche in Sherman Oaks. The Kongfrontation ride was essentially born over that lunch. We started tossing around what we might do with a full Kong ride. In Hollywood, we only ever had the upper-torso of the monkey. That wasn't going to be enough this time. I said, '*If we're really going to do this right, we need an establishing shot that shows a big-ass gorilla in full. He's got to be ferocious.*' Then Peter says something like, '*Yeah! And he can be attacking the tram on the 59th Street Bridge in New York!*' And then I go, '*Exactly! Except you're actually on that tram and you're headed straight for him! And you have helicopters flying around shooting at him!*' That was all one lunch conversation. Then I went back to start drawing that idea up and Peter started writing it. All we had to do then was convince Lew and Sid that it was a good idea.

The 1990 ride's kill shark platform raised out of the water during programming.
(Photo courtesy Tom Reidenbach)

Jaws was born much the same way. We had to figure out how to put guests in an experience as close to what was on the screen as possible. In Hollywood, Jaws just comes up alongside the tram as the air canons blow water. It's a little goofy, honestly. We knew we couldn't do that again. Everyone already knew that Jaws. If we were going to trump Disney in Orlando, Jaws had to bite the boat! Guests have got to be on that boat and he has to be grabbing it and shaking all of them. This was not a drive-by. This was an all-out attack! And, of course, Jay always loved fire and explosions, so we had to get those in there too. Ultimately Steven Spielberg helped us coin the phrase, '*Ride the movies*'.

**Which opening day attraction was most challenging to create?**
Everything was equally challenging. Here's what you have to keep in mind. Epcot was now open. There had been people who left Imagineering and were now running their own businesses. This was getting to be a small industry. But Disney was telling all these people, '*If you do any work for Universal whatsoever, we'll never hire you again.*' That caused us to have a lot of trouble getting access to people who had done these kinds of things before. Fortunately, some really key Disney guys started their own show engineering and animation company, Sequoia Creative. Bob Gurr is an industrial engineering Disney legend. Dave Schweninger and Tom Reidenbach joined Bob and they built our first King Kong animation in Hollywood mid-eighties, which was really instrumental for us. Nobody in our company really knew about animation engineering. And if we didn't know how to do that, we surely didn't know how to make a shark bite a boat in water. That was a whole different ballgame. We were heading into a world that was totally foreign to us, which made rides like Jaws an exceptional challenge.

**When did Universal Studios Florida start to ramp up as a project?**

We got things kicked off in early '87 and we opened in June of '90. The typical theme park takes five years to design and build the right way. Yet there we were, a bunch of people who had never done this before in our life with neither the resources nor experience to really do it. And we're trying to do it in three-and-a-half-years! I mean, how does that strike you? I'll tell you how it strikes me! It strikes me as, '*Houston, we have a problem!*' We kept moving the date all around too. I actually have pins in my drawer that say, '*Universal Studios Florida Opening April 1989!*' And that obviously didn't happen.

**As someone who was so personally vested in the park, what was June 7, 1990 like?**

You dream of that day being one of the most special days of your life. For me, opening day was... turbulent. The days running up to that were also tough. We were getting pummeled from every direction. We were also working 24/7 just to get things operational. Most of the rides were operational, just not consistently operational. It was also unfortunate that we had this great advertising program that talked up our marquee attractions like Kong, E.T., and Jaws. We had like eighteen attractions but most of the focus went to the big six or seven that were not consistently working. The remnants of that day surfaced in the following day's newspaper headlines. Michael Eisner told the press that week we would probably close in two years.

On opening day I found myself aboard a Jaws boat with Sid Sheinberg, his wife, and a number of celebrities when the boat itself broke down. We were out there for thirty minutes before they got a rowboat to come get us. Let me tell you, the conversations that went down on that boat would pulverize any drill sergeant that I ever knew. (laughs) Meanwhile, we had to get off that ride to go do another upbeat interview. It felt like hand-to-hand combat. All the while, Sid and Lew are saying to Jay, '*This is on you! This is your fault! You talked us into this mess, you idiot!*'

**When did you feel that the park had survived the chaos of its grand opening?**

I'd say about six months after we opened. That's when Jay Stein wrote a note to Lew and Sid talking about creating a second theme park. This was even before we had bought the property to the south of us to expand. Everybody thought Jay was crazy for making that suggestion, but it was just him still being passionate about a vision for an even greater Universal destination. That's when I got involved in the bigger vision of Universal Orlando and started focusing on things like the second park, the hotels, Citywalk, and everything else. I knew by then that both we and I had survived the opening day mess.

We were all really proud when we were able to successfully launch Back to the Future: The Ride in the spring of '91. That was terrific. We had a great time coming up with ideas for that. Peter was very involved in that one. At one point, Steven Spielberg thought it should have been a rollercoaster experience. We told him, '*Steven, you can't tell stories on a rollercoaster. This has to be bigger than a rollercoaster.*' And that's how it evolved. Like with Jaws and Kong, we had to ask ourselves where would guests want to be if they could step into a Back to the Future movie? And it was obvious. They'd want to be in the DeLorean. So that's where we put them. Back to the Future quickly surpassed Disney's Star Tours attraction and set a whole new attraction experience benchmark for the industry.

**What was your impression of the Jaws ride when it worked as intended?**

I loved it for the same reasons that everyone else loved it. It did have its limitations, of course. Both Jaws and Kong will always be near and dear to me because they were part of the original DNA of Universal Studios Florida. They were both present on the studio tour long before there was ever a Universal theme park anywhere. They were such key attributes in launching the Florida project. Once we got the park opened, we closed Jaws in order to redevelop it's show and ride engineering. I got involved in that for about a year-and-a-half. Ultimately, I was proud of what we were able to do with it. Together with Oceaneering, we found ways to breathe new life into Jaws that allowed it to live out a reasonable life over time. It became clear to me during the redesign that Jaws was going to be one of those attractions that wouldn't always be there. Some things last many years while others get turned into something else. Kong is now Mummy. Back to the Future is now The Simpsons. Jaws simply wasn't going to last.

**Why did you feel that Jaws wasn't going to last?**

It just wasn't built that way. If we could have demolished the whole thing and started over brand new, it might have had a chance at lasting forever. But we were so vested in what had already been spent and in the ride layout that was already there. Our redesign had to fit within the framework of what was done on the first Jaws. We did not have a blank slate. The technology was also an issue. With something like Back to the Future, the hardware and media of that ride was very upgradeable, which allowed it to become The Simpsons. The marine technology we used on Jaws was not upgradeable. For all those reasons, I knew Jaws was going to have a certain life expectancy to it. Had we been able to start over from scratch with our redesign, it might have been able to last forever, especially considering everything we learned the first time around. But we weren't really able to apply all of what we learned because we were still working with the old attraction layout. It's also about remaining relevant with your audience. Guest expectations change generationally over time greatly influencing attraction content.

**As someone who worked on both versions of Jaws, which was your personal favorite?**

The original Jaws ride will always have a special place in my heart. Unfortunately, we didn't have the technology, experience, or money to do it correctly at the time. It was such a cool idea, though. I never felt the second version captured the same thrill of the first when the shark grabbed the boat. The second version came close to achieving it, but it never fully did. Of course, the second Jaws ride seemed to have a primary goal of reliability over creating those kinds of memorable moments. That was certainly important so that it wasn't broken down all of the time. In the end, I enjoyed both versions.

Bob Ward in his office surrounded by relics from his remarkable career. A model of the iconic Universal Studios archway sits on a high shelf. (Photo courtesy Bob Ward)

Boathouse signage from the 1990 attraction created in tribute to Jay Stein, whom Bob Ward credits much of Universal Studios Florida's early success to. The boathouse would later change owners to Quint for the 1993 re-opening. This sign would be retired to the queue. (Signage courtesy Jeremy Homan)

# CREATING AMITY IN ORLANDO

an interview with

## TOM REIDENBACH

### Owner, TRA Architects
### Jaws Ride Design Team 1988 - 1991

From laser-shooting dragons to man-eating sharks,
Tom Reidenbach has seen it all. (Photo courtesy TRA Architects)

**How did you come to join the design team for Universal Studios Florida?**

It was through an evolution of projects I had been involved in. I had done several things for Universal throughout the '80's including a huge effect for The Adventures of Conan, which was a live action stage show on the studio tour out in California. My contribution was, with our team, to design, build, and program a twenty-five-foot-tall fire breathing, laser shooting dragon. It was one of the biggest pieces of show animation ever done at that time. I did that through Sequoia Creative, a company I had with Disney legends Dave Schweninger and Bob Gurr. And Conan was a very successful show for Universal Studios, California.

After that, I helped them add King Kong to their studio tour. Universal always had it in the back of their mind to do something with Kong but they never settled on an approach they liked. Keep in mind that this was going to be part of the studio tour and not a standalone attraction. The ride vehicles for the tour consisted of multiple trams not unlike a train. Altogether I think they held around two-hundred-and-eighty people or so. They would go throughout the backlot and occasionally stop at a soundstage where a show had been set up such as Conan Swords and Sorcery. The guests would disembark, watch the show, and then return to the trams. Kong wasn't going to be like that. We were going to have the guests remain on the tram as it drove into the soundstage. Universal originally wanted people to see Kong twice, first from a distance full-size and then right up close. The problem was that the view from the left side of the tram was quite different than from the right. I suggested along with Bob and Dave that Universal actually have two different scenes with two different Kongs, one full scale for the faraway view and another just from the waist up for the close proximity encounter.

We pitched that to Sid Sheinberg, Lew Wasserman, and Jay Stein in a big presentation with show models and a ten-foot-tall, fully animated King Kong head. I fought like hell to get them to do two Kongs but they wouldn't go for it. They ultimately decided to have a partial Kong to be seen in close-up. We went with that and staged a lot of special effects around him like a crashing helicopter and electrical sparks. It was terrific. The show opened in June of '86 and was so massively popular that studio tour attendance tripled. They even did a television special on it with comedian Jonathan Winters. He interviewed all of us who worked on it.

Around that time or shortly after, Universal finally decided to move forward on the Florida project due in no small part to the success of the Kong attraction. They had already purchased the necessary land years earlier but couldn't decide if they truly wanted to do it or not. Lew and Jay were the most active ones on the Florida project. Lew was not at all convinced it was a great idea. Actually, Lew wasn't even convinced we should be doing King Kong in California. But I think Kong's huge success ultimately led them to go forward with Florida. And, of course, they later used our two Kong approach for Kongfrontation in the new park.

**What attraction did you work on first for the Florida park?**

I was initially working on the E.T. Adventure. I designed the chase scene where the bikes fly over the police car, which was right out of the movie. I also designed the false perspective model of Hollywood that you fly over. Those ride vehicles were designed by Bob Gurr. I actually took myself off the E.T. project after a while due to some creative differences I was having with Universal. Fortunately, Peter Alexander had asked if I would do some concept work for Earthquake around that time so I moved on.

**If you don't mind me asking, what were the creative differences?**

Remember when E.T. takes you to his home, the green planet? Universal wanted that environment to look entirely organic. I thought to myself, '*Wait a minute. These advanced aliens have built this marvelous space ship that has traveled billions of miles to earth and their home is basically a sweet potato!? Give me a break!*' I laughed about it. I didn't think they were serious. We actually had words over it. I thought that guests should arrive on his planet through a space station with all sorts of creatures hanging about. It would have somewhat resembled the cantina scene from Star Wars. We drew up some fantastic looking concept art for it but Universal ultimately decided E.T. should be living in a sweet potato with vines and flowers everywhere. They were supposed to be this advanced civilization and they were basically living in a rainforest.

**How did you come to join the design team on Jaws?**

Peter Alexander and Bob Ward asked me to take a look at Jaws because their team was so swamped figuring out the rest of the park. They were having to outsource work to other companies like Gary Goddard Enterprises. The original plan was to have Universal Studios Florida open by 1989 which of course didn't happen. Moving the opening to 1990 still had them under a tremendously tight deadline. They had wanted to get the park up and running in about two-and-a-half years, which I and many others knew to be an impossible time frame. That's why their grand opening was such a disaster with so many attractions not operational. It was a horrible day in their history. I know there were some really ugly confrontations between guests and ride operators. The Orlando Sentinel had a field day with it as did Disney. However, when Disneyland opened in California, their opening day in 1955 had similar problems.

Jaws was set to be the largest attraction of its kind ever built, far bigger than Disney's Jungle Cruise. The ride occupied around twelve acres and featured a six-million-gallon lagoon. It was clear that Universal absolutely did not have the personnel available to work on it. They asked if I'd consider helping them out architecturally and assigned me three buildings to do - Amity Church, Mayor Vaughn's house and the Harbor Master's. These turned out beautifully if I do say so myself. Peter, Norm Newberry, and Bob Ward came back to me and said, '*These are really great. Can you do the whole thing?*' So I reached out to my consultants who all agreed to do it. I brought them together under a company I had started years earlier called TRA Architects. I then went back to Peter, Norm, and Bob to say, '*Yeah, we can do the whole thing. In the words of Alan Shepard, "Let's light this candle!"*'

Amity under construction. (Photo courtesy Tom Reidenbach)

I told Universal that TRA and its consultants would handle all theme architecture plus structural, electrical, and mechanical engineering as well as civil and water treatment elements. At one point, we had up to thirty-five people working literally day and night on twenty-one buildings and the six-million gallon lagoon systems. TRA also did the show design and engineering elements for the dark ride portion in the boathouse. We also created show design and storyboards for the meat machine effect in the final scene. In short, we did everything but the boats and the sharks. It was during this time that Bob Ward also asked if the TRA Graphics Department could help with signage for the ride, surrounding Amity area, and Metropolitan Street. Working with the Universal design, TRA created over a thousand signs and graphics. We were also in charge of construction administration which meant we had to check everything when the contractors put in for a payment to make sure that the work had actually been done. Beside myself, two to three days a week, I had three separate project managers on Jaws, one of whom was an architect and two of whom were construction superintendents. It was quite a lot to oversee.

**Wow. You very quickly went from "helping out" to handling several huge aspects of the attraction. How did you not lose your mind with that kind of workload and the associated pressures?**

Who says I didn't? Actually, I absolutely loved the work I was doing and looked forward to the challenges it brought. Every day was something new. One day I was working on Quint's shark house, then I was working on the dark ride feature, and then the shark meat machine. I never looked on any of it as work. I also had some great people I could rely on as my project managers and designers. They had as much enthusiasm as I did for this kind of stuff.

Top: Mini-Jaws takes
a bite out of Tom.

Right: Tom poses with the dragon
head from the Conan show.

(Photos courtesy
Tom Reidenbach)

**Did you ever suspect that the Jaws ride might not be ready by opening day?**

I knew right from the start they were going to have problems with it. The sharks were made by a company called Ride & Show Engineering who were quite capable in their abilities. Some of the people that were building the sharks had previously worked on Kong and really knew what they were doing. Mechanically, however, it was all experimental. This stuff had never been done before. I'll tell you some of the problems Universal encountered with Ride & Show's work but understand that I don't blame Ride & Show entirely. They were on a tremendously rushed schedule to do something that had never even been mechanically proven to work. Also, due in part to the chemicals in the lagoon water to create turbidity, the shark skins were deteriorating.

One big issue was that Ride & Show were so squeezed for time that they never once tested those sharks in water out in California. They waited until they got to Florida to check them out in water. Consequently, the sharks didn't work properly once installed in the lagoon. Another huge problem involved the hydraulic connections to the pumps. We did all the pumps and gave them a tap out wherever they requested one be placed. Because Ride & Show were in such a hurry, they used what are called quick disconnect couplers on the hydraulic system. This meant the hoses going directly to the sharks were also quick disconnect. Those things were leaking forty gallons of hydraulic fluid an hour. This meant the fluid wasn't going to the sharks where it should have been but into the lagoon where it shouldn't have been and it really messed things up, not the least of which were the filters.

The boats were also terribly designed. Those things had Volvo engines in them and were way overpowered. They could push the boats up to fifteen miles per hour despite them not needing to go anywhere near that fast. They were overpowered and therefore overheated all the time. It was like driving a Ferrari down the highway at five-miles-per-hour. They were bound to burn up and that's exactly what happened. But again, I don't entirely blame Ride & Show. It's one thing to build a fire breathing dragon or a giant ape, but everything changes when you're working underwater. That's when it gets really tough. My whole discontent with the situation was that I told them in no uncertain terms, '*You've got to stop this and tell Universal you're not going to have this ready by opening day. It is literally impossible.*' And they refused to do that. Testing is part of the development of every ride. You have to test all the mechanisms and they didn't. Maybe they couldn't. They were speeding toward a horrible deadline.

**Did you experience any unforeseen technical challenges on Jaws as Ride & Show did?**

Most everything we did for Jaws worked well. Mechanical, electrical, structural, and plumbing systems were A-okay as was the queue, load, and unload areas. The themed architecture and landscaping created New England in Central Florida beautifully. We did have some issues with the meat machine where the shark explodes. I always had a problem with that concept. You're supposed to be going on this peaceful boat tour around the island, right? How many people are going to get on the boat if the guide's got a bazooka?! Universal, they were great at overkill back in the '80s and they said, '*Well, we want to have a big explosion at the end and this is how we plan to do that.*' So all this shark meat goes flying up into the air and lands back in the water to be caught by a partially submerged net. Then the net retracts and the meat is collected back into the machine. The shark pieces were basically weighted pieces of foam. We had a time getting that to work right. But fortunately we were able to rehearse and perfect it.

**What was your impression of the original Jaws ride when it worked as intended?**

Not taking pride of authorship, I thought it was very well conceived. Don't get me wrong, the original Jaws was great when it worked. The post ride interviews were terrific. People absolutely loved the attraction. It was a little intense for small children, no question about it, and even for some adults. I thought it was miraculous that it ran at all during those few months it was open. Maintenance was always there waiting as soon as the last boat came in at closing. They would be doing the same things each night such as blowing out the hydraulic lines. They would work right up until the boats went out again the next morning. Universal knew it was only a matter of time before Jaws failed, so they ran it as much as they possibly could until it broke.

**Did you have a favorite scene on the attraction and if so, what was it and why?**

Probably the boathouse because I got to design that scene. Initially they were going to have the boat come in to hide and the skipper would eventually go, '*I think the shark's gone. It's probably safe to go now.*' And they would continue onto the next scene. I said, '*Let's take advantage of this being in the dark and do something scary.*' So I came up with the idea of the shark banging on the outside of the boathouse wall, which was a fairly easy effect to pull off. On the third bang you would see light start to shine through as if the shark had broken through the wall. Then Jaws himself would pop up on the right side of the boat. That was just a head that jumped out, not a full shark. Universal had originally wanted to duplicate an existing head from one of the other sharks, which were proportionate to their bodies. I suggested instead that we really emphasize this particular shark and make the head about a third bigger than it ought to have been since it was so close to the guests. They went with that. I thought it was a pretty terrifying scene.

**How much of your work carried over to the second Jaws ride that opened in '93?**

All of the architecture did. They didn't tear down any buildings to my knowledge. They just added a fuel dock outside the boathouse. All of the buildings around the island were still there like Quint's, Chief Brody's, Mayor Vaughns and so on. With regard to the lagoon elements, I would say eighty-five to ninety percent of our work remained in the attraction. Universal really only took out the sharks and boats.

**Of TRA's many contributions to Jaws, which one are you most proud of?**

Without a doubt, I'm most proud of the island's overall atmosphere, that feeling you got once you were through the queue line and getting ready to board the boat. In that moment you couldn't see any other part of Universal Studios Florida. You didn't even feel like you were in Florida anymore but in a quaint New England fishing village. I'm so proud of the visuals we created with things like the lighthouse and the church. You really felt like you were setting out on an adventure, like you had somehow been transported to another place. If I had to point to one building in particular, I'd say the boathouse was a very special structural achievement. I also like Quint's place, which I thought looked just like it did in the motion picture.

Top: Mayor Vaughn's home, Chief Brody's home, and the Harbor Master's.

Bottom: The load platform under construction. (Photos courtesy Tom Reidenbach)

# AMITY UNDER CONSTRUCTION

Opposite top: Amity Church
Opposite bottom: Lighthouse Cove
Top: Maintenance boathouse
Middle: Quint's Shack
Below: Queue Interior

(All photos courtesy
Tom Reidenbach)

# A CLOSE-UP LOOK AT
# THE MEAT MACHINE

One of the more unique parts of the original Jaws ride was something called the "meat machine," which simulated the shark's gory death by grenade explosion in Scene Five. This effect was invented by attraction producer Craig Barr and fabricated by TRA Architects. Rubber shark chunks would be shot out of the lagoon using pressurized air concurrent with the release of red dye into the water. The resultant effect was right out of the 1975 film's ending. These chunks would then splash down into a sloped net that would guide them back into the shooting mechanism in preparation for the next explosion. The effect would also activate a diffuser mechanism as the boat departed to rid the water of any lingering red dye. The meat machine could reset in as little as seventy seconds.

(Photo courtesy Tom Reidenbach)

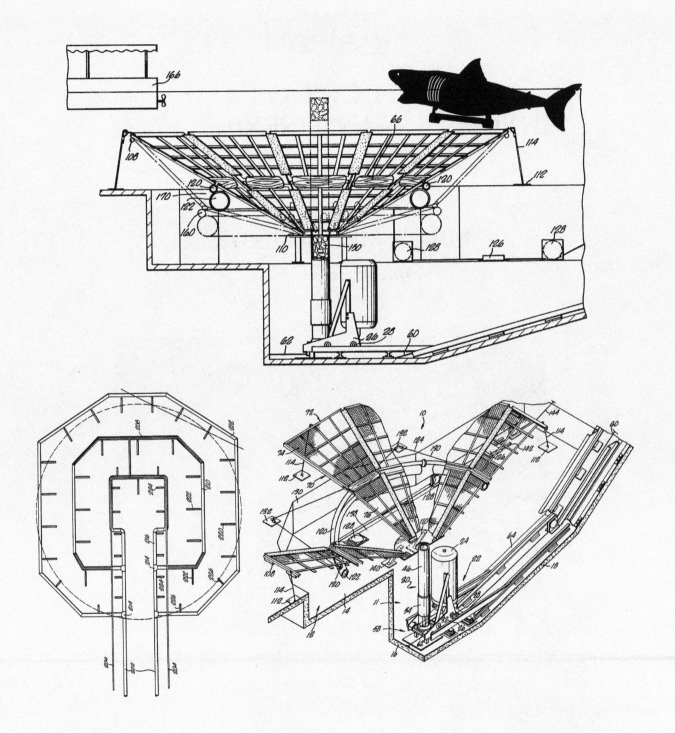

# A PERFECT STORM OF
# INNOVATION AND INEXPERIENCE

◆━━━━━◆◆◆━━━━━◆

### an interview with

## MARK MESSERSMITH

### Director of Marketing
### Ride & Show Engineering Inc.

"Boys, oh boys…. I think he's come back for his noon feeding."
(Photo courtesy Mark Messersmith)

**How did you become involved with the Jaws ride?**

I was hired by Ride & Show Engineering around '88 or '89 to be their director of marketing. To them I was an outsider. They thought it would be a good idea to hire someone who understood marketing that didn't necessarily come from the same Disney mold like everyone else at Ride & Show had. They were in the midst of several projects for Universal when I first walked through the door. The big ones were Jaws and Earthquake. Universal Studios Florida was being planned as a billion dollar project and those were two of the star attractions.

It was enormously impressive to walk through the shop at Ride & Show and see pieces of Jaws and Earthquake coming together. They had these giant mechanical sharks that were so articulated and could move in all sorts of ways. The sharks didn't even have skin yet but they were incredible to see in action. The founders of Ride & Show - a couple of guys named Ed Feuer and Bill Watkins - had been top engineers at Disney previously and were responsible for much of Epcot. They had tremendous ability and experience building complex ride systems.

Ride & Show's main contribution to the Jaws ride involved the design, construction, and installation of the sharks and boats. The sharks moved through the attraction on these gigantic underwater motion bases. We're talking motion bases that were fifteen or more feet tall that had to move these giant steel objects through water at very fast speeds. In one infamous scene, the shark had to actually interact with the boat while both of them were in motion! It was breathtaking to see and much more complex than I think anyone expected it to be. As you might expect, that scene alone required a tremendous amount of testing and fine tuning, which we weren't really given the time to do. Universal was quite aggressive in pushing the limits of the attraction. Contractually, they could do just about whatever they wanted with it and they certainly did.

**How much, if at all, did Universal's inexperience at running a world class theme park complicate the launch of a cutting edge attraction like the first Jaws ride?**

It absolutely complicated it. They weren't Disney. They didn't have fifty years of theme park experience under their belt nor were they used to operating large scale ride systems. Universal did hire on some really great project managers to open their Florida park, but most of them came from other industries. They didn't know much about ride engineering, which is a really complicated thing. Universal just wanted their rides to be 'Wow!' by any means necessary. Could the sharks swim faster? Could they move around more? Could the boats rock harder from side to side? Being so new to this, Universal didn't always understand what exactly they were asking for with these kinds of requests. We would try to reel them back in from taking any more risks with the equipment but we weren't always successful. I think that was probably the ultimate demise of the attraction. There was so much underwater force being transferred through the sharks and the boats that the steel couldn't handle it all. Even the concrete substrate couldn't take all the forces at work! But it was sure impressive while it lasted.

**Both the Jaws ride and Earthquake were mandated to open with the park on June 7, 1990. Was the pressure of that deadline felt by the staff at Ride & Show Engineering?**

It most certainly was. I was fortunate in that I was a young marketing guy, so I wasn't actually responsible for any of it. But I did have a front row seat to watch this thing come together over more than a year or so. The specifications on Jaws were so cutting edge and innovative. That alone made it a really complex project. When you slap a hard deadline on something like that, it becomes exponentially more complicated because you're now racing against time to get it ready. Like I said, Universal Studios Florida was a billion dollar project. That kind of money puts a certain pressure on everyone involved. The money people were saying to us, '*I don't care what you do or how you do it, but Jaws had better be ready by opening day!*'

I can honestly say that there's a valuable lesson to be learned here. I stayed in the theme park business another twenty years after this but I never forgot it. Jaws taught me about something called "test and adjust." It's a crucial phase that must occur before a ride is ready to go. It's ultimately up to the park as to whether they want that to happen in front of the public or not. It doesn't matter to the ride itself. But you can't put a date on a calendar and demand that a ride be perfect by that date simply by edict. No ride is ever going to work flawlessly right out of the gate. You need extensive testing first, especially if you've changed anything at all from the initial planning and engineering. Test and adjust is all the more important on projects that are complex or revolutionary. Those never work perfectly right away. There are bound to be surprises you have to adjust for. Again, whether or not you want guests to see that process is up to the park. In the case of Jaws, it was a very public phase.

**What was your impression of the first Jaws ride when it worked?**

It was positively breathtaking. I thought it was incredibly realistic. When the shark swam up and grabbed onto the boat, the ride vehicle actually jerked up and moved with the shark. I mean, you know you're at Universal Studios and that it's obviously fake, *but still*. When you see a shark headed straight for you and it's not stopping and it rams your boat, it's exciting! Everybody would hold on and scream in those moments. We actually had to manage how much of an impact those movements had on guests to account for younger and older riders. When Jaws worked, it was an extremely fun attraction.

**Did the ride's opening day troubles come as a surprise to Ride & Show? Or were they somewhat expected?**

We knew there would be issues long before the park opened. It was such a unique thing to have two huge motion bases interacting with one another and spinning around in unison. I don't think anyone at Ride & Show expected that effect to work right away but we were optimistic that we'd figure it out at least before opening day. Things got fairly contentious between us and Universal the closer we got to the park's opening. The pressures were increasing exponentially by the day, which was not a great environment to be making smart decisions in.

Top: The Shark Fin #3 platform raised out of the water for maintenance.

Bottom: Is that Amity Three sinking? Nope! It's Tours Three from the original ride.

(Photos courtesy Jeff Clay)

**How about Universal's eventual decision to shut down the ride? Did that come as a surprise?**

Not really. Universal had begun taking control from us little by little in the months before it opened. They were hiring their own people to oversee engineering and design modifications. We were slowly losing control of our own project. It was tragic what ultimately happened on Jaws. It was never given the proper time to test and adjust. Plus Universal was trying to operate it at such a high level. I think they ultimately closed it out of sheer frustration. The conclusion they reached seemed to be, '*These motion bases are just too big and too powerful. They are literally tearing up the concrete floor of the pool. No more fixes or repairs. We need to start over from scratch.*' And that's what they did.

I think their goal with the next version of the ride was success by any means necessary. And so they simplified it as a means of achieving that goal. Jaws was a completely different attraction when it re-opened. The second version had much smaller motion bases that behaved much differently toward the boats. It was nowhere near as complicated as what we were trying to do, as though Universal just said, '*Let's get a shark and a boat that can move through the water and we'll call it a day.*' It wasn't bad by any means. It was just less ambitious.

**How difficult did the Jaws ride's highly publicized troubles make your job as director of marketing?**

Very difficult. Universal tried to blame all of their problems with the park opening on Ride & Show. If you go back and read all of the stuff that was going on at the time, you'll see that we were just one of many vendors that were struggling to meet their demands.

**So you thought Ride & Show was being used as a scapegoat?**

I did, yes. Here I was this new guy in marketing and I get a phone call from the Wall Street Journal saying, '*Universal is blaming Ride & Show for the park not being ready by opening day.*' It's in that moment I take a very deep breath. I pray about these kinds of things, you know. I go, '*Look, we're a small company out in California building a couple of attractions for them. To say we have that much influence over a billion dollar theme park would be fairly complimentary. We're just not that influential to anybody.*' I would then direct them to speak with Universal's other vendors who were also struggling with them, various companies, food suppliers, and unions. I thought it was hilarious that people thought we were that significant, but we weren't. And I got quoted all around the world. It made them look a bit silly.

**That sounds like a pretty diplomatic way of making your point.**

Thanks. Again, that's why I pray about these things so that I don't wind up saying the first thing that pops into my mind. I think the reality of the situation is reflected in a famous quote about MCA Universal from the LA Times in the early '90s. It said something to the effect of, '*Universal sees their legal department as a profit center.*' I think that spoke volumes as to how they saw their relationships with vendors. The irony is that I only worked for Ride & Show a little while longer before I was hired by Intamin in 1992 as a sales manager for their ride systems. The next thing I know I'm involved in the second version of Jaws and also Back to the Future! I told them right away, '*I probably shouldn't be involved in anything having to do with Universal Studios. Don't even tell them I'm here.*' Intamin's engineering was all done in Switzerland, so those ride parts were all fabricated there and then sent here. I really had nothing to do with the construction aspects of those attractions.

For the next year, I wound up being the project manager for the MGM Grand Adventures Theme Park in Las Vegas. That park was only around for three years or so before MGM decided to plow it over and put a sports facility in its place. This was back when Las Vegas thought family friendly attractions were the way to go. Turns out that wasn't a great way to grow the market. People want to escape their kids in Vegas, not bring them along!

**It's rumored that MGM purchased the original Jaws ride boats for their Backlot River Tour. Any truth to that?**
Yes, that's true. MGM had six attractions and the Backlot River Tour was one of them. And yes, we recycled the boats from the original Jaws ride on that attraction. We took them to a local fiberglass guy who had them fixed up and repainted. MGM was big on things like that because it saved them a lot of money. The first monorail between Bally's and MGM was an old Disney monorail that had been sitting in a warehouse for a decade or more.

**Did you ever go back to ride the second version of the Jaws ride?**
No, I never did. I typically tried to keep my distance from Universal after that. I was surprised that Jaws lasted as long as it did in the park. It was a heck of a concept. To Universal's credit, they were committed to doing something very impressive. While I would not support how they got there, they did get there and invested to keep it working for many years. Jaws was ultimately an amazing attraction. There was a time in the '90s when Universal Studios Florida was arguably the best theme park in the world because of rides like Jaws. That's just my observation as a customer.

The original 1990 boat fleet as later seen at the MGM Grand Adventures Theme Park.

# WHAT SANK THE ORIGINAL JAWS RIDE?

an interview with

## ALAN J. ARENA

### Head of Engineering
### Ride & Show Engineering Inc.

Logo insignia for the Jaws ride's 1990 design team, which adorned construction hats and t-shirts.

**How did you become involved with the Jaws ride?**

I was head of engineering for Ride & Show at the time. Ed Feuer and Bill Watkins had started the company back in the '80s. They had been high up in Walt Disney's engineering department and left to start Ride & Show shortly after Epcot opened. That was when Disney decided they didn't want to have their own ride engineering and manufacturing departments anymore. So you quite suddenly had an explosion of engineers leaving Disney to do their own thing. Universal saw that as an opportunity to upgrade their park on the hill out in Hollywood, which they did. They also saw it as an opportunity to compete head to head with Disney in Orlando. Feuer and Watkins did several things for Universal's backlot tour including upgrading the old Jaws gimmick and adding the Earthquake tram stop. They built a great reputation with Universal on these projects. This was about the time I joined them as head of engineering.

I can remember being in Florida working on the Norway Pavillon for Disney when I first heard that Universal was going to be opening something in Orlando. Disney initially thought it was just going to be another park on the hill, no big deal, just a studio tour or something. They weren't much concerned about it. Then the details came out and they were quite surprised that it was going to be a full fledged theme park, something that could directly compete with them. It was an interesting time.

**What was the early development like on the Jaws ride?**

We first had to show Universal proof of concept, that we knew how to move a mechanical shark through water. There was some early testing that occurred in Hollywood. They had a pond way in the back where we set everything up. This wasn't the Jaws pond on the tour but another part of the lot that was off limits to guests. We installed a test track and a full body shark to show we could do some of the basic shark movements that Universal was wanting. And it worked great. It wasn't guest ready or anything, but it proved that we could do it. So we won a contract to do the ride along with Earthquake. Bill Watkins was so energized for the ride and really went after it. They had an amazing concept for the Jaws attraction, especially the big attack scene. It was going to be state of the art. No one else in the world had an attraction like this at the time. The project was so ambitious as first described to me that I had some initial concerns about it.

**In your eyes, how did Jaws compare to Universal's other opening day attractions?**

I'd say Jaws was probably the most ambitious of them all. Certainly Kong and Earthquake were big envelope pushers in their own right, but Jaws was so much more complex because it involved water. There was so much we had to figure out on our own. No one knew much about the dynamics of moving mechanical sharks through the water or the life span of the materials we were using. It was all new. No one had ever done anything even remotely like this before, particularly the shark-bites-boat scene.

The 1990 ride's notorious boat-chomping shark lifted out of the water. (Photo courtesy Jeff Clay)

**Tell me about the infamous attack scene.**

The engineering on that was complex. Basically, we had a shark on one track intercepting a moving boat on another track, all happening in water. Those two moving things would have to lock onto one another in order to achieve the desired effect. Yet we also had to design it in a way so that the ride could recover and move on if the shark and boat failed to hook up, which happened quite often.

We later came to realize that the shark-bites-boat effect worked best with the more aggressive ride operators. We simply assumed that the operators, the skippers I mean, would have the throttle wide open until the shark appeared and then back off the throttle. This was too often not the case. Many of the operators would, in anticipation of the shark, ease off the throttle too early, which meant the boat would arrive in its designated spot too late. When that happened, the shark would fail to lock onto the boat and the gimmick wouldn't work. We eventually suggested to Universal that we switch to an autopilot system but they didn't want to do that. They wanted to leave control of the boats to the ride operator, so the scene became very hit or miss. If you rode Jaws and had a more aggressive ride operator, you got the full effect of that scene. If you had a less aggressive ride operator, the boat slowed down, never connected with the shark, and the scene didn't work.

We did a dry run of that scene in the shop at Ride & Show and it did work. Granted, it wasn't in the water but we had the track, the shark, the whole set up. At no point did someone stop and say, '*You know, we might get an operator that's going to back off the throttle here*.' That was never even a concept for us. We had extensive plans, paperwork, all kinds of documentation. We had Universal come out for a formal sign-off on the test saying it was okay to ship this to Florida for installation. But the human factor complicated things as did last minute changes Universal requested.

**What last minute changes?**

There were several changes very late in the project, changes that ultimately sank the ride. As someone with a background in engineering, aerospace, and weapons systems, I knew the importance of having the right contract documentation figured out and signed beforehand. The original Jaws ride contract said that we were supposed to have clear water in the lagoon, so we designed the materials to work in a filtered pool water environment. Somewhere along the way, Universal decided that they didn't want clear water because that would allow you to see down below the surface to the boat track and shark pits. So they added a suspended clay to the water to give it that murky look they were wanting. It was such a late change that we didn't have time to react to it and it wound up causing a lot of grief with all the mechanisms. We had underwater sliders that were supposed to be moving in clear water, not murky water. The underwater seals we had used weren't strong enough to keep the clay from getting into places it shouldn't have been. As a result, the sharks wouldn't move right or they would get stuck in place. It was a decision that hugely impacted the quality of the ride. You can't re-do the engineering on something that late into a project.

**Were some of these essentially beginner's mistakes on Universal's part?**

On some level, yes. But we had just gone through something like this with Disney on the Norway Pavilion. Disney made a lot of these same mistakes because they weren't accustomed to having an outside contractor do the upfront engineering. They never had to worry about a contract before. They would just load up their money cannons and shoot them at a ride until it was ready. When there's a contract involved, there are lawyers that want to hold the contractor accountable to that contract. Then when you start to have changes, it becomes all about money. Who's going to pay for those changes? Unfortunately, these two projects happened so close together that we weren't able to apply what we learned on Norway to Jaws.

When you're doing something that's never been done before, you need to have design reviews along the way. That's where you put the smartest minds on a project in a room together and they tear apart the design. When they're finished, they should all agree on what the best approach going forward will be. When you do that, you've got ownership on both sides, the customer and the contractor. Disney understood that. Universal didn't. When both sides sign off on a design review, it keeps the customer from coming back a month later and going, '*Why isn't this working perfectly? You're the expert. You should've known better. You now have to pay the full cost to fix this!*' That's what Universal tried to do. You're talking big dollars when you try to re-engineer a project that far along. That we didn't have design reviews and shared ownership is, I think, a big part of what killed the original Jaws ride. It very quickly became an '*us versus them*' thing, which was a poor situation to be in.

**It's been well documented that the filmmakers had trouble with the mechanical sharks on the Jaws films, particularly the original. Were your challenges on the ride similar at all to those of the filmmakers?**

I see why someone might wonder about that, but no. The way you would attack a problem in filmmaking is entirely different than how you would in a theme park. On a movie, the goal is to have something work once or twice, however many times they need to shoot it. On a ride, you need that thing to work and then reset itself every twenty-five to thirty seconds only to go again. That's a whole different design criteria. It's one of the reasons people who do show action equipment for rides typically stay out of filmmaking and special effects because the engineering behind them is just so different. You can do things on a one time basis pretty easily without much planning or research. That's not the case on a ride where you've got to consider so many different aspects, things like fatigue analysis to make sure an effect is going to live forever if need be. On rides, you have to build show elements much more robustly because of their application.

**Were you ever able to actually experience the original Jaws ride?**

Sadly, no. I never got to ride it because I wasn't in Orlando for the installation. Our version of Jaws had closed by the time I was able to get down there. I was very disappointed about that because all its engineering had been done on my watch. I knew what it was supposed to do and it would have been phenomenal. I just wish we had been able to correct the two big things that Ride & Show had not foreseen, which were the ride operators and the quality of the water. Had we fixed those issues, I think the first Jaws ride could have stayed there forever.

Truthfully, the whole Jaws project was a bittersweet set of events. I ultimately left the company over it. I left just before the installation started but after all the testing had been done. I tried to tell the owners about the problems I was noticing. One of them said, '*Yes, I understand that but there's nothing we can do.*' And the other one said, '*There's nothing wrong with Jaws. Everything's fine. If you really believe something's wrong, you should leave.*' So I left. I couldn't be in an environment where I saw problems coming and no one would address them. I heard from others after I left about all the problems that went on. From what I was told, it was not a pretty scene.

**If you could go back and tell yourself one thing heading into Jaws, what would it have been?**

Hmm... I think I would try to convince myself to bring a different perspective to the project. We were too focused on the guest perspective. At one point, we even arranged our chairs in a meeting like we were on a boat in order to visualize the ride from their standpoint. We should have also been looking at things more from an operator standpoint. We missed on that. I would also have told myself to push the design a little further so that the ride system could handle any kind of water, not just pool water. But that's hindsight.

Opposite Top: One of the 1990 boats at the load dock. Captain Jake's original fleet was distinguishable from the later '93 ride vehicles by their rounded canopies and pontoon bumpers. (Photo courtesy Jeff Clay)

Opposite Bottom: The 1990 kill shark in the drained lagoon during installation. (Photo courtesy Tom Reidenbach)

# THE MAIDEN VOYAGE OF AMITY BOAT TOURS

an interview with

## JEFF CLAY

**Opening Team Skipper (1990 version)**
**Attraction Lead**

Skipper Jeff strikes a pose by the hanging shark.

(Photo courtesy Jeff Clay)

**How did you become a part of Universal Studios Florida's opening team?**

I was living in Baltimore at the time. A guy I went to college with had moved down to Orlando and told me I should move down too because Universal was opening up. He said, '*They're going to have actual studios down here. You can get production work even if you just work in the park.*' That sounded good so I said, '*Why not?*' I moved down to live with him just as Universal was doing all their hiring right before the park opened. I think the starting rate for Ride & Show positions was $5.35 an hour. I got the job and began training a few weeks later. I had to work at Olive Garden until the Universal job started up.

**How did you prepare to become one of the first Jaws ride skippers?**

Training started about three months before the park opened. We opened in June 1990 and training began around March. They were dead serious about the first Jaws crew. For whatever reason, they wanted all male skippers, so the opening crew were all guys. On top of that, they wanted the better looking guys from the Ride & Show Department, so it was kind of a cool thing to be chosen for this. Every day we would walk around the unfinished park. They were still building the roadways and sets. It was essentially one big construction site. We spent a lot of time in a classroom with an acting coach who would teach us how to act out the spiel. Then we had lifesaving classes at the local Aquatic Center where the Olympians trained. Universal felt that was necessary since some of the shark pits were going to be quite deep. We had to dive to the bottom of this fourteen foot pool, pick up a heavy brick, and bring it back to the surface. We trained on every aspect of the ride from the story to the mechanics. We felt like we were ready about a month before the park opened so we spent our remaining days watching Jaws the movie over and over again. We'd sometimes watch it twice a day and then go find odd jobs to do around the park.

I was one of the original Jaws skippers but I didn't stay a skipper for very long. We had three leads when we opened, which were like managers. Those three were very quickly promoted to supervisors around the park, so I moved up to become a Jaws lead almost right away. As you probably know, Universal's opening day was pretty disastrous because Jaws wasn't ready nor was King Kong. I think Earthquake might have been running intermittently that first week. Needless to say, people were pretty disappointed. We got really good at handling angry customers on a daily basis and doing what we could to make them happy.

The original opening crew was all male but that soon changed. Several women began complaining until someone finally asked human resources, '*Why can't females work on Jaws?*' And, of course, there was no good reason why they couldn't so they soon joined in. One of the first to break that barrier was a skipper named LisaMarie Gabriele who complained to the right people in order to get hired on at Jaws.

**What was your impression of the original Jaws ride?**

When Jaws worked, it was awesome. The original ride was different from the one most people experienced with all the explosions. The beginning and boathouse scenes were exactly the same. I think they jazzed the boathouse up a little in the second version. The big change was when you left the boathouse. Originally, the shark would bite onto the boat's pontoon and drag it around. That required the mechanical shark to actually latch onto the boat. The problem was that your latch rate on most days was around fifty percent. If you were out there spieling and the shark didn't latch onto the boat, you basically floated through that scene in a very strange way. There was nothing you could really do to cover in that situation. People could usually tell that something that was supposed to happen didn't happen.

The ending was also different. In our version, the skipper would eventually fire a grenade into the shark's mouth. The shark would then go under the boat, rocking it back and forth. The skipper would ask the crowd, '*Did I get him? Did I get him?*' and then on the other side of the boat there would be this huge bloody explosion. Meat pieces would fly up into the air and the water would turn red. People loved that! Again, when it all came together and worked, the ride was awesome. When one or more things broke down, it wasn't so great.

**So you preferred the original version of the ride?**

I did actually like our original version better than the re-tooled one. I thought ours was creepier. It was a little more shocking with the shark's appearances. People were blown away when it would grab onto the boat and drag it through the water. That was such a great ride to spiel on when you had a full boat because people had so much fun with it. You figure they probably had to wait a long, long time to ride Jaws standing in the summer heat. That was an outdoor queue, so it got very warm in there. If you're a guest and you wait ninety minutes to ride a six-minute ride, you're going to have fun whether you actually like it or not. Fortunately, the Jaws ride could deliver. People were always so responsive to it - screaming, laughing, and cheering along with the action.

**In your experience as a skipper, what effect was most likely to fail on the original ride?**

The biggest issue that I recall just happened to involve the best scene in the entire attraction, which was the shark latching onto the boat and dragging it around. Fortunately, that took place halfway through the ride so a failure to latch didn't necessarily ruin the entire experience because you still had more shark appearances beyond that one. It just meant you had to deal with an awkward thirty-second dead space in the middle of the ride. The exploding shark finale was still an exciting finish regardless of whether or not we latched.

Failure to latch wasn't the only problem with that scene, though. I can remember being the skipper on the first official run through of Jaws the night before the park opened. This boat was full of journalists, photographers, and their families. One of them snapped a photo that wound up on the front page of the Orlando Sentinel's local section. If you look closely at that photo, you can see that the shark has almost no teeth left. Not only was the latch effect hit or miss, but it would latch on so hard that it would knock the shark's teeth out from impact with the boat! It's hard to be scared of Jaws when Jaws doesn't have any teeth. We had another name for that particular shark. He was Gums to us. Gums the shark.

Skipper Jeff aboard the Orca as originally docked outside Quint's shack.
(Photo courtesy Jeff Clay)

**Did you ever have a celebrity guest on one of your boats?**

Yes, several. But there was one I'll never forget. The park was still open but the Jaws ride had closed for the day. There were only a few of us working to cycle boats so the engineers could work on the ride. I was about to send the next boat through when I hear the guy running the control board come over the radio. '*Hold up. There's a couple of VIP's coming through. They want you to take them around the ride.*' I said, '*Okay, sure.*' Then I see Steven Spielberg and Peter Alexander, who was a park executive at the time, walking up. They take a seat in the back row of my boat. I'd seen plenty of celebrities at Universal before and never gotten star struck, except for maybe Charlton Heston, but Spielberg had been my idol growing up. Suddenly, I was paralyzed! He was so nice too. He said, '*Hey, how are you doing? I really want to see the ride because we're thinking of changing some things. If you could just take us around and do your regular spiel, that'd be great.*' When you hear that, the first thing you think is, '*Holy crap, this is Steven Spielberg! If I do this really well, he could make me a star!*' (laughs) Sadly, it did not work out that way. It was not easy taking him around the ride. Doing Jaws with a boatload of people was easy because their reactions made it fun. But when it's just you, Steven Spielberg, and Peter Alexander, it's so nerve wracking! I think we did actually latch up that time. Spielberg was also kind after the ride and said, '*That was really good. You did a great job. Thanks a lot.*' And that was it. I never became a star! (laughs)

The shuttered Jaws ride entrance circa 1990 (Photo courtesy Jeff Clay)

**Did you ever have any crazy guest experiences in your time at Jaws?**

We had one major event. I wasn't driving the boat that day but I was there as a lead. Someone hit the emergency stop over on the far side of the lagoon where the main scene was. I'm talking about where the shark bites the boat. That's where we had the biggest, deepest pit with the most machinery in the entire lagoon. It was the absolute last place you would want to fall overboard. Apparently, a guest fell hard against the safety bar when the shark latched onto and shook the boat. And apparently this safety bar had either a missing pin or a broken pin because it came off altogether, which sent the guest out of the boat and into the water. I was so proud of the skipper for immediately hitting the e-stop, which shut down the entire ride literally one second after the guy fell over. They grabbed him and pulled him right back into the boat, so he was only in the water for a few seconds. The skipper then brought the boat to unload and the guy was totally fine. That was the biggest emergency I can remember. The far more common emergency we faced involved people passing out in the queue from dehydration or from the hot sun.

**At what point did you start to realize that the kinks in the ride weren't being worked out?**

Not for a while, actually. The engineers had things working pretty well at first. You'd have several weeks of almost everyone latching up in Scene Four. You can quote me as saying that the ride ran well for a very brief period in time. Obviously I'm not an engineer, but I got the impression that the fixes that were in place were not going to be long term solutions. The underwater machinery just wasn't going to be able to handle all of the abuse from the latching and the water pressure and forcefulness of the shark's movements. They knew it wasn't going to hold up forever. I will say that I'm really glad for the thousands of people that did get to experience the original version of the ride because it was definitely the hit of the park. Kong was certainly a big hit as well but there was something about Jaws that people just loved so much more. It was fun while it lasted.

**You worked at Jaws and King Kong? Why did you get to have all the fun?**

It *was* fun! It was so much fun. There were a considerable number of people in the Ride & Show department so getting to be a Jaws lead in particular was pretty special. All the girls wanted to date the Jaws guys or at least that's what my girlfriend told me at the time. Being a lead is kind of like being a manager, but you still have your turns in the rotation. I loved it. I could've spieled that ride thirty times in a row. People were so excited and energized getting on that ride.

**Did you ever get to ride the second version of Jaws?**

I did. Although I moved back up to Baltimore after I left Universal, I did eventually come back down to visit the park while on vacation with friends. And of course I had to see how they changed the attraction. It was a little strange hearing the boat drivers do the spiel because it was still kind of familiar to me. Half of it was, anyway. They made some major changes to the final scenes of the ride. Jaws was, in my opinion, still a really fun attraction to go on. I re-visited the ride several more times over the years as well.

**How much of a disappointment was the ride's closure in 1990?**

It was very sad. The thing about the first Jaws crew is that we all really liked our jobs. There were no limits on overtime back then, so we were working sixty to eighty hours a week by choice and we loved it. I was working at Jaws so much that I literally began to dream about the ride. I still remember the lagoon water. It was dyed dark during operation but otherwise it was clear, particularly when they were working on the ride. They had these white square things called diapers that would float around and soak up the excess hydraulic fluid. I'll never forget waking out of a dead sleep in my bed and thinking the t-shirts on my bedroom floor were diapers in the lagoon. I was still half in my dream trying to find the boat throttle in my bed. That's when I realized I was probably working too many hours on the ride.

# HOW TO KILL THE SHARK USING ONLY YOUR BOAT

an interview with

## LISAMARIE GABRIELE

**Opening Team Skipper (1990 Version)**
**The First Female Skipper**

Skipper LisaMarie takes aim with the grenade launcher.

(Photo courtesy LisaMarie Gabriele)

**How did you come to join the ranks of Amity Boat Tours?**

Prior to Universal, I worked at another theme park as an entertainer. The company that I worked for was a contract company. When they were released from their contract with the park I was consequently released from my contract. I initially auditioned as an entertainer at Universal but wasn't hired on. So I applied for a regular position and was hired into the Ride & Show Department. When I went in for my final interview, they asked me where I wanted to work. I immediately told them I wanted to work at Jaws. The guy's response was, '*You can't work at Jaws because there won't be any women hired on at Jaws.*' I was a little surprised by that. I asked him why and he said, '*Uh, we're going with the time period in which the movie is set and back then there weren't any female boat drivers.*' My response to that was, '*What about all the other positions within the attraction?*' He said they work in a rotation system where you switch positions throughout the day and eventually you would have to rotate onto a boat.

I remember the discussion very well. The more he tried to explain to me why women couldn't work at Jaws the more uncomfortable he became. I think he came to realize from his own words that the whole idea was pretty stupid. He eventually said, '*I'll tell you what. Let's send you over to Jaws temporarily until we can place you somewhere else and we'll see how it goes.*' Keep in mind, this was about a week before the park opened. I agreed to that and went over to the wardrobe department to get my skipper uniform. Unfortunately, they didn't have any female uniforms because they hadn't planned on having female skippers. They gave me one of the guy t-shirts and some pants from E.T. Adventure. I still remember walking up to the ride that day. There was a group of young men sitting on a boat with a woman who was training them on their script, basically an acting coach. Their conversation stopped as I approached. One of them said something to the effect of, '*What is SHE doing here?*' I immediately turned on my acting abilities and said, '*Oh, I'm only here temporarily just to observe.*' And then they all relaxed.

**Whoa. Was this 1990 or 1930? Never mind that the last Jaws movie had a female lead killing the shark.**

It was 1990, believe it or not, but there weren't going to be any women at Jaws. Some of the men were very put off by the thought of having female skippers. And it didn't matter to them what happened in the last Jaws movie because the ride was based on the first one. That was their reasoning.

**What made you choose the Jaws ride in the first place?**

I remember going to see Jaws when it was first released back in the '70s. My father took me. I was probably eleven years old. He would go to the movies every week. This was back when you could see a double feature for $1.25. He thought I would enjoy this new movie coming out called Jaws, not realizing I was going to have nightmares for months. My mother was so pissed! I became very intrigued by the movie as I grew older, the magic of the special effects and the filmmaking techniques. When I went to work for Universal I wanted to be a badass, plain and simple. I wanted to be the badass female boat driver that blew up the shark.

**What was training in that kind of environment like?**

It wasn't easy. I would sit in the back of the boat and listen to the guys working with the acting coach. I tried my best not to be noticed, but I listened and learned. They never even gave me a script. I memorized the spiel from listening to everyone else. This went on for a week until the park opened. Then we got to opening day and the ride never actually opened to guests. It wasn't ready. I was assigned to be the person standing outside the queue next to a sign that said, '*The Jaws ride won't be open today*.'

**I hope they gave you a bulletproof vest for that position. Or at least some kind of shield.**

I remember thinking to myself, '*If I'm ever gonna be a badass, now is the time!*' I stood out front and greeted countless angry people one after another the entire opening day. I turned on the charm and steered them toward what was open, which wasn't much. The only big ride that was working was E.T. Adventure. Nothing else was ready! Kong wasn't ready. Earthquake wasn't ready. Jaws wasn't ready. Back to the Future wasn't even built yet. There were a lot of very angry people. One guy even spit on me.

There was another man who started yelling at me from halfway down the street. He saw this diminutive female standing next to a sign outside Jaws so obviously it was not open. He was hollering and cussing. As he got closer, I could hear what he was screaming. '*We flew all the way from New York for this ride and you're saying that it's closed!?!*' I very calmly looked at him and said, '*Do you mean to tell me that you and your family got on an airplane and flew all the way to Orlando just to ride Jaws?*' And he screamed, '*God damnit, yes!*' And I very calmly said, '*What a silly thing to do.*' He looked at me confused, like '*What did she just say?*' I took his map from him and started showing him everything he could do in the park that day and pointed him in those directions. Most of his options were shows and not rides, but by the time I got done talking to him he hugged me, so I think I did my job that day.

**How justified do you think that opening day anger was from guests?**

Fairly justified. When people come to a theme park, they don't come just to see shows. They want to go on rides. Universal had advertised a whole new state of the art theme park experience that they simply were not ready to deliver on. These were not roller coasters or merry-go-rounds. These were simulator rides, the kind that had never been done before. Disney didn't have anything like this. On Earthquake, Universal was giving you the feeling of what it was like to be in an actual earthquake. On Jaws, Universal was giving you the feeling of what it was like to be attacked by a great white shark. Yes, we all knew it was fake, but it was still incredible. People would arrive so excited for these experiences only to be told that they couldn't ride them.

There was one point on opening day where a rumor went out across the park that they were finally going to open Earthquake. Guests literally bolted from every direction to the attraction because they were so desperate to ride something. The Earthquake attendants and supervisors had to form a human chain to keep the crowd back. It was getting to be riot status. The guests were trying to push their way onto the ride, which wasn't going to open because the rumor was false. I had a supervisor friend who got his arm broken that day because they were pushing so hard on the human chain. That's how angry people were over this. It was quite a day.

The 1990 boat fleet lined up at the unload platform. (Photo courtesy Jeff Clay)

**In your opinion, should Universal have pushed the opening date back?**

They already pushed it back. The park was originally scheduled to open in May. They knew they weren't going to be ready then so they pushed it to June. Universal was going to open the park in June come hell or high water so they did. And it was certainly hell. The technicians were working twenty-four hour shifts trying to get these attractions up and running. They just needed more time.

**Opening day was disastrous. What was the next day like? Any better?**

It was a little better because Universal realized they had to do something to appease the guests. They knew that by the end of the first day. People planned entire vacations just for this grand opening. They spent a lot of money to come through those gates and were left incredibly disappointed. Before closing on the first day, the upper echelon decided that they weren't going to refund everyone's money but that they would issue passes for people to come back. They told guests, '*This pass can be used indefinitely. It does not expire. If you come back tomorrow, you'll experience the same thing you experienced today. But if you come back in a month or next year, you can use this ticket to get in and things will be working then.*' That helped a lot. Anyone who came that first week got a free return ticket. Guests were still frustrated and annoyed but they knew they had that free ticket.

**So you made it through training and opening day. How did you finally wind up getting on a boat?**

By pure happenstance! One of the skippers called in sick which left them short handed. They were going to have to pull one of the boats offline if they didn't put me into rotation. That would've made for even longer lines, so they let me onto a boat and spiel. We had been open for several weeks by then.

The shark must've eaten the canopy off this boat. (Photo courtesy LisaMarie Gabriele)

**What was your impression of the original Jaws ride?**

It was exciting but not always in a good way. I thought the original Jaws was an excellent idea that, unfortunately, was not very well executed. One of the problems involved the boats. Universal had wanted to make Jaws as realistic as possible. Consequently, the ride had actual free floating boats. These were not ride vehicles on a track but real boats that traveled along a pit underneath the water. We as skippers controlled the boat's speed and direction, though we couldn't steer outside the designated pit area which was quite narrow. This gave guests the impression that they were actually riding out on the open water. The downside to this realistic approach was operator error. When you give an inexperienced ride attendant the ability to control a boat but you need that boat to be in a certain position at a certain time for the ride to work... they're going to screw that up. We soon came to realize that it didn't take much at all to screw things up at Jaws. That's simply what happens when you put the control of a boat in the hands of people with no experience controlling boats.

I'll give you an example. Your boat had to be in a certain position for the shark effect to work right when you left the boathouse heading into Scene Four. The effect would not engage unless the boat was maneuvered perfectly. If that happened correctly, the boat would click into position with the animation unit. Then we would let go of the wheel and the animation unit would take over. The original Jaws ride didn't have any pyrotechnics or explosions in that scene. Our Scene Four had the shark swimming up and chomping on the boat. The pontoon would deflate and the shark would shake its body, rocking the boat back and forth. Everybody would scream. It was terrifying. If you didn't maneuver the boat just right to make the shark latch on, none of that scene would go as planned.

**Do you remember your last tour around the lagoon?**

I do, unfortunately. Not only was I the first female skipper on Jaws, I was also the skipper who caused the damage that permanently closed that version of the ride. This incident involved the shark I was just talking about. My boat was heading into Scene Four and I was moving into position to connect with the shark. What I didn't know was that my boat had snapped off an underwater latch and coasted a little too far forward. As a result, we came to a stop on top of the animation unit. Somehow it still engaged, which caused the scene to play out with the boat resting on top of the shark's head. The hydraulics were trying to propel the shark out of the water but couldn't because there was a boat in the way. Our ride vehicle starts shaking and suddenly there are nuts and bolts everywhere. I knew right away something had gone horribly wrong. We eventually pull into the unload dock and I tell the young man working there, '*You need to call the supervisor. I just killed the shark.*' And he looks at me and laughs. '*Of course you killed the shark. You're supposed to kill the shark. You're the hero. Yay!*' He got all of the guests cheering for me. I looked at him and said, '*No, no. I mean I really killed the shark! This ride is no longer operational!*' Then the next boat pulls in and the skipper goes, '*What in the hell happened to the shark in Scene Four?!*'

I just knew they were going to fire me over this. I had no idea how much damage had been done but I was convinced it was all my fault. I didn't know at the time that the underwater latch had snapped off. I thought I was going too fast or wasn't steering the boat right. It wasn't until they closed the ride and lifted the animation unit out of the water that they saw what had gone wrong. That was also the day they announced that Jaws would be closed until further notice for some serious repairs.

**It's ridiculous you had to handle the boats considering you were performing and keeping an eye on the guests.**

Exactly. It was too much responsibility for someone who had never done anything like this before. We tried hard to get it right. We trained for weeks at night after the park had closed. We would run practice boats to make sure we could engage the effects just right because it was a huge responsibility. This was a multimillion dollar attraction that depended on us getting it right. But something was bound to happen and it did.

**Did you stay on at Universal after Jaws closed?**

Yes, I did. To my surprise, they did not fire me. They instead moved me over to Earthquake where I sat in the technical director's booth. My job was to make sure all the effects happened safely. I knew when every effect was supposed to happen from the ceiling falling to the wall caving in to the water rushing over the stairs. I had my finger over the emergency stop button in case any guests decided to climb out of the ride vehicles. Keep in mind that the guests were not restrained on Earthquake, so if someone wanted to climb out of the train while all this was happening they could. Fortunately, they never did. At the end I would walk out with a bullhorn like I was the director of a movie and say, '*Cut! That was great! That's a take! Print it!*' And the guests would cheer like they had just been in an actual movie.

They then decided to promote me to lead, which is one step below supervisor. They moved me to Kongfrontation where I did things like make sure guests were flowing through in a timely manner, make sure the ride was clean, make sure all the attendants got their breaks. I did that for several months before I started to feel burned out on the whole theme park thing. I had gone from Jaws to Earthquake to Kong, all of which had their share of technical issues. I finally asked if I could be moved somewhere else before I had a breakdown and they moved me to the Nickelodeon Studio Tour, which was so awesome! I loved that job. All I had to worry about was making sure each tour went in on time. It was a very relaxing position. I did that until the day they told me they were almost ready to re-open the Jaws ride.

**This would be about 1993, right? Did they want you to be a skipper again?**

Yeah, only I wasn't sure that was what I wanted so I asked to be put on the night shift while they worked on the ride. They needed someone to cycle the boats through overnight, which was a very boring position, but that's what I did. They hadn't even installed the sharks yet. I brought a book along to pass the time. I very quickly came to know exactly when the boat was supposed to shake and pitch so I would read my book up until those points, observe the boat rocking, and then continue my reading once it stopped. I did that for several months. So boring!

**But did you even want to be a skipper again on Jaws II?**

At one point, yes. I was planning on following through to the re-opening of the ride, but I didn't want to be a skipper again after having been a lead at Kongfrontation. That was like going backwards. By this point, I had gotten a certain reputation with management for speaking my mind. I know they didn't always like hearing critical feedback from a subordinate. Consequently there were certain managers who did not like me at all, one of whom was going to be over the new Jaws ride. He called me into the office one day and said, '*It's never going to happen. I'm going to make sure you're never a lead on this attraction.*' At that point I was like, '*Thank you. You've just helped me make a major life decision. I quit.*' And I quit. I don't put the blame for that on the whole management team, just that one guy. I know my outspokenness can be a little off putting at times, but I wasn't willing to accept being a spieler again.

**Did you ever go back to ride Jaws II?**

I did! I went back years later with my boyfriend, who is now my husband. That happened to be the weekend he proposed to me, though I didn't know that was the plan. We went to ride Jaws and come to find out when they re-opened the attraction they named one of the boats after me! It said my name right on the front! I asked the attendant, '*Do you know why they named the boat the LisaMarie?*' She told me, '*I heard she was someone who used to work on the ride but got killed.*' (laughs) I was like, '*Well, that's sort of true but not really. Killed in a weird sense of the word, but not physically.*' Then I introduced myself to her. She thought that was the coolest thing ever. I came to find out that the technicians were the ones who got to name the boats on the ride. I had befriended several of them working night shifts just before I left the company and one of them suggested my name. How cool, right?

Top: Good to see that Bruce and LisaMarie are no longer trying to kill each other.

Bottom: The "Lisa Marie" boat from the 1993 ride. (Photos courtesy LisaMarie Gabriele)

# THIS WAS NO BOAT ACCIDENT

## an interview with

## JAMES E. ADAMSON

### Engineering Consultant
### Kinetix Inc. / Perry Tritech Inc.

The 1990 boathouse shark awaiting oral surgery with a duct-taped snout.
(Photo courtesy Tom Reidenbach)

**How did you come to work on the original Jaws ride?**

Around 1987 some friends and I started a company called Suntech Engineers. We did general engineering kind of stuff and in the process discovered that we could do things at the theme parks in Orlando. So we did some new and remedial work at both Disney and Universal Studios, which was just then being built. We ultimately came to realize that we were better engineers than we were businessmen so we folded that venture. In the meantime, we had done some work for a company called Kinetix. After we closed Suntech, the president of Kinetix, a guy named Glenn Burkett, offered me a job as a project manager. They were right in the final throes of their opportunities at Universal Studios during this time. Kinetix had been involved in control systems not only for Jaws but for many of the other rides as well. As it turned out, they were owned by a company called Ride & Show Engineering who were themselves responsible for many of the rides at Universal. Jaws was one of those.

Right as I came on, Glenn and the principles at Kinetix decided that their goals didn't align and Glenn went his separate way. Meanwhile, Kinetix was in the process of troubleshooting some of the problems on Jaws. As soon as they figured out I could do engineering stuff, they assigned me to help repair and redesign Jaws instead of project managing like I was hired to do. I started working on the attraction six months before the park was set to open. There was a scramble to try and get all the attractions working so that the park could open on time.

**In your opinion, how ambitious was the original Jaws ride?**

Quite. My sense was that Universal was attempting to do something incredibly ambitious with Jaws. The mechanical implementation of what they were going for was very difficult. Kong and Earthquake were also hugely ambitious for their time but I thought Jaws was the most ambitious of the three. The most memorable scene within the attraction and also the most difficult to execute was the attack scene where the shark grabs the boat and moves it around.

**Did you that think the ride's problems could be fixed by opening day?**

I'll put it to you like this. When the gentlemen at Ride & Show asked me to help them out on Jaws, I told them I would do it under the condition that my name never get attached to it. I insisted on that because I thought the ride was fundamentally flawed in many ways from the very beginning. There were certain aspects of the original Jaws ride that were not done well at all. In my judgement, they had done a poor execution of an already difficult concept.

**Jaws, like all other attractions, was mandated to be ready by opening day. How did that affect your work?**

We were under a clear deadline which made things very stressful. Universal would feed us on the park grounds so that the only time we really needed to leave was to sleep. We would usually get at least six hours of sleep, sometimes eight. I remember when we *cut back* to one hundred hours one week. That was us cutting back our hours! We thought we were cruising along pretty well at that point but even then it was tense.

**What was your impression of the ride when it worked? I assume you rode it?**

Yes, I rode it a few times. More than a few times, actually. I rode it before the park opened and then again during the celebrity opening. It was a wonderful ride when it worked. I also rode it with the skippers because of the difficulties they were having engaging the latch in the attack scene. I would often coach them on how to best handle that. As a concept, I thought it was a great attraction. I brought my wife and young children to the park to ride Jaws after it opened. I told them ahead of time when and where the shark would appear and they were still terrified despite knowing exactly what was going to happen.

**Did you continue to work on Jaws after the park opened?**

With that many flaws, we might never have finished our work on the project. But I stayed around to oversee Jaws for about a month after the park opened. I left Kinetix at that time to go work for one of my old employers, Perry Tritech. It's kind of strange but the Jaws ride seemed to follow me to my new job. Universal wound up asking Perry Tritech to send a team to help assess some of the difficulties on the ride and whether or not they could ever be truly fixed. And so we did. We had three or four guys go out to the ride for six weeks or so. This was just before they permanently closed Jaws. Our guys helped Universal assess a very disastrous fatal flaw in the attack scene that I think may have been the final nail in the ride's coffin.

In my opinion, the mechanism that engaged the shark in that scene was not robust enough. The whole concept wasn't robust enough in my judgement. The fact that the skipper had to do anything with the boat at all was a flaw in the whole concept of the attraction. As drivers, they had to position the boat in a certain way for the shark attack to engage. If they didn't, it wouldn't work. Not only that, but the mechanism in that scene was already terribly stressed by the ride's opening. The effect was probably under designed because of the original designer's unfamiliarity with doing things underwater.

**I've heard others echo that position, that the skippers shouldn't have been responsible for the boats at all. Some have suggested the first Jaws should have been fully automated as the 1993 version was. Do you agree with that?**

I agree wholeheartedly with that position.

**Did you expect to eventually have to tell Universal that their signature attraction was basically unsalvageable?**

I didn't tell them that right away but I suspected it was the case all along. We did a thorough assessment of the ride and kept discovering one thing after another that was fundamentally wrong with it. We didn't make the decision to close it. That was on Universal to decide. We just gave them our best assessment of the attraction which was thoroughly negative. Honestly, I think it would have been a major improvement if we had switched the ride to an autopilot system. That way the skippers didn't have to do anything to engage the mechanism in the attack scene. The rest of the issues were just a problem of putting all the steel in the right places where things needed to be strengthened.

The grenade shark platform rasied out of the water. The also raised boat-chomping-shark platform can be seen in the distance. (Photo courtesy Jeff Clay)

The final difficulty we discovered happened when we put a couple of divers in the water. The maintenance concept for the attack scene was that the whole foundation rose up so that it could be serviced above the water. This was a giant steel platform that had flotation on it. The flotation also had some problems though we were able to fix those. One day our guys swam underneath the platform and found cracks in nearly every single weld joint. This giant platform was supposed to be welded to the base of the lagoon but the welds were barely holding together. This was a massive problem involving the most basic framework of the ride. The structural foundation of that scene was ready to fail at any moment. I told our guys to get out from under the platform and drain the lagoon immediately. That was the last time the original Jaws ride had water in it. Not a fun day.

That entire platform weighed many, many tons, which made it beyond deadly. The ride technicians would not have ordinarily been swimming underneath it. The whole idea was to not need to put divers in the water that often. Our divers were just doing inspections. Of course, it would've also been bad if you had been on top of the platform above the water and it had failed. You would've gone down with the ship.

**Could those welds have been fixed? Would that have helped the long term reliability of the attack scene?**

Nothing is ever impossible but by then you're typically past the point of making those kinds of changes. The platform could have been repaired but at great cost to Universal. That would have required taking the entire scene apart, foundation and all. You'd need to gouge out and re-weld all the welds. Even if we did that it probably wouldn't have run perfectly as there were other problems affecting that scene.

**Are you saying that the platform wouldn't have been able to remain in place above or even in the water?**

Exactly. The platform would have broken up and gone under. It's hard to say exactly when that would have happened but it definitely would have. With something that big, there was just no way it wasn't going to flex a little bit each time it floated up to the surface. The cracks in the welds would have grown bigger every time that happened. It was truly a disaster waiting to happen. With something like this, I think somebody during the fabrication phase should have looked at somebody else and said, *'My goodness, we're not getting any welds to the bottom of these structural members.'* It's totally conceivable that a structure like this could have been designed and fabricated similar to how they did it, but it needed a bit more care, I think.

**How do you look back at your time working on Jaws?**

I have mixed feelings about it. It was certainly a professional challenge so in that sense it was fun. I will say that I had many more grey hairs after Jaws, that's for sure. I also made lots of lasting friends working on it. Some of the folks that had worked with me on Jaws I still keep in touch with.

**If you had a time traveling DeLorean, what would you go back and tell the 1990 Jaws ride team?**

In my experience, Universal in those days seemed so very interested in their rides and shows. They were also far less risk averse than other theme park companies I had dealings with. In that sense, their attractions were almost always more exciting to ride as a park-goer. Unfortunately, this also made their projects far more challenging from an engineering point of view. I would caution them against that because it can and sometimes does result in a bad ride. I would also encourage them to make sure they gave all their rides the proper engineering and management budgets. They would sometimes skimp on budgets for projects that posed enormous engineering challenges. That's never a good thing.

Top: Tall fences surround the attraction as Jaws closes mere months after opening in 1990.

Bottom: The grenade shark from Scene Five raised out of the water during programming.

(Photos courtesy Thomas Meyer and Tom Reidenbach)

# BONEYARD BRUCE FROM JAWS THE REVENGE

(aka the other shark in the park)

Amity Boat Tours wasn't the only place to find Jaws at Universal Studios Florida. He could also be found hanging out at the Boneyard from 1990 to 2008, which is now the Universal Music Plaza Stage. Guests could take photos with a full shark and fin from 1987's Jaws: The Revenge. Unfortunately, opportunistic fans soon made off with all of Bruce's teeth, resulting in an entirely toothless shark! These props were so badly weathered from the elements by their 2008 removal that Universal discarded them altogether.

Jaws the Shark

Gums the Shark

(Photos courtesy Thomas Meyer)

# REVENGE RELICS

## (aka the queue boats)

The Boneyard sharks weren't the only items from Jaws: The Revenge to be found in the park. The Jaws Ride queue housed two vessels featured in the 1987 sequel - the Amity Police Launch and Neptune's Folly complete with reconstructed bowsprit since the actual one was used to spear the shark in that film's finale. These boats remained outside Jaws from opening day to its closure in January 2012. Unfortunately, they were severely rotted out by then and therefore discarded by the park.

Amity Police
Launch

Neptune's
Folly

# DESIGN ENGINEERING
# THE SECOND JAWS RIDE

an interview with

## BRUCE FARBER

### Mechanical Engineer
### Eastport International

Mayor Vaughn asks that you ignore the legs sticking out from the shark's mouth. (Photo courtesy LisaMarie Gabriele))

**How did you come to work on the original Jaws ride?**

I was working as a mechanical engineer for the Eastport International office in Ventura. Universal had approached Eastport due to its reputation for creating underwater robotic devices for the military and navy. The new Jaws ride was going to be using technology similar to those devices. I first heard about it when the Maryland office asked us to put together a proposal for the project. We were told that the ride had already been built once before by a company called Ride & Show but that there were numerous problems with it. Ride & Show had experience doing theme park attractions but were unable to solve the challenges posed by the Jaws ride. Apparently, they were having to re-weld the ride several times a week just to keep it operational. Universal eventually decided to just close it down and start again. That's when they reached out to Eastport for help.

**What kind of time frame were you working with on this project?**

Eastport spent a lot of time negotiating the Jaws contract with Universal, which I was not a part of. We did do some preparation work in anticipation of winning the contract, however. We looked at what the computer hardware and personnel needs would be to support a project like this. That process dragged on for some months. Then we finally won the contract the week before Christmas 1991. The Jaws ride was originally planned as an eighteen-month project. We spent almost an entire year negotiating it and, unfortunately, they never amended the project's due date to reflect that negotiation time. That meant we only had about six months to design and build the first shark! Plus, the first deliverable we had to prepare for Universal was due two weeks after Christmas, which was going to be an animation showing what that first shark could do. In the meantime, we had to take delivery of the computer hardware, install the software, get trained in the software, hire people, and produce a crude video that would demonstrate the first scene with the shark.

The first piece of software was Pro/Engineer, which was a solid modeling software package that was quite popular at the time. It was very expensive and required a $25,000 machine to run on. We used Pro/Engineer to design the steel structures that transported the sharks through the water. Using that, we ultimately decided upon an approach that included dynamic analysis of the shark's movements. It's sitting there acquiescent underwater and then the scene starts. That scene might last ten or fifteen seconds where the shark moves across a set distance. It would have to accelerate up to a certain speed to make it look as though the shark was already swimming before it broke the surface. There would also be movement of the head, jaws, and body. Then the shark would go underwater again. All of that had to be analyzed for the forces and pressures involved in order to figure out things like how big the hydraulic cylinders had to be or what kind of steel would be needed.

One thing Eastport knew a lot about was added mass. Anytime you accelerate something underwater you're displacing the water that it moves through. So if it's moving at a steady speed like a submarine, all you've got is drag against the hull. But in the case of the Jaws sharks, they were accelerating from zero to seven feet per second in the space of two feet. That is very rapid acceleration. You're displacing tons of water in that half second that it's accelerating. That in turn provides a lot of resistance to movement, which is something Ride & Show failed to account for in their calculations. And Universal always wanted the sharks to move faster. The structures that Ride & Show built were just not set up to do that.

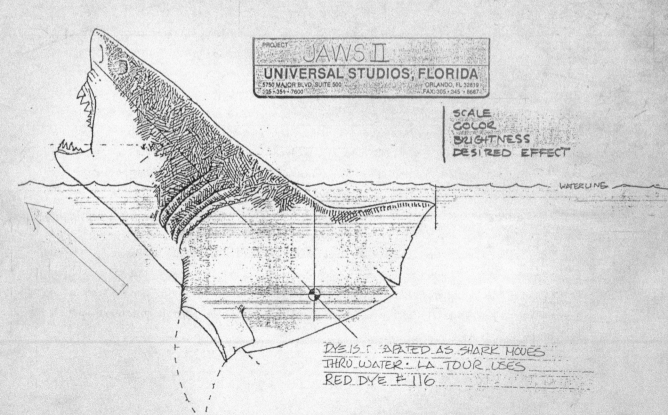

PROJECT **JAWS II**
**UNIVERSAL STUDIOS, FLORIDA**
5750 MAJOR BLVD, SUITE 500   ORLANDO, FL 32819
305·351·7600   FAX·305·345·8687

SCALE
COLOR
BRIGHTNESS
DESIRED EFFECT

WATERLINE

DYE IS SEPARATED AS SHARK MOVES
THRU WATER · LA TOUR USES
RED DYE # 116

We had three very sophisticated and relatively new pieces of software that had to work together and talk with one another, one of which was Pro/Engineer. The salesman we spoke with prior to getting the contract assured us that all three of those programs could do that. When we finally got the contract, we called that salesman back and asked, '*Okay, where do we start?*' And he said, '*I don't know. We haven't actually done what you're trying to do.*' And so we said, '*Okay. Give us the name of a company that has done it. We'll hire them as teachers so they can walk us through it.*' And the salesman goes, '*Well, no one has ever done it before to my knowledge.*'

**Oh, God. That does not sound like a good conversation to have after you bought the software.**
Yes, it was quite stunning to us. So here we had about ten days left to give Universal Studios the first shark animation video and no one on our staff knew how to make these three pieces of software talk to each other.

**Can you break down the three pieces of software you were working with?**
I already mentioned the first, which was Pro/Engineer. It could generate a computer graphic, the kind you see all the time now in commercials and such. It was kind of like assembling the mechanical sharks in the computer before we actually built them. The second piece of software was DADS, which stood for Dynamic Analysis Design Software. That allowed you to put in a bunch of engineering equations in order to see what happened when these structures accelerated and stopped. This was the first time we had used this in an underwater application. The third piece of software was Finite Element Analysis Software, which we used for structural analysis. It showed how far materials could bend and all the different stresses in a given structure. If those stresses become too great, things will bend too much or break altogether, which is what happened to Ride & Show's work.

So we developed a model for the shark animation in the ten days we had left. We knew how big the shark needed to be from talking with Universal. We ran it through the DADS modeling and were able to put in some position versus time data from a LOTUS 123 spreadsheet. We somehow managed to animate the shark moving along a path. It was very crude. I actually brought my video camcorder from home and pointed it at the computer screen because we didn't have the capability to export the animation direct to videotape. We then mailed that to Universal. They came back wanting to know how much power would be needed to move the sharks. We crunched those numbers and the energy requirements were huge. Universal said, '*We don't want the lake to heat up from powering the sharks but we also don't want to have to build a nuclear reactor on site. Show us what we can do within reason.*' They expected to wait another two weeks for a new video but we did it overnight simply by tweaking some things to reduce the energy requirements but still give the sharks the motion Universal wanted. They saw that and replied, '*This video is now the contract document. Build that shark!*'

Opposite: The seldom seen and far less grisly left side of the dead shark and corresponding concept artwork.
(Photo courtesy LisaMarie Gabriele)

With three sharks, Scene Five was the most populous shark pit in the Jaws ride 2.0 (Photo courtesy Jim Beller - JawsCollector.com)

**I take it these pieces of software weren't standard use for most theme park engineers at the time?**

Right. Most of the engineering that was happening at the time would have used some kind of solid modeling software. That was the best way to make sure things fit together correctly when you built them. Structural analysis had been around for decades but was just then being integrated into solid modeling software. The new part in all this was the dynamic analysis. Prior to this, most engineering had been done using hand calculations. You would solve equations on your notepad, which would sometimes take days to produce a single result. We didn't have that kind of time. We had to turn around new results in hours because we were doing this on the fly. We had six months to develop the shark models. That meant figuring out how to build them, weld them, bolt them together, and power them. It's amazing what we accomplished in those six months. It really should've taken us a year or more. But we were confident in what we were doing.

**By this point, we're well into 1992. Wasn't Eastport acquired by Oceaneering International around this time? How, if at all, did that affect your work on the Jaws ride?**

It didn't really affect us in the Ventura office. Frankly, it didn't even affect the Maryland office all that much at first. Oceaneering was wise to listen to Eastport during the transition. They had wanted Eastport for its technology and engineering capabilities. We were more of a fabrication company, which helped to round Oceaneering out a bit.

**Was it important for Eastport to understand why exactly Ride & Show's version of Jaws hadn't worked out?**

Very important. We had discussed that extensively during the proposal phase. Universal had informed us as to how Ride & Show's engineering fell short. Needless to say, we had to make sure that all of the equations not accounted for in their version were accounted for in ours. I was put in charge of the analysis team on Jaws that spring. There were so many things to consider. For example, we came to realize that the shark is actually out of the water for part of the ride. The parts of the sharks that were above the water would not have the same buoyancy, drag, or added mass during those brief moments. So we had to work closely with the DADS software team to come up with new algorithms and equations to model when the sharks were underwater, partially underwater, and then back underwater again. That became critical to consider because the forces were highest when the shark was fully underwater. The forces above the water were quite different. That's also when the shark's head and jaws were moving back and forth. So it was a challenge to model that correctly in the software. To the best of my knowledge, it was the first time something like that had been done before.

**What could've gone wrong if you hadn't taken that into consideration?**

It's possible that the motion would not have been as controlled. The sharks might have moved more like a machine and less like an actual living thing. The vertical forces also changed when the shark popped out of the water. Even a piece of steel weighs less in water than out of water. We had to find small ways to keep the forces down on the sharks. One way we did that was to limit the shark's head movements to when it was out of the water. That helped a little bit.

**This all sounds incredibly complex. Was it a challenge or just another day at the office?**

We were challenged on a daily basis and constantly scratching our heads trying to figure out if what we were doing would make sense in the real world. So you do lots of hand calculations to check your work, make sure you don't have a factor of two off somewhere. This kind of complexity in structural analysis had been done before, but not on the scale and magnitude of the Jaws ride. Toward the end of that spring, we were even modeling the friction of the oil moving through the hoses because it affected how big the pumps needed to be. It was very sophisticated stuff.

**How soon did fabrication begin after those six months of design?**

In some cases, fabrication happened concurrent with our work. We would release certain parts of the structure as we felt confident enough that they were finalized so that the fabrication team could start building it. Everything was built and assembled before being taken apart and trucked down to Orlando and reassembled on site.

**When did you feel confident your team's work had paid off?**

The first test happened in July of that year in Orlando. We sent a team to supervise the fabrication and installation of this particular shark. They installed pressure and flow sensors on the sharks in order to see how close our calculations were to the real world. The data from that first test showed that our predictions for the hydraulic pressures and flows were within 10% of the actual numbers. I was ecstatic over that. It was far better than I'd hoped for. I would've honestly been happy with just being 25% off. At that point, I knew we had predicted the motion and forces correctly. We had designed the whole structure to those same forces, so therefore, the design of the structure was correct. I slept very well that night for the first time in many months.

Some months after that there was an industry conference for Pro/Engineer where thousands of its users would get together to learn about all the different things that had been done with it that year. I had been persuaded by my office manager to go and host a presentation of how we had used their software on the Jaws ride. I figured on being in a room with maybe fifteen or twenty people that would be interested in esoteric stuff like design analysis. I put together some slides to show on an overhead projector. Ha, remember those? When I got there, I found that not only was the room packed with over sixty people but it was standing room only and the conference had to set up monitors outside the room so that additional people could watch! Needless to say, it was dry mouth time and I became very nervous. They later told me there had been about two hundred people in total watching my talk on Pro/Engineer and Jaws. It turned out to be one of the largest presentations at the entire conference. How we used this software to design the Jaws ride was apparently of interest to a lot of people. I got phone calls for months afterwards with people asking me all sorts of questions on how to do this and that. I guess I hadn't realized just how groundbreaking what we'd done was.

**The second version of the Jaws ride ultimately ran for nineteen years before closing for good in early January 2012. Did you expect it would last that long?**

Our goal was for the sharks to have a ten year lifespan doing one-hundred-and-fifty shows a day, seven days a week. Nineteen years? I'm proud of that. We did a good job. The entire company did a good job. Truthfully, we were hoping to get more business out of Universal and some of the other various theme parks. Animatronics were getting to be a big thing in theme parks, especially with Jurassic Park right around the corner. Unfortunately, we knew what it cost to make those the right way and the low price bidders usually won those contracts.

Opposite: The gas dock shark explodes out of the water.
(Photo courtesy Christopher Lord)

# JAWS VERSUS THE
# TEENAGE MUTANT NINJA TURTLES

an interview with

## DAN ROBLES

### Mechanical Engineer
### All Effects Company

Looks like the Ghost of Captain Cutler is loose in the boathouse again. Better call Mystery Inc. (Photo courtesy Colin Peterson)

**How did becoming an engineer lead you to work on the Jaws ride?**

At the time I was just an engineer shopping around for jobs in California. It's sort of a rotating industry out there. You don't really work for anybody. You're contracted so you get a call for a project, work on it, and then it's over and you go find another project. That's what I was doing. I was a young kid in California living the life. If you had an engineering degree and at least some talent, you never suffered for work. It was a fun time. I had gone to work for the All Effects Company, who had been hired to do certain effects on the Jaws ride. All Effects had been doing a lot of animatronic and related effects for movies before and during this time period. Universal had reached out to them to handle certain mechanical effects for the Jaws ride. Not the sharks, but things like the grenade launchers, the flame bar, the exploding barrel, the breakaway dock, things like that. We handled basically anything that moved or had to be reset after the boat drove past. I did all of my work on Jaws at the All Effects workshop in California. I didn't actually experience the ride until I went to the park years later. All things considered, I played a pretty minor role on the Jaws ride but I'm happy to discuss it. I'm just flabbergasted that people are still talking about the ride.

**What would you consider to be the All Effects Company's biggest contribution to the ride?**

Probably the flame bars for the big explosion scene. We over-designed those for reliability purposes. The effect would activate when the boat traveled over a certain knob on the track. The effect would then deactivate when the boat rolled over another knob. With this design, the flames could only be triggered when the boat was actually present. We also installed these protective shrouds that would cover the flame bars as the boat traveled overtop them. That way even if the gas somehow ignited underneath the boat, the flames would travel far away from the guests and not cook anyone. Obviously an effect like that comes with a lot of safety concerns. We did a lot of research on the materials that went into that effect. We chose materials that wouldn't corrode, things like stainless steel and polyurethane. We knew we weren't going to have a chlorinated environment in the lagoon but rather a brominated environment, so we had to know what reacted with bromine. Our main goal was safety but we also wanted to provide something that would last for many, many years with very little maintenance on Universal's part.

**Is that design challenge as daunting as it sounds? Because you're essentially making guests feel as though they're about to burn up in a gas dock explosion without actually burning anyone.**

Not really, no. I was a test engineer on the space shuttle. *That* was daunting! This was really nothing compared to that. Well, not nothing. I thought working on the Jaws ride was really cool. We just took great care to make sure the flame bars ignited near the guests and not actually the guests themselves.

**Tell me about the grenade launchers.**

Did you happen to see the flamethrowers that Elon Musk was recently selling? They were essentially modified roofing torches. We did something similar with the grenade launchers on Jaws. The grenade launchers were a modified propane nail gun. On remote sites you'd have roofers using these propane powered guns that would shoot the nails into wood. If you took that apart, you'd have a combustion chamber and a cylinder that drives the nail. If you removed that and made it a big exhaust port, you'd get an extremely loud noise when you set it off. That's how we did the grenade launchers. Back then, there was a big thing about cars getting stolen all the time. So a lot of cars had these after-market car alarms. We used to go set the grenade launchers off in the back alley behind the All Effects shop. The bang would set off not just one but all of the car alarms. It was hilarious! Shortly after that, they decided that the grenade launcher was a little too loud and asked us to modify it to make it more quiet.

**Interesting. Those props were often silent by the ride's closure.**

They could've run into safety concerns or regulatory problems and switched it off. The props could have worn out. People might not have known how to do upkeep on it. I do know that it was incredibly loud when we made it. We delivered a very loud popping device that let out a huge pressure wave. You felt this thing going off.

**You teased in your e-mail that the Jaws ride had a strange connection to the Teenage Mutant Ninja Turtles...**

Yes! On Jaws we used these programmable logic controllers that were made by Allen-Bradley. They worked from a relay that would switch certain things on at certain times. This was a precursor to having a computerized system. They're used all over the world for different mundane devices. Elevators use them as do water pump systems in high rise buildings. Every time one of the Jaws effects switched on there would be something called EMI or electromagnetic interference. Any sensitive radio driven object near one of these effects would get a static crinkle.

It just so happened that the All Effects Company was working on another project concurrent with the Jaws ride. We had been contracted to do the animatronic turtle masks on Teenage Mutant Ninja Turtles III. To make the expressions on the turtle's faces, they would use the same kind of controllers you would find in a remote control airplane. Off screen you'd have a team of guys working these controllers in order for Raphael and Donatello to move and be expressive. They could remotely move their mouths or blink their eyes or wiggle their noses.

Our problem was that the EMI's coming from the Jaws effects were messing with the turtle masks, which would send them into these insane contortions. So they'd be working with Donatello's face and suddenly he would start making these indescribably funny movements. The puppeteers later tried to duplicate these expressions and couldn't. They were just random electronic impulses from the Jaws effects. These two projects were happening in the same building at the same time and neither could be put off or moved. We eventually had to lay this big metal screen between them to seal off the EMI. It was a pretty hilarious time to be in the shop. Here we are, trying to make these flame bars safe, keeping in mind "Thou shalt not kill," while nearby we've got these ninja stunt guys learning how to do flips with giant shells on their backs!

**Could the reverse have happened? Could the masks have affected the ride effects?**

Oh no, not at all. The effects they were using for Jaws were high voltage whereas the little controllers in the masks were 2.5 volts or something. It was a crazy time at All Effects. They had Johnny 5 and the Energizer Bunny rolling around the shop as I'm trying to work on these Jaws guns!

Above: The thrilling gas dock explosion in Scene Four. (Photo courtesy Colin Peterson)

Right: The All Effects Company's mask work in Teenage Mutant Ninja Turtles III: Turtles in Time.

# PAINTING THE HEAD, THE TAIL, THE WHOLE DAMN THING

an interview with

## LUKE SAWH

**Shark Painter**
**Kinetix Inc.**

Sawh's striking work can be seen at Universal and Disney theme parks throughout the world. (Photo courtesy Luke Sawh)

**How did you become involved with the Jaws ride?**

I grew up in England and always had an affinity for art, model making, and special effects. After college I started working for a few companies doing various things from sculpting to animatronic prop making. Around 1991, I had an opportunity to come work in the United States and actually had a company sponsor me to come over. As of April 1992 I was living here in Florida working for Kinetix. At the time, they were creating the skins for the sharks on the Jaws ride as it was being built. They decided to use me to paint those skins. It is astounding to me that I'm able to get involved with these projects, especially Jaws. I was a huge fan of the original movie when I was a kid, so it was so cool to see my work on display at the ride. Jaws has turned out to be just one of many theme park projects I've been involved with over the years.

**How many sharks did you end up painting?**

I forget the exact number. Weren't there like seven sharks in the entire ride? Some of them were just fin sharks, which consisted of only the tail and dorsal fins. Those didn't have much of a body to them so there wasn't much to paint. The far more interesting sharks to work on were the ones that were full bodied and animated. Those bigger sharks had latex skins that were 3'8 of an inch thick, so pretty heavy duty stuff. It would take several people to drag these skins over the mechanical shark armatures in order to install them. A lot of the skins I painted were badly fatigued or destroyed during the early testing of the ride.

Speaking of that early testing, I'll give you an interesting tidbit about the gills of the shark. Originally, there were actual gills cut out on the molds for the big sharks that appeared in the boathouse and later attack scenes. These areas seemed to be suffering the most amount of grief as far as the stress from the mechanics. They were often failing and getting tears in them. Universal decided to address this by getting rid of the gills entirely, so we filled them in on the mold. I would then essentially paint gills onto the flat area where the gills had been. One of the best compliments I ever got was a guy who came over and said, '*I thought we were supposed to be removing the gills!*' (laughs) With the right light, my gill painting really did look three dimensional. That helped alleviate some of the problems they were having. I ended up painting four or five skins for the boathouse shark alone because they were going through so many during testing. There were still some issues around where the jaw would open and close but we solved that by reinforcing those areas.

**Was it strange getting called back constantly to paint additional shark skins?**

I was working full time for Kinetix, so I was always there whenever they needed another one. We kept a lot of skins mounted on these fiberglass plugs to help them keep their shape. We would just pull a skin down whenever we needed another one. I'd climb up on a ladder and start painting it. These sharks stood about five feet tall, so I had to almost climb on top of them to paint them. They were shipped on something of a shark mannequin. It was so laborious putting them onto the sharks but also kind of odd. They used giant bolts and washers to hold the skins in place once they were installed.

**Did painting the sharks become easier with repetition?**

Exactly, yes. I didn't get a lot of direction or photo references for the first shark I painted. The art director would come in and give direction as I was working. One thing he mentioned was wanting a little more speckling in the transition from grey to white, so I would use a sponge to get a more realistic transition between the colors. Another thing I remember the art director saying was that the shark needed to have a few more scars and marks on it. He then literally took a two-by-four, dipped it in some brown paint and started smacking the shark with it. *'There. That's what I want!'* So I did exactly that. The idea was that the shark does barge through the wall of the boathouse so these scars and marks would be evidence of that behavior. The teeth were painted separately and installed with the skin. I'd paint them like a giant pair of dentures.

**From blank skin to finished product, how long would this process take?**

I could paint a full shark in about two days. The blank skins, which were raw latex, had kind of an amber color to them. After the skins had been primed with a special primer that would accept paint, I would use basically an air gun like you'd use to paint a car. The painting system we used was a tricky business because we needed a paint that would stick to the latex but still be flexible enough so that it wouldn't crack. Yet it also needed to be able to survive the harsh underwater environment. I forget exactly the type of paint we used, but it was a polyurethane product from a company out in California. I would spray on the base coat for the two halves, the grey half and the white half. Then I would mix different colors together to get the darker and lighter shades for sponging in.

**Was there ever a concern about the paint holding up underwater?**

Not that I remember. We didn't worry about the paint cracking as much as we worried about the latex skins themselves cracking. Certainly the water was something to consider but a much bigger problem was the hydraulic fluid that leaked out into the lagoon. There were always leakages and that fluid would deposit itself on the skins, so there was a certain amount of cleaning that had to be done from time to time. That was less a problem with the paint and more a problem with the contamination of the lagoon.

**Did you ever ride Jaws to see your work in action?**

I did, very much so! Being fairly new to Florida at the time, I would have a lot of family come to visit. Being proud of the shark skins, I would often take them to Universal to show off my work. I think I was most proud of the dead shark, which was a purely fiberglass shark. It was essentially the same paint scheme as the latex skins but applied to a fiberglass shell. I also got to work on applying the burn texture around the shark's jaw where it had chomped down on the electrical cable. It was fun attaching pieces of latex skin in certain areas to show evidence of death by electrical shock. Looking at that grotesque image, you knew the shark was well and truly destroyed.

Opposite: A close-up of the fierce looking boathouse shark
(Photo courtesy Luke Sawh)

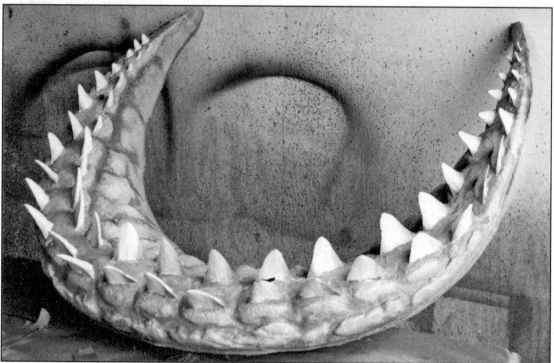

Above: Jaws the shark awaiting his jaws.

(Photos courtesy Luke Sawh)

**Were you ever present on site for the installation of the skins?**

I was. I would sometimes have to go out and do touchups and additional painting once the skins were installed. I'll never forget working on the shark near where the gas dock explodes. They were constantly testing the explosion effect while I was out there. I was a safe distance away from that area but the flames made it incredibly hot. This was in July 1993 so it was already terribly hot to begin with. The heat was so bad that there were only certain times of the day I could paint the sharks because the sun would overheat them, which would negatively affect how the paint went on. Working in that sun with the additional heat from the flame bars was intense. It was kind of exhilarating and a little scary at the same time.

**Do you recall the last time you rode the attraction?**

It probably would've been a few years before it closed. I've been involved with Universal on other projects. Whenever I'm there for a meeting I'll usually try to sneak over to the park afterward and ride the rides. I remember the last time I rode Jaws the skins must have been replaced because they looked different. I left Kinetix at the end of 1993 so I'm not sure if they continued the contract to provide Jaws skins. I know more skins would certainly have been needed over the years. The ones I saw the last time I went looked different.

**Let's be frank – the later skins were rough items and nowhere near as artful as what you created back in 1993.**

I think those later skins were probably a combination of budget, time, and knowing how much they were going to get soiled from the contaminants in the water. Universal probably felt it wasn't necessary to go to the same degree of paint as I did. You only see the shark for a few seconds and it's gone again. I'm guessing the decision was probably made to not put the same level of detail into the latter skins.

**How does Jaws compare to other ride characters you've worked on over the years?**

I've done a lot of skins for animated characters over the years. One of my biggest projects back in 2009 was for Harry Potter and the Forbidden Journey. I actually got to design the mechanism, sculpt, and produce the skin for the dragon on the ride. That was a very cool project. The thing about animated figures in theme parks is that they need to be able to last a long time, which is why parks often get nervous about using skins. They would much rather something be completely fiberglass without any wear points. For the dragon, I presented an idea that the head and jaw could be fiberglass but that the neck could be a silicone skin. That wasn't completely out of the question because they were already using silicone skins for the T-Rex over at the Jurassic Park ride. It's a shame that you only see it for a fraction of a second in the scheme of things. I'm very proud of it. I love to tell people '*That's my dragon!*' when they tell me they've ridden it. I also did some work for Diagon Alley, though it was mostly animated propwork so I didn't have to spend too much time out at the park like I did on Jaws.

# SWIMMING WITH (MECHANICAL) SHARKS

an interview with

## ADAM BEZARK

**Show Director (1993 version)**
**Voice of Amity Base**

Bezark has worked on some of Universal Orlando's most iconic shows and attractions over the years. (Photo courtesy TeaConnect.org)

**How did you become involved with the Jaws ride?**

I was working for Landmark Entertainment at the time. They're not around anymore but they were a legendary theme park design company in the '80s and '90s and a regular vendor to Universal. They did some pretty great stuff. Through them I worked on the Ghostbusters show and also did concept artwork for things like Terminator, Spider-man, and Jurassic Park. We had just finished a rehab on Ghostbusters when we got the call about Jaws. They were in the middle of fixing the attraction and said they needed someone to do a week's worth of programming. I went out there and found that Jaws was a bottomless pit of work. A one week job snowballed into something like six months of work. I came on pretty late in the game which was unusual for me as a show director. Ordinarily I would have been involved from the earliest stages. Not only had the first version of the ride been built and closed by the time I arrived but the second version was well underway in construction. It was Phil Hettema who called me to work on the project. He was one of the creative leads at Universal.

I joked to my friends at the time that it was like being asked to direct a movie where the script is already written, the sets are already built, the actors are already cast, dressed, and in place ready to say the lines. Even though they had already built so much of the ride, there were still a ton of things that needed attention. I worked on the script, the soundtrack, the lighting, the programming – things like that. I turned out to be a lot more useful than anyone probably thought I would be. The job was a lot of fun.

**What was your understanding of why the first version of Jaws didn't work out?**

As I understood it, the original Jaws ride was a very technically ambitious concept. I don't think the technology at the time was ready to do what they were wanting it to do. There were three things that went wrong with the original ride: the boats, the sharks, and the boats versus the sharks. As I recall, the first ride had actual floating boats like on Jungle Cruise. That wasn't precise enough for what they were wanting to do with the timed effects, so sometimes they were in the wrong place at the wrong time. The original sharks also didn't behave well underwater. My recollection of what I was told is that the first round of sharks were made by a company who didn't take into account how much tougher it is to make these things work underwater. Bad things would happen when those sharks would suddenly lunge out of the water with great force. Either the skin would tear or the shark would break altogether. I heard they tested great on dry land but not so well in the water.

The most difficult part of the original ride was a moment I thought was brilliant. The shark was supposed to swim up and actually bite the boat! Its jaws would clamp down and the shark would swing the boat around in a big circle. They had built this gigantic contraption on what was essentially an oversized turntable. It was such a cumbersome thing that it so often did not work. It became one of the issues that ultimately sank the ride. They messed around with it for months after the park opened but were never able to get it working reliably. That led to Universal's decision to scrap the attraction and start over. They got rid of the boats, the sharks, and all the related effects. The only things they kept were the lagoon and the island itself.

**What kind of pressure were you under walking into that situation?**

The pressure was out of control. I think Jaws was the only new thing Universal was working on that year so it got a lot of focus from the top brass. You also have to keep in mind that the guy behind fixing the Jaws ride was Jay Stein who had been running things since the very first Universal Studios tour opened way back when. He had overseen the construction of Universal Studios Florida and was getting ready to retire. Jay was determined that he was going to fix this darn ride before he left, so he took a very hands on interest in making sure it got fixed and fixed right. He was even involved in writing the new ride script. Jay was a famous character in Universal history because he was the opposite of most business executives. He was loud, foul-mouthed, and would yell at people, but he was also very good at telling you what he wanted. I think it was important that the second version of Jaws not embarrass him as he got ready to retire. So the entire team was under a whirlwind of intense pressure from top management.

**What do you think was driving that pressure? Money or reputation?**

I really don't think money was an issue for Universal. I think it had more to do with pride and reputation. This was the one giant lingering piece still leftover from their disastrous grand opening. They had gotten all the other rides working fairly well and fairly quickly - all except for Jaws.

**Were you working toward a deadline to have the ride open by?**

No, I don't think so. If we did have a date, they didn't tell me about it. I just remember one day we started letting people on the ride once we felt we had nailed it. It was different back then because we didn't have legions of fans like there are today. No one was showing up at the park every day expecting the ride to suddenly be open.

**What was it like programming the ride? Did you have a favorite scene?**

All the scenes were great but my favorite was the boathouse. I thought it was the most cinematic and also the most Spielberg-ian. We had more control over the lighting and atmosphere because that scene was indoors. We tried to light it as dramatically as possible. I messed around a lot with how the skipper would interact with the searchlight. I eventually had them spin it around so that it would backlight them as they spieled. Shining the searchlight back onto the audience seemed to be a very Jaws-like thing to do. I loved the drama of that scene. The hardest scene to program was one that might seem like the simplest. Remember at the beginning when the shark goes under the boat? We had so much trouble getting the timing of the boat rocking to line up with the sharks. We needed the boat to shake at exactly the right moment between the shark's appearances on either side of the boat. That drove me crazy.

The most fun scene to program was the gas dock scene because I would go out in a rowboat and sit where the boat was going to be. Ron Griffin, our pyro expert, would trigger the fire sequence and each time I'd say, 'Can you turn it up some more?' and he'd go 'Okay!' And eventually I had to say, 'Okay, my eyebrows are now burned off so that's probably high enough.' We decided between the two of us that the right amount of fire for that scene was just enough

Opposite: Chomping on the power cable in Scene Five. (Photo courtesy Christopher Lord)

so that you felt like you were going to burn up but you didn't. So we went as high as we dared and then dialed it back just below the pain threshold so that the flames would be as spectacular as possible. And we loved that scene.

We had some dumb luck with the electrocution in the final scene. Our original plan was for the shark to simply hover above the power cable because it had never occurred to us to put the cable in the shark's mouth. One day it just swam up and grabbed the cable in its jaws and we were like, '*Uh... is this okay? Can we do this?*' So we tried recreating that effect and each time the shark would very politely swim up to position, grab the cable in its mouth, thrash around, and gently let go of the cable as he sank down. We thought he might have torn the cable off but he never did. So we made that part of the scene. You would think we spent a lot of time trying to program that but it was all luck!

**That's crazy considering you're essentially recreating the ending from Jaws 2 where the shark bites the cable.**
Right? We definitely took that from Jaws 2 but we never thought we could pull it off in its entirety. We had planned on covering the shark's mouth with sparks and smoke to hide the fact that he wasn't actually biting the cable. But he did and it worked out fine. He bit the cable very happily for something like eighteen years after that. Dumb luck!

**You mentioned working on the soundtrack. Would that have been with David Kneupper?**
Yes, I thought he did a really excellent job of taking the John Williams themes from the movie and scoring them to fit the ride. There were a couple of times where we worked together to make the music just a little more powerful theatrically for the story we were telling. I can think of two times off hand. One was in the fire scene with all the explosions. Originally, Dave had music playing all through the explosions and into the next scene. I said, '*Why don't we stop the music here? Let the explosion take over and happen on its own?*' It was very powerful without any music behind it. That kind of thing is a common movie trick. Coming out of that scene Dave would kick the music back in with that big drum solo and it continued on. I thought it worked awesome.

The other piece I remember us working on quite a bit was the finale. We had planned for the musical score to end with the burnt shark. The last piece of music would have played as it lunged at you. The boat would then motor back to the dock in silence. That wasn't Dave's idea. That was something Universal had asked for. I came back and asked Universal to pay him to create a final piece of music to bring us back to the dock. That gave us the idea to do the '*Call off the marines, we're coming home!*' That's a triumphant moment at the end of the ride. The whole idea was that if we did our jobs right the audience would want to applaud after surviving a killer shark attack. There was no moment like that in the script. Originally, the shark blew up and then you got off the ride.

Do you remember the movie Yellow Submarine? If you have the original soundtrack album, one side of that is just the orchestral music used in the movie. There was this great cue, the triumphant return of the Beatles in the film that starts off quietly in the distance and gets closer until it swells into a huge, happy, heroic song. I played that for Dave and said '*Do something like this but for the Jaws theme.*' And he did it! That's the final song as you ride back to the dock. It was this grand whoosh of music with trumpets and the Jaws theme. The hard part was finding something to match that energy for the last line of the ride. One of the trainers suggested the final line of ride the day before we opened. The skippers would go, '*We got him.... didn't we?*' And that got a last minute chuckle.

**What condition was the ride script in when you arrived on the project?**

The script was finished and perfect because Jay Stein said it was finished and perfect. He was the boss at Universal and had personally overseen the writing of it. He might even have written some of it himself. Going into rehearsals, I could already see that it was going to be tricky. There were parts of the ride script that just weren't written for human mouths to speak. It looked good on paper, but it wasn't easy to say those lines. I had to suck it up and go back to Jay and ask to adjust the lines to make them more speakable. And I had to do that without changing the intention of what he had labored over. Fortunately, he was okay with it. The final script was not one that I wrote but one that I massaged and doctored to make easier and more fun to read for the skippers.

**How important were the skippers to the attraction?**

Everything. They were everything. It was all about the skipper. It would've been a pretty boring ride if you rode around without them even with the sharks and explosions. The whole ride was centered around the skipper's performance. I can't remember who said it, but someone said the Jaws ride was like Disney's Jungle Cruise on steroids and that's true. Jaws revolved around the skipper's ability to deliver the material. Unlike Jungle Cruise, there wasn't much room for improvisation or kidding around. I always thought the best skippers were the ones who didn't treat it like a joke, the ones who really did it intensely like their life was on the line. It was so much fun to watch. There were some who did it seriously and some who did it sarcastically and certainly it worked both ways. I performed it a million-jillion times because I was trying to figure out the timing. I would also be the one who had to do it for the top brass before we had the real skippers trained and ready to go.

Amity Six heads for Lighthouse Cove. (Photo courtesy Christopher Lord)

**Did you ever have anyone fall into the Jaws lagoon?**

I fell in once! (laughs) It was stupid. We were riding around in the boats pretty close to opening. Have I mentioned that they're not really boats? They're trucks driving through the water pretending to be boats. They were driving on a track but they were also on a motion base so they could rock back and forth when the shark bumped them. We actually had to program them to be more fluid and move like boats, which was a lot of work. The guy responsible for that was Marc Plogstedt.

So back to the story, he and I were programming the boats just before the park opened. On this particular day all of the seats on the boat are filled with sandbags equal to the weight of the park guests that would be on the ride. These sandbags took up all the space in the seats. I was standing at the back of the boat and for some reason I needed to get up to the front. Like an idiot, I tried to walk around the side of the boat hanging onto the canopy for support. Halfway to the front, I started to slip and everything went into slow motion. 'Ooooooh shiiiiiiit!' And into the water I went. I was surprised at how hot the lagoon was. This was May in Florida. Marc was still in the boat and hit the emergency stop right away so I wouldn't be chewed up by the ride. The skippers came and helped fish me out. I was covered in yucky lagoon water with hydraulic fluid and crap all in it.

**When did you know you had it perfect? Did word come from upstairs?**

I knew we'd gotten it right when they stopped yelling! There wasn't any big congratulations. I just remember that the yelling stopped. Unlike some of the projects today that were opened with a big event, Universal just wanted this one opened as fast as possible. I stayed another week or two after that and everybody seemed happy. Crowd reaction was good. The cheers were great. A bunch of Universal execs came and rode it too. Legends like Lew Wasserman and Sid Sheinberg. When they went away happy, we knew we were done.

**You helped launch the second Jaws ride at Universal Studios Japan. What was that like?**

That was an interesting experience. I went over to train the skippers for that version which is almost identical to ours. I had to teach the Japanese skippers to perform in Japanese when I had no idea what they were actually saying. I was flying blind. So my instruction was more about body language and energy levels with their acting. One funny thing about working on the Japanese ride was seeing some of the same people again. For the Orlando version, the sharks were built by a company called Oceaneering. They had a project manager back then named Mike Hightower, a great guy. I was always asking Mike to make the sharks do things differently or things in an entirely new way. And he would always go, '*No, the sharks can't do that because it's not in the warranty.*' Not long after that, Universal hired Mike as one of the top executives at Universal Creative. Nine years later, we're both in Osaka going around their Jaws lagoon together and there's a new project manager from Oceaneering working on the sharks. So I ask the new guy to do something different with them and he goes, '*No, the sharks can't do that. It's not in the warranty.*' And Mike shouts back, '*You can't use that line on us! I know that trick because I invented that trick!*' (laughs)

The gas dock shark from the ride at Universal Studios Japan. (Photo courtesy Christopher Lord)

**Did the Jaws ride's closure surprise you at all?**

In a way, I think it surprised even Universal. When they first went to Florida to build their first big theme park from scratch, they spent a lot of time picking the movies they wanted to base their rides on. They settled on classics like Jaws, King Kong, E.T., Earthquake, and Back to the Future. The word they used a lot in those days was "evergreen." They believed these movies were such classics that they would never go out of fashion, that these rides would be the equivalent of Pirates of the Caribbean and Haunted Mansion. I don't think any of us realized that simply wasn't going to be the case. Even great movies like E.T., Jaws, and Ghostbusters eventually fade from the public eye. Today they're just not as relevant to audiences as they once were. I think it surprised Universal one by one as they realized that people were going to those rides less and less. They're still movies we all love but kids don't know them and teenagers don't care about them. I was astonished when they closed E.T. because there was a time when that was the biggest movie of all time and yet kids today don't know who E.T. is.

Jaws is something that still lives on in the hearts of film lovers everywhere. But the average kid has either never heard of it or doesn't care. So that Universal is kind enough to keep both the film and ride's legacy alive in their parks is great. I'm referring to the hanging shark that's still there. I appreciate that. Even if they can't justify keeping an entire ride based on an older movie, they can at least keep a piece of the attraction and I'm glad. It makes us dopes who make these things feel like someone actually remembers and cares about what we did. Even the guys that are tasked with building replacements for these classic rides truly care about the older attractions and that's a great thing.

# PROGRAMMING A SHARK ATTACK

◆━━━━━◆◈◆━━━━━◆

an interview with

## MARC PLOGSTEDT

### Chief Technology Officer
### ITEC Entertainment

Working with giant apes and killer sharks - it's all in a day's work for Marc Plogstedt. (Photo courtesy ITEC Entertainment)

**How did you come to be involved with the second Jaws ride?**

I was one of the original founders of a company called ITEC Entertainment whom Universal had contracted to work on Jaws. Most of the people at ITEC had previously worked at Disney doing various projects mostly related to Epcot. Up until that time Disney had been handling most of their rides and attractions internally. After Epcot they made the decision to downscale and that resulted in an awful lot of skill and talent getting cut loose. You'll notice that a lot of companies in the industry got started around the same time. I saw this as an opportunity and decided to start a business with some other people, which is how ITEC came to be. We focused on creative design, technical design, and production management work. Some people know us for our creative stuff or our technology but we offer a whole range of services. For example, we did Revenge of the Mummy for Universal over in Singapore. We completely turn-keyed that attraction for them so it just depends on the needs of the customer and project as to what we do.

**Was the reimagined Jaws ride your first project with Universal?**

No, it wasn't. At the time we had been providing technical engineering services to a company called Landmark Entertainment. They had done the original Ghostbusters show for Universal here in Florida. So we became somewhat known at Universal and wound up getting asked to do other stuff there. We did some work on the re-tooled Ghostbusters show and also on Earthquake: The Big One. We were invited to work on Earthquake just after the original opening of the park. We specifically focused on the subway train, which was the main ride vehicle of that attraction. The ride control system we put together for Earthquake led Universal to look on us favorably when they started to think about redoing Jaws.

**Adam Bezark called you a "technical sorcerer." Is that an apt description for what you do?**

(laughs) Technical sorcerer? I don't know. Maybe. Adam and I go back quite some time. He's a fantastic individual to work with. That was one of the great things about the Jaws II project. Universal didn't just assemble any old team. They brought in only the best companies to redo that attraction, many of whom they had already worked with. So the team they put together for Jaws II was really a top notch group of talented individuals. Adam was a terrific part of that team. He and I have done so much stuff together over the years.

**How important was it for the new team to go back and learn why the original Jaws ride had failed?**

Very important. We needed to look closely at both the creative and technical aspects of the failed attraction. Fortunately, we had an endless amount of technical information to pour over as Universal had done an extensive postmortem on the first ride. Everyone involved in the redesign had a pretty clear understanding of what had gone wrong. Knowing why certain things proved unreliable the first time helped to guide some of our technical choices on the second version. It also helped that Universal brought in a company called Eastport International which is now Oceaneering. They were serious experts in deep sea robotics and submersibles, so they did all the sharks and underwater platforms. Those people had a really strong understanding of what would be needed on a project like this. Their expertise was going to help ensure the new ride worked reliably and as intended.

**It's interesting that Universal chose not to simply recreate the original ride scenes but to stage entirely new moments like the gas dock explosion and the cable-chomping-shark.**

That decision stemmed from conclusions that were drawn following our full assessment of the original ride. There were certain creative choices on the first Jaws that, in retrospect, were either risky or simply not the best. Having the shark bite the boat, while impressive, was a really difficult thing no matter how you approached it. Realizing that, Universal decided to go in a completely different direction with that scene. The technical aspects of this particular attraction had a strong influence on the creative direction. Universal had to seriously consider what it was going to be like to maintain this attraction for what they hoped would be many years to come - just as you would on any attraction.

There's an old saying that comes to mind with all of this. You know in Hollywood how they say you never want to work with kids or animals? In our industry they say you never want to work on boat rides because they're notoriously more difficult than other types of rides. You have so much more to consider on a water attraction, things like water chemistry. Plus, you can't really manage or control water. Water is going to do whatever it wants to do.

**How would you summarize ITEC's contributions to Jaws?**

Our job was to provide the ride control system for the entire attraction. That ultimately took us into some other aspects of the ride, but the control system was our main task. I usually tell people that we're like the director of an attraction. On a film, the director tends to give a lot of creative input as to what's going to happen and when. That's basically what we do. It's our job to execute the intent of the ride and work with other companies in doing so. For starters, we were responsible for everything that happened with the boats. We didn't build them but we controlled how they moved throughout the lake. Adam and I sat out there for an eternity going around and around in those things. And they weren't really boats. They were machines. It was our job to make those big mechanical devices feel like boats. That was the black magic of what we did.

We configured the entire ride to work based on the locations of the boats. Different event sequences would trigger depending on your boat's position. That was then overlaid with a whole bunch of safety related stuff. The Jaws ride had elements to it that were inherently dangerous, which is true of most attractions in one way or another. Take the gas dock explosion for example. If your boat was in the wrong place or the wind was blowing too hard, you could easily wind up with an unsafe situation for guests. The ride control system would make the decision to either trigger or not trigger the fire effect based on what it knew to be safe. It was all computers and programming.

Our ride system ultimately helped bring everything together to make you feel like you were being attacked by a shark. When you hear the shark slamming into the boathouse wall, that's not really happening. That's a computer triggering a series of sounds and effects in a certain order to give you that impression. Sure, other companies made the sharks and fire effects but our system was responsible for triggering them in the right order at the right time. These systems really are the glue that holds an attraction together.

The boathouse shark attacks!

**What was your favorite scene to program?**

My favorite scene was the parking lot whenever we got to go home, which was rare! Like I said, we spent an eternity going around that lake. If I had to pick a favorite scene, I'd probably say the boathouse. I thought it was a spooky and effective scene. I liked that it mostly stayed the same whether you rode Jaws during the day or at night. The shark also came up right alongside the boat in that scene, which I think was jarring to most people. Everything about that scene was intense. I liked it.

You know that Adam's voice is in the ride, right? Adam is the radio operator that calls in from time to time, the one the skipper radios to for help. They were desperate to add some more voices to the ride and asked if I would help out. If you'll recall, there was a cannery just past the load platform. I was one of the worker voices making God knows what kind of comments when the boat went by it. So maybe I'll take that as my favorite scene. It's the only time I ever got any stage time in a ride.

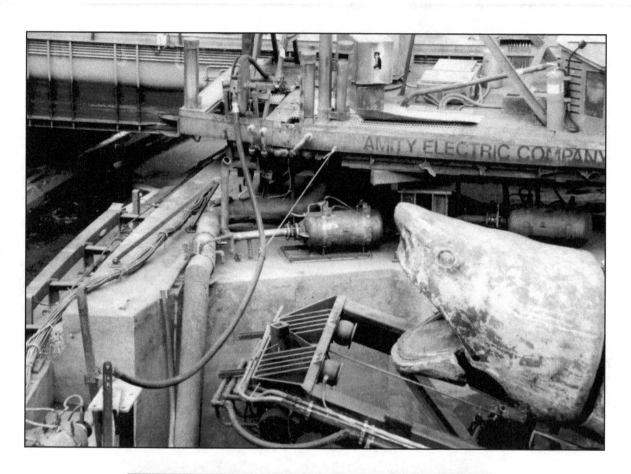

JAWS
RIDE CONTROL SYSTEM
MONITOR DISTRIBUTION BOX
MD050

Top: The kill shark armature during one of the ride's many refurbishments.

Bottom: Signage from the attraction's ride control system. (Photos courtesy Jim Beller - JawsCollector.com)

**What then was the most difficult scene to program?**

All of it. Our senior vice president for entertainment technology, Steve Alkhoja, was responsible for the sharks so I'm sure he would say programing the sharks was most difficult. I don't think people have a good appreciation for how complex that whole system was, especially for that point in time. There was a ground computer, so to speak, that would tell the boats where all the other boats were on the track. Each ride vehicle would then make its own decision to go ahead based on whether or not the next scene was clear. There weren't any physical barriers or brakes in place. It was all electronic. Getting that system to work smoothly and be transparent to the audience was a challenge. Say you were heading into the boathouse scene and everything was going as planned. That's great. But say you head towards it and the doors don't open right away because there's some delay ahead. It was our job to have the boats be able to respond to that delay and even pause if need be without ending the entire ride right there. We did a lot of work with predictive analysis to make that all feel natural.

The most difficult part about programming these motion profiles into the ride vehicles was that we couldn't ever stop and back up ten feet to see something again. We would have to go all the way around the lagoon to see any changes we made, so it was a very long and laborious process. We would try to be as efficient as possible by working on multiple spots along the track at once, but we tended to focus on just one spot which took a lot of time. We went around that lagoon thousands of times.

**It sounds like you left your sanity in Amity.**

Oh we so did. There's no question that we had long lingering effects from that experience. Adam and I would focus on something we wanted to change, make that change, and then wait several minutes until the boat came back around to that part of the ride. We'd do looney things to pass the time. You'd slowly go insane and start acting out random scenes from shows and movies. I'm sure if someone looked at us from outside the attraction we'd have been arrested and thrown into a rubber room.

**As an industry outsider, I found it impressive how Jaws worked with a full boat rotation. One boat left a scene just as another enters, all while the effects reset to go again. There was an incredible efficiency to that process.**

We spent many thousands of hours trying to make the ride work that way. Whenever you do one of these attractions, you have to think of it in a couple of different ways. Obviously there's the creative side. The second part is the operational side. You can't spend millions of dollars on an attraction that only ten people can ride per hour. These attractions come with certain operational expectations in place, which everyone is made aware of well in advance. These requirements help drive what happens in each scene and also which technology is chosen to make those scenes happen and reset. We put a lot of thought and effort into making these attractions run as efficiently as possible. A big part of that is looking at how long it takes each effect to reset. If a scene lasts thirty seconds but it takes thirty-five seconds to reset, that's not good.

One thing we learned early on was that adjusting the velocity of the boats during a slow down was more efficient than stopping them altogether. That was because stopping a ride vehicle meant you had to start it up again which took more time. It was far better to slow the boats down by 5% until the delay happening ahead of them was resolved. The great thing was that this all happened automatically. The boats were programmed to do this all by themselves.

**I've read where ITEC also worked on Kongfrontation. Was that before or after Jaws?**

Kong was after Jaws. That was another one of the Universal's opening day attractions that was supposed to debut with the park but didn't for numerous reasons. They did finally get it up and running but it was a difficult attraction for them to maintain. They eventually took it down for an extended rehab to work on everything from the ride vehicles to the monkeys. That's when they sent us in to improve upon the ride system. We applied several of the concepts we learned on Jaws to Kong. The whole idea was that more intelligent ride vehicles made for a more robust system. Previously on Kong, the entire ride would come to a complete stop whenever something unexpected would occur. The problem was that the system couldn't restart until all of the ride vehicles had been cycled through back to the beginning. The old system wasn't smart enough or robust enough to handle that kind of a stop. This meant the reliability for the attraction was a lot lower than what Universal wanted it to be. The original Kongfrontation was very sensitive to any kind of issue, which lowered its ability to run efficiently. We changed that.

**Kongfrontation eventually closed in 2002. Did that come as a surprise to you?**

Not really. You expect it on just about anything in this industry. You'd always prefer that the attractions you work on last forever like It's a Small World, but classics don't happen all that frequently. Pop culture keeps moving onto something else. Parks change. Audiences change. Kong was always an interesting attraction to me because of how terribly complex it was. Unfortunately, that kind of complexity didn't translate well to the audience. People got a much bigger thrill out of the boat rocking back and forth on Jaws than they ever did when Kong dropped the tram they were in. If you watched Kong drop the tram from the ground, you'd be looking up going, '*Holy crap, that's really impressive!*' But when you rode it, it was somehow a less dynamic experience. People would go, '*Eh, it's alright.*'

**The second Jaws ride lasted nearly two decades. Do you consider that a decent run for a water attraction?**

I do. You know, anything will deteriorate over time if you don't maintain it. Universal does a great job of keeping these rides in good shape. With the sharks, they would often replace the skins and mechanical components. Both Universal and Disney are at the top of the game in terms of proactive ride maintenance. Even so, I don't personally think the longevity of a particular attraction has to do much with that. It has to do with audiences. Maybe the best example of that I can give you involves my own kids. I have four daughters in college right now. They weren't even born when I worked on the Jaws ride. Just before the ride closed, we all went out to ride it one last time. We get to the end and they go, '*Yeah, it's okay, Dad.*' It doesn't mean as much to them. The newer attractions are much more impactful to young people because they know those films. Jaws probably means the most to people who can remember when that film

Old banana breath tearing through New York City in Kongfrontation.

first came out. That movie scared the crap out of people! Yet you play it today and you don't get anywhere near that kind of reaction because the audience is totally different. Their own perceptions of what they can and can't tolerate are totally different. Attractions based on movies are a similar deal. It's an easy argument to make that Harry Potter is simply more relevant to today's young people. It doesn't mean that Jaws wasn't good or that the Jaws ride wasn't good. It's just about perception and awareness. The Jaws ride is still quite popular in Japan, which is great to see.

**You're one of several people that worked on the Jaws ride that also worked on Diagon Alley, aren't you?**
Yes, I did. That one is a little newer so we're still restricted by non-disclosure agreements on it. We did stuff inside of the ride vehicles on the Hogwarts Express, mostly related to the technology of it. It was quite complicated and a lot of work. I'm not sure we actually did anything in the actual alley of Diagon Alley.

# DA DUM, DA DUM, DA DUM

an interview with

## DAVID KNUEPPER

### Music Editor (1990 version)
### Composer (1993 version)

**I know you scored the 1993 Jaws ride, but you were also involved with the 1990 version, right?**

The 1990 Jaws ride used an edit of the film soundtrack for music, so my involvement was limited. There were some things about that ride that we loved, such as the meat cannon, but it was clear during programming that something was wrong. I don't remember the specifics, but I think the ride operated just a few months after opening before being shuttered for the update.

**How were you approached to score the 1993 ride?**

My old partner, John Miceli, put the Jaws project together with Universal, pitching us to the do the music and sound. To this day, I'm very proud of him for landing that job for us. The big design theme for Universal back then was '*ride the movies*', so the basic creative idea was to evoke the film through a series of near-death encounters with the shark while on a pleasure cruise around Amity Island.

**Were you able to ride it at all prior to scoring?**

Like most ride-based attractions, the music for Jaws was composed to a timed script while the ride was still under construction. The Jaws script was excellent in its detail, in particular the timings. The source music to draw from was legendary, so the write was a lot of fun. Our first ride on the boat happened during programming, which was exciting. I still remember that first pass, not breathing as the music for each scene was triggered. I remember that, after hearing the music in the show, I re-wrote the boat house escape and the ending as we return to port. Otherwise the original pass of the music held up surprisingly well. I made a handful of changes to better match show timings, but there was very little drama in creating the music for Jaws.

**Was there a pressure to draw from or work with John William's music?**

John Williams composed one of the most iconic horror scores ever written, so naturally the main idea -- the requirement -- was to adapt the Jaws soundtrack to the ride. It was a fabulous honor of course. Because of the script and show timings, very little music was actually lifted in its existing form from the film soundtrack. Rather, I used the themes, melodies, and chords to construct a semi-original score that hit all the dramatic beats of the show. Some scenes, like the boathouse escape with the drumming music, were more original than others.

**How was your work on Jaws different, if at all, from your work on Kongfrontation or E.T. Adventure?**

All three of those projects were very different from one another. Kongfrontation was an original score, and my first big scoring project for a theme park ride. I was originally only contracted to do dialogue and sound design. I stepped in at the last minute to compose new music when the original score didn't work out. For E.T. Adventure, John Williams adapted his own score for most of the ride. I was brought in to write just one cue, the crazy, everything-but-the-kitchen-sink celebration music when E.T. returns to his home planet. It was supposed to be instruments not found on earth, so it became a riotous percussion pandemonium, with the main E.T. theme woven in throughout.

**What was your reaction to news of the Jaws ride's closure in late 2012? Do you recall the last time you rode it?**

I've been around long enough that, unfortunately, the Jaws closure wasn't the first attraction I'd worked on to close. Many attractions have a ten-year life expectancy, so for Jaws to last twenty-two years is an amazing accomplishment. It had such a loyal fan base, and the camaraderie of the boat captains and others who worked on the ride was unlike anything I've ever experienced. Jaws has a vocal community of supporters, and interacting with them made the closure feel much more personal. The Jaws closure felt like the end of an era, both for the park and for me.

Retired Studio Directory signage for the Jaws ride (Photo courtesy Jim Beller - JawsCollector)

# IT'S A SHARK THANG

an interview with

## BING FUTCH

**Opening Team Skipper (1993 version)**
**Director - "It's a Shark Thang" Music Video**

Skipper Bing out front in Amity Circle. (Photo courtesy Bing Futch)

**How did you come to work for Universal Studios Florida?**

My theme park history goes back all the way to 1984. My first job in the industry was at Knotts Berry Farm out in California. I did mostly odd jobs but eventually got into ride operation. Then I went to work for Six Flags. I've always loved theme parks. What kind of workplace could possibly be more fun than a theme park, right? Several years later I applied for a position at Universal Studios Hollywood. It was a grueling audition but I made the cut and wound up a tour guide on their backlot. I did that from about 1989 to 1991.

**If you did studio tours, then you already had experience with mechanical sharks prior to the Jaws ride.**

That's right! The backlot shark wasn't anywhere near as good as the ones in Florida. The Hollywood shark was quite laughable when I look back on it. So I began work as a tour guide in Hollywood just prior to the opening of Universal Studios Florida. It was exciting that there was this east coast spinoff of our park about to open up. Most of us considered the studio tour to be kind of threadbare and a bit silly, so of course we were mind blown at what they were building in Florida with huge rides like Jaws, King Kong, and Back to the Future. They were obviously putting a lot of money into this project. I had been living in Los Angeles for a while and I was getting pretty sick of it. Some of the other Universal tour guides expressed interest in moving out to Florida to work at the new park. The reason behind that was many of them were wanting to break into the film industry and thought the new park might give them that opportunity. We heard that Universal Studios Florida was going to have several brand new soundstages so there would be plenty of production work available. I thought this sounded like a great idea and decided to head east.

I got out of my lease and moved to an apartment in Kissimmee. Unfortunately, they were no longer hiring at Universal by the time I moved out there. I found work instead as a ride operator for Seaworld on Mission: Bermuda Triangle. Universal did eventually start hiring again. My background as a tour guide helped me land a job in ride operation pretty easily. They initially had me working over at Kongfrontation.

**How did working at Universal Studios Hollywood compare to working at Universal Studios Florida?**

There were some similarities. If there's one thing you learn in ride operation, it's to always be ready for a ride to break down. With rides that don't have a spieling component, that's just a matter of standing out front and deflecting guest questions. It's a bit different on a spieling attraction where you're providing the dialogue. In that situation you've got to be ready with an alternate game plan if your ride breaks down with people still on it. No one likes to be broken down. No one likes to sit in silence. And no one likes to not know what's going on. By Kongfrontation, I was quite experienced at having breakdowns because my first summer at Universal Hollywood had seen the addition of Earthquake to the studio tour. Earthquake was absolutely amazing when it worked but often times it didn't work. Because it was Universal's star attraction at the time, they wouldn't want you to bypass it on the tour even when it was broken. So the trams would wait until whatever was broken got fixed so they wouldn't have to issue rainchecks.

So picture it. You've got one-hundred-and-fifty people on your tram for a three hour tour. You're wrapping up the middle break and about to get going again. Heading out of Tram Plaza, you look down into the valley and all you see are tail lights. There must be twenty trams lined up waiting to go through Earthquake. In that situation, you're going to burn through all your regular material very quickly waiting to get through that traffic jam, so you have to find other things to talk about. That was the best preparation for Jaws in particular because on Jaws you had to keep talking whenever that ride broke down. I'd talk about the park or how they made the Jaws movies, anything to break up the silence. You couldn't clam up because doing so could easily cost you your job.

**How'd you go from the mean streets of Kongfrontation's New York over to Amity Island?**
Universal was just about to open the second Jaws ride when I started at Kongfrontation. They were very clear about only wanting the best spielers to work at Jaws since they had spent so much money on rebuilding it. I'm talking the crème de la crème of spielers. I hadn't been at the park very long but I thought my history as a tour guide might help me switch over to Jaws. The area manager was Bret Hyler who was six foot two, had perfect hair and was always dressed suave. I went over to audition for Jaws skipper and Bret said, '*We're looking for the very best ride operators and we're not sure you've proven yourself yet. Why don't you come back and try us again sometime?*' So I said, '*Alright*,' and went back tail tucked to Kongfrontation.

One night shortly after that we had a bad breakdown on Kong. We were stuck right beside him near the bridge, which was a long way from unload station. They had to get a maintenance guy to climb down onto the roof of our gondola from the catwalk and manually bring the vehicle back into the station. Oh man, the ride vehicle just crept. We had a good twenty minute crawl back to the station. I couldn't be silent during that, so I went into the phases of production and talked about the original RKO production of King Kong. I discussed things like the stop motion animation effects and kept it flowing as best I could. Keep in mind that the headset I was wearing was real. The control tower could hear everything I was saying. We finally get back to the station and our tech jumps off the roof to manually open the door to let guests off. As we're unloading, I'm finishing my talk about filmmaking and I see Bret Hyler leaning off to the side smiling at me. He's got this Cheshire Cat smile. As I help the last guest off, I see Bret walking away. About an hour later, I'm in the breakroom at Kong and I get a phone call. It's Bret and he says, '*Come to my office tomorrow morning. I've got a script for you.*' And that's how I began my career as a Jaws skipper.

**What kind of training did you undergo for Jaws? And was the ride finished enough for you to train on the boats?**
We were able to train on boat but we initially spent a lot of time in classrooms giving tours to each other. We called them "pencil tours" because we would talk into pencils instead of headset microphones. By that time, the lagoon had been filled with water but not all of the effects were online yet. ITEC was in the process of programming everything. We did eventually get to rehearse on a boat that would go a full loop around the lagoon. The trainer would sit in the back of the boat and give us notes. As I recall, they were still figuring out some things like the blocking. Blocking refers to the skipper's position on the boat and when exactly they grab the grenade launcher and where they stand when the shark appears throughout the ride.

Timing was a big part of being a Jaws skipper. We worked to improve our timing through endless repetition. There were several parts of the ride that required you to have impeccable timing or they wouldn't work. One of those involved the transmissions from Amity Base. In order for those interactions to sound real, you had to nail the timing. The grenade launcher also required you to be on point. The skipper controlled the loud firing noise but they still had to fake the recoil. Those had to line up with the preprogrammed explosions that would happen in the water.

**What was your general impression of the Jaws ride 2.0?**
There was nothing else like it anywhere in the world. It was a state of the art attraction. People got so into it and just loved the experience it gave them. Celebrities and VIPs would always want to visit the ride when they came through the park. I remember one time we had a visit from both Peter Benchley, who wrote the original Jaws novel, and Carl Gottlieb, who wrote the movie adaptation. That was incredible.

**The first Jaws ride was infamously unreliable upon its 1990 debut. How reliable was Jaws 2.0 in 1993?**
The boats were very reliable. There were certain shark animations that would go down from time to time. The hard part about that was how into our spiels we would get. The skippers were all generally excited to be sharing this incredible ride with guests and so we'd get psyched up in anticipation of certain moments. We would ramp up our energy heading into the boathouse expecting that great scare that would happen inside there. Then we'd hear something over our headset, '*The boathouse shark is down!*' Now all of a sudden we have to somehow distract our guests from the fact that nothing was actually lunging up out of the water in that scene.

Skipper Bing hanging out with the sharks of Scene Five. (Photos courtesy Bing Futch)

The far worse thing to have happen was what we called a popsicle shark. That's when a shark would get stuck in place above the water. Every once in a bad while, you'd come out of the boathouse and find the gas dock shark just hanging out above the water not moving at all. That's when you had to play it off because there wasn't much you could do with it. '*Uh, look at that, folks. I've never seen anything like this before. Looks like we got him!*' Then you cruise by and hope the kill shark doesn't show up in Scene Five because then you have to go, '*Look! It's the shark's sister!*'

**Did any non-shark effects ever break down on the ride?**

I remember that the flame bars in Scene Four wouldn't work right every so often. In that scene, you shoot the grenade launcher and set off the gas pumps, which explode and create a wall of fire between you and your escape route. You would get incredibly hot going through that scene as though you were in a sauna. And then miraculously, the flame bars would extinguish and the boat would cruise through to Scene Five. There were several times when, for whatever reason, the flame bars didn't extinguish and we sailed right through the flames. Guests on boat would be stunned thinking it was somehow part of the ride. That's when I would get on the radio as discreetly as possible and say, '*Flame bar is not extinguishing! Repeat, flame bar is not extinguishing!*' There was always a weird smell whenever the boats would drive through the flames, a smell that wasn't supposed to be there. Maybe something had gotten torched.

**Yikes! Would you continue spieling through that or would the ride essentially be over?**

You'd have to split the difference. There would be this brief moment after the flame bar where the music starts back up as you're driving to the electric barge. It was just enough time to let tower know about the problem without missing any of your spiel. That the flame bar wasn't working properly was too important to wait until you got back to tell someone, especially if you had a seven-boat rotation going. That meant a new boat would be entering the scene just as your boat left it. Two more boats would have driven through the flames if you had waited until you got back to tell someone. They wouldn't have stopped the ride over it, but they would have disabled the flame bars from the tower. They never, ever wanted you to break away from your spiel if you didn't have to. They didn't want guests knowing something had gone wrong if they could help it.

We always remember and talk about when the ride didn't work, but I thought Jaws actually worked really well. It had a few bugs upon opening, but it soon came to be a well-oiled machine that ran like clockwork. At one time, I think it was among the rides with the lowest downtime in the entire park. It became much more reliable as time went on. They did have to constantly replace the shark skins in Scenes Four and Five over the years because the hydraulic fluid would eat away at them. The later skins weren't anywhere near as good as the skins that opened the ride. They made the shark look plastic, though they were much more pliable and could withstand for longer periods.

**Tell me about "It's a Shark Thang." How did that come about?**

The opening crew was a pretty great group of people. A lot of us were veteran tour guides and ride operators who really wanted to be on this ride because Jaws was a status ride. It was *the* ride to be on. We would often party after work at each other's houses. I threw a Jaws party shortly after we'd opened and everyone was there including spielers, maintenance, leads, and even a supervisor. We had burgers, beer, and all four Jaws films playing on television. One of my fellow skippers was a guy named Mike Lupia who was also a video producer. He had made this music video based on "Amazing" by Aerosmith, which we were going to debut at my party. In Mike's video, this kid is playing a virtual reality game and gets sucked into an alternate reality where he's a Jaws skipper. It was really cool.

I wanted to do something similar to that, so I wrote "It's a Shark Thang," which was going to be the inside story of working at Jaws. I recorded the song with my buddy, Casey Dodd, who also worked at the ride. Casey had come out to Florida from Hollywood with me and another skipper named Steve Shirie. We then decided to make a video for "Shark Thang" that would show you the day to day life of a Jaws skipper. At the time, Universal was offering us a lot of overtime. Around this same time, they had drained the ride lagoon and needed people to help clean it, so we three signed up. We took a video camera along for those extra shifts and got some pretty rare shots of the ride without water. We incorporated that footage into the video for "It's a Shark Thang," which also had footage from the ride while in operation. Our video was a hit with everyone who saw it. People loved it! Every so often, I'll go online and post the video to a Jaws fan group and they'll be all over it. I think ultimately the only people who really appreciate it are either theme park nerds or those who really loved the ride.

The drained lagoon reveals half-sharks and ride track. (Photos courtesy Bing Futch)

**Did you ever have any agonizingly slow crawls to the unload dock like on Kongfrontation?**

Oh yes, a number of times. It was pretty much the same thing. The difference was that the skipper could put the boat into manual mode and get it back to the dock. On Kong, someone had to drop onto the top of your ride vehicle and take you back. The worst breakdowns on Jaws were when you had to unload your guests somewhere other than the unload dock. Heaven forbid you had to unload at the steam barge where the shark gets electrocuted. The clearance wasn't great there and we had to lay out these wood planks for people to walk across. I only remember one time when things broke so badly that we had to use it for unload. We just kept our fingers crossed that no one slipped and fell into the lagoon because it would've been a lot of paperwork and possibly even litigation.

**Did you ever have to hit the emergency stop button?**

Fortunately, I never did. There was one guy named Derek who accidentally caused an e-stop once. All skippers were attached by lanyard to a kill switch on the boat. If we ever fell overboard, it would activate the kill switch and immediately shut down the entire ride so no one got run over by a hydraulic shark or a boat. Derek was a fairly new skipper and got a little too excited at the edge of one particular show scene. Sure enough, he fell over into the drink and stopped the ride. I don't think we ever let him live that one down. As far as I know he was the only skipper at that time to fall into the lagoon. His guests probably thought it was part of the show!

**In 2002, Kong closed. Did that surprise you?**

Not terribly. What surprised me was that they brought Kong back recently with a new attraction at Islands of Adventure. I wasn't too surprised about Kongfrontation closing because it was such a slow loading attraction. It was way behind the times in terms of guest experience, although a lot of people still found the sheer scale of it all quite amazing. Universal was always looking at ways to get more guests into the park and through the rides. The hourly capacity on Kong was among the lowest in the entire park except for some of the smaller shows. The Mummy certainly improved upon that.

## Find Skipper Bing online!

**In addition to having been a shark-slaying tour guide for Captain Jake, Bing Futch is also a world-renowned, award-winning master of the mountain dulcimer!**

**Visit him at BingFutch.com!**

# IT'S A SHARK THANG!

## LYRICS BY BING FUTCH

Well I'm workin' as a skipper on a ride called Jaws.
It's a cool little ride but it's got some major flaws.
We cycle and we program through the dead of night,
hoping in our wildest dreams that we'll get it right
(It's a Shark Thang!)

So early in the morning we be cleanin' dem boats.
In the winter coffee's necessary, so are peacoats.
It's 9'o'clock and time for us to have a little fun
when Boat Seven loses power and we go 11-1.
(It's a Shark Thang!)

I've been on this boat for hours and I've got a boring bunch.
My bump must be in Cleveland and I want my lunch!
I'm in a seven boat rotation and I've lost my voice,
but half the crew went to a football game. I've got no choice!
(It's a Shark Thang!)

I got my lunch and I'm feeling okay,
but Joe Rogers changed rotations for the fifth time today.
Scene Four is getting violent. I think I burned my face.
And worse than that the boathouse shark is frozen in place.
(It's a Shark Thang!)

## WATCH IT ON YOUTUBE!

**"It's a Shark Thang" - Directed by Bing Futch**

http://youtube.com/BingFutch

A day in the life of a skipper on the JAWS attraction at
Universal Studios Florida.

# BEWARE THE LANDSHARK!

❖

an interview with

## JOHN WISER

**Fabricator / Transportation Coordinator
of the LandShark Promotional Vehicle**

John Wiser posing with a 1911 American LaFrance Speedster.
(Photo courtesy John Wiser)

**How did you first get involved with Universal Studios Florida?**

I already had a lot of production experience before I started at the park. I believe I was one of the earliest employees hired for Universal Studios Florida. I first worked on the motion picture side of things, but I was also closely involved in the building of certain aspects of the park. One of my first projects when Universal opened was the Flintmobile, which was one of the Flintstones vehicles. It didn't take me too long to do that one. After that, I built something called the Biplane for the Rocky & Bullwinkle Show they were doing, which was a large cartoon airplane that the characters could come out and interact with during the show. And Universal loved it. From that point on, I started doing more and more projects for them.

**How did Universal approach you for the LandShark?**

This was around 1993 just before they opened the second version of the Jaws ride. Mark Woodbury was the guy in charge of creative at Universal. He called to ask if I was in town, which I wasn't. I was up in Ohio. He said, '*I need you to take a look at a drawing of something and tell me what you think.*' By that point, I had good enough credentials with the park that they would trust me with top secret things like this. Back then if they liked you and trusted you, they would keep coming back to you. Mark sent me a drawing of the LandShark on a piece of paper about the size of a napkin and said, '*I'd like you to handle this.*' So from that drawing I built a scale model that we could look at and touch. Scale models are helpful in that they can tell you a lot of things about a project. Once we agreed on the look, I just had to build it on a bigger scale. The vehicle's plans were drawn up by a guy named Reid Carlson. And the final product matched those plans very closely.

**What were you told about the vehicle's purpose?**

The LandShark was going to be something they used to help promote the park and the newly re-opened Jaws. The best vehicle to compare it to would be the LiMOUSEine, which Disney had built for the MGM Studio theme park. I thought that was a very successful promotional vehicle, but I was told that the LandShark needed to be better than that. It was going to be a no holds barred kind of project. Whatever it took to make the LandShark look like a great white shark, they said.

**Where do you even start on something like that? And how long did it take?**

It was difficult. I told Mark, '*I don't even know how to bid on a project like this.*' But you have to put a number on it because it has to have a price. I assembled a small team of people and we built it in ninety days, which is a really short amount of time. The shark exterior is made of polypropylene honeycomb. I built that entire body, every single panel of it. Underneath, the frame of the LandShark is really just a Pettibone off-road fork lift called the "Super 6." We had a V-8 Chrysler turned around backwards put in as well. Ultimately, the LandShark was a giant vehicle with huge sixty-seven-inch tires. And it was street legal too. All my cars are street legal. They've been on many streets all over the country for parades and such.

**What was the interior like?**

Fred Bernstein was the head of marketing at the time and he wanted the inside to be like the belly of the beast. Functionally, the inside was a real working radio station that could broadcast wherever the vehicle went. It also put out one-hundred-and-fifty decibels of sound, which is fifty points above deafening, so it was quite loud. The vehicle sounded as incredible as it looked. We would often let people come inside the LandShark at our appearances, especially young people. The whole park was about young people so we wanted them to enjoy this too. They loved it.

**So you built the LandShark - then what happened?**

Universal wanted it to go on tour around the country to promote the park. They asked me, '*Would you mind driving it around to these different appearances?*' And I said, '*Sure, I'll take it anywhere!*' And I went on tour with it. I traveled with Rodney Fox, one of the filmmakers from the original Jaws, and Peter Benchley, who wrote the novel. It was an exciting time. Universal booked an entire year of appearances every day of the week except Saturdays and Sundays. Out of 365 days, I think we put in just over 300 days of appearances and we never missed a date. We took it to museum openings and industry conventions, all sorts of things. I would put the LandShark up on a semi-truck for traveling between appearances and then bring it down once we got there. I can tell you that we caused more than a few traffic accidents with people trying to drive alongside us to get a better view of the thing. Drivers would run into the car in front of them because they were too busy staring at this giant shark vehicle instead of the road.

**What happened to the LandShark after your year on the road?**

It toured internationally some, though I'm not sure where all it went. I know it went to Germany at one point. They kept it at the Florida park while they were building Universal Studios Japan in Osaka. Once that opened, they took the LandShark out there for that Jaws ride. It's still there today. I would love to go out to Japan to see it again because it does kind of feel like my baby. I know every part of it very intimately.

LANDSHARK SOUVENIR TOY

# LANDSHARK

The LandShark on tour!

(Photos courtesy John Wiser)

# PRIDE AND PRESTIGE
# IN AMITY

an interview with

## TOM CROOM
### Skipper (1994 to 1996)

"Ten minutes?? We'll be shark bait in ten minutes!!!"
(Photo courtesy TomCroom.com)

**What made you want to become a Jaws skipper?**

To answer that we have to go back to the early 1990's. My parents were suffering from a slight case of get divorced, get remarried, and then get divorced again. My life was kind of spiraling. I had grown up in a small beach town in Southern Florida and never even finished high school. My kid sister eventually went to live with my dad, who got a job offer to move back up to Atlanta. This was about 1993. I said, '*That's not going to work for me. I've been there before and I'm not going back*.' I decided to move to Orlando to live on my own. My mom suggested I take my cousin Jim with me since he was trying to get his life back on track, so I did. I immediately started applying for work once we got to Orlando and Jim wound up applying everywhere I did. One of the places I applied to was Universal Studios Florida because I was a big fan of theme parks. We went into the interview together. I was a surfer kid, just turned twenty-one, with blonde hair and a tan. Jim had spent his entire life growing up in New York and still had a Jersey boy accent. The HR lady immediately goes, '*You should work at Jaws and you should work at Kong*.' We were hired into two of the key rides at Universal. This was sometime in 1994.

**What was your training like to become a skipper?**

First you had your core training about the history of Universal. Then you had water safety training which was specific to Jaws. That was in case a tourist ever thought it would be a good idea to go swimming with a giant mechanical shark. In the off chance that happened it became your job to pull them out of the water. The next part of training involved learning to spiel, which was a veiled way of avoiding having to pay an actor's fee to the skippers.

**Isn't that designation kind of ridiculous, though? Because the skippers were acting their asses off all day long.**

For sure. I knew what acting was. I had done professional theatre down in South Florida and even one professional film production. The second they started talking to me about spieling I said, '*Wait a minute. You know this is acting, right?*' And they came back with, '*No, no. It's not acting. You're merely conveying information in a ride script*.' I knew right then they were skirting the grey hard on this one. They were going to carry that torch as far as they possibly could strictly for budgetary reasons.

I eventually got together with a handful of other employees and put together a presentation to compel the Ride & Show Department to increase pay for the spielers. I pointed out that I was making as much money standing in the hot sun all day blowing out my voice as someone pushing a button indoors with air conditioning at the Funtastic World of Hanna-Barbera. We made the exact same amount of money. I was on the committee that eventually created something called spiel pay, which was a paid differential for spielers. It was $0.35 in the beginning. So if you worked at Jaws in regular rotation then you got an extra $0.35 an hour to do that. If your voice was blown out and you were stuck in tower or unload all day, you didn't get the spiel pay. It wasn't much but it helped those of us who worked at spieling attractions like Jaws, Kong, and Earthquake.

**Why work at a spieling attraction at all? Why not just push buttons over at Back to the Future?**

You have to understand that there was a level of prestige there, especially in the '90s. If you were hired to work at Jaws, it meant that you were the crème de la crème of the park and that your goal was to eventually not work at Jaws. A lot of people who started there wound up jumping into management. Look at Michael Aiello. He started at Jaws and now he's creative director at Universal Studios! It was kind of like taking your lumps to move onto something greater.

Another reason was that the culture and community of Universal was very much an '*us against them*' kind of thing, us being Universal and them being the mouse down the street. Everything was about competing and showing how we were better. There was a sense of camaraderie in that we were the underdog. And when you're the underdog and you're succeeding, that's an incredible buzz that you never want to wear off. You feel like you really belong to something. There was also the more localized competitiveness of it, which was '*My ride is better than your ride!*' There was no greater rivalry at Universal than Jaws and Kongfrontation. The Kong spielers were constantly reminding you how shitty your life was because you're standing outside in the hot sun without air conditioning. And the Jaws spielers were constantly reminding them how shitty their life was because they went home smelling like bananas. The pièce de résistance were the attraction parties and the quest to see who could throw the cooler party.

Why did people want to work at Jaws? Because it was so often a springboard to something greater. Because it was part of an ecosystem of young people who felt in competition with other rides and attractions, not to mention with the other parks across town. There was this huge sense of pride and community throughout the entire park. Universal was still ramping up in the '90s. It was a special time and place to be there.

**Looking back, it does seem like a special time. Why is that, though?**

It was special for several reasons. I personally liked how they were all about customer service back then. They had this employee empowerment program where the goal was to provide the best guest experience possible. If I ever saw that a guest was having a bad time at Universal Studios Florida, I could comp or spend up to $50 on that guest. And I didn't need management approval to do it. So maybe your kid was upset that they got wet on Jaws and now they're crying, even though you knew it was a water ride. We would buy that kid a new t-shirt. Or if you dropped your ice cream, here let's buy you a new ice cream. You could just do that back in the day. But like any other system like that, give it five or so years of being in place and it becomes an abused system, so it went away. But it was great. You were granted empowerment for the sole purpose of making someone's experience a better one.

**What was your favorite scene on the Jaws ride?**

That question has a qualifier because it depends on what time of year we're talking about. If we're talking from October to April, the fire scene was our favorite because it warmed us up! It doesn't snow in Orlando but it can get damn cold. Keep in mind that you never wore jeans on Jaws if you were smart. You always wore shorts. If you wore jeans and got wet, your legs would be soaked for the rest of the day. You could always see on the cameras whenever the boat went past the fire scene, the skippers would have their hands outstretched toward the fire. During the summer months, I'd say my favorite scene was the boathouse because it was so much cooler in there. It made for a nice break from the heat.

**What was the hardest part about being a skipper?**

I'd say the two hardest parts of being a skipper were things that most guests never saw. Number one was that being an opener meant getting there at four in the morning to clean the boats. Man, we hated opening. It would be freezing cold. This was pre-proliferation of Starbucks so you're drinking whatever crappy coffee you can find to keep yourself moving in those morning hours. You would clean each boat row by row with these huge buckets of soap. Opening was a shit job but we all did it.

The second hardest part was truly horrible but yet also good from a money-making standpoint. Universal would have to close the Jaws ride every once and while for maintenance. They would drain the entire ride down to nothing so that we could go in and clean out the residual hydraulic fluid. The filtration system could only pick up so much of that while the ride was in operation. If you were a boat skipper, you either took shifts at other attractions or you put on a hazmat suit and went down into the ride trenches to clean the hydraulic sludge. You'd scrape it into buckets and haul it off. It was the worst work in the world. The upside was that there was no limit on overtime for sludge work. You could work until you were dead if you wanted because the sooner you finished, the sooner Universal could open the ride back up. And having an attraction like Jaws closed was a huge detriment to the park, so they wanted it back open as soon as possible.

Skipper Tom on boat (left) and posing with a guest (right). (Photos courtesy TomCroom.com)

Missed again! (Photo courtesy TomCroom.com)

**What was the most difficult show element to cover for when it was missing or malfunctioning?**

Whenever the shark would get stuck in the up position! Everything else you could cover for. I'll tell you some of the very worst ones, however. Number one – leaving the dock and realizing you forgot your grenade launcher. Everyone did it at least once whether they admit it or not. How do you handle that? I saw it handled several ways. One was to just point your hand like it's a gun toward the explosions in the water. I saw another guy go, '*Oh, no! We're under attack! Don't worry, I have the power to summon the elements!*' Then he would raise his hand like a sorcerer just before the grenade explosions and go, '*I summon the power of water!*' And for the gas dock explosion he would say, '*I now summon the power of fire!*' Then the explosion would happen. It was so bad. The worst one I ever saw may or may not have involved a hangover. One skipper told the crowd, '*I have amazing powers... in my stomach!*' Then he would lean his butt over the edge of the boat and pretend to fart in the direction of the explosions in the water. I won't name names of who all did these, but I can confirm that they all happened.

**That sounds pretty off script! Did you ever improv or stray from the spiel script?**

All the time! I could do the entire script in Christian Slater's voice, which was pretty funny. I also had an impeccable Jim Carrey version that involved climbing up the side of the boat whenever the shark appeared. Some deviated more than others and, yes, some were caught. Getting caught usually involved lectures and paperwork. We all knew what lines not to cross. My thing was almost always doing caricatures of famous people. I had an Arnold Schwarzenegger version too. '*We ahh here to kill de shaaak.*' Our direct parallel in the theme park world was Disney's Jungle Cruise who did the exact same thing. Were they ever supposed to go off script? God, no. But did they? Absolutely. The most important thing on Jaws was that the skippers could do the show properly and flawlessly if summoned upon to do so. We frowned upon people that didn't know how to do the actual script perfectly.

Little known fact: Before hosting his Graveyard Revue, Beetlejuice was a Jaws skipper!

**When and why did you eventually depart from Amity Boat Tours?**

I left to become a lead at Beetlejuice. Whenever a lead position opened up in the park, there was a seventy-five percent chance they were going to fill it with someone from Jaws. If you could survive Jaws, you could survive anything. It was my turn to move up, so I became second full-time lead there. Our cast included a Wolf-man played by Joey Fatone. I remember him telling me about some band he was starting called N'Sync. I told him, '*Give it a rest, Joey. The New Kids On the Block already happened!*' One year later I was feeling like an asshole.

**Do you remember your last time spieling around the lagoon?**

Yes, but it wasn't my regular last day as a skipper. Flash forward to the late '90s and I'm working as an entertainment coordinator. I run into an old friend of mine, a Ride & Show manager named Bret Hyler. I asked him how things were going out at the mistake on the lake, which is what we jokingly called Jaws. He said, '*We're having a huge issue right now. The entire class of skippers we just brought in failed water safety training.*' And I said, '*You're kidding me!*' He goes, '*No, really. It's much harder now than when you did it.*' I laughed it off but they were having real staffing issues because of it. So I said, '*If you get desperate enough, I still remember the spiel. But considering what I make hourly, you probably don't want to do that.*' I made that little joke and went on with my life.

A few days later, Bret calls me and goes, '*What are you doing tonight? Because we really are that desperate.*' I couldn't believe it. This shift put me past overtime into double-time. Basically, I was about to get paid a ridiculous amount of money to work a regular theme park job. I went back along with another former skipper that had gone into the Entertainment Department named Larry. We had a great time spieling again. It only took a few days of that for the rumor mill to circulate that we were each making hundreds of dollars per shift doing regular rotations on the ride. Of course, we were the first ones to get cut when things got slow. The leads really grumbled about having us fill in but we bought them enough time that week to get a new class of skippers through safety training.

**Were you surprised by the announcement of the ride's closure?**

I knew it was coming through my continued professional relationships but I wasn't happy about it. My biggest problem has been that Universal Studios Florida was originally intended as a vehicle to promote their movies. I'm one of those old school guys that thinks there is an important legacy in motion pictures. Universal Studios Florida was built around that legacy. The fact that they were taking out a ride based on one of the best known movies of all time and replacing it with a licensed property was just awful. I was openly pissed when they added Rip Ride Rockit. What does a high speed rollercoaster that plays loud music have to do with Universal? Why couldn't that have been themed to Fast and Furious? I felt that Universal had lost its creative vision.

But obviously they've done an incredible job with the Potter stuff. You could speak the glories of it all day long. I was recently in Los Angeles and I took the Warner Brothers studio tour while I was there. The tour guide goes, '*You see that way over there? That's Hogwarts from Harry Potter over at Universal Studios. We technically own that but Universal sends us a nice check every single month.*' I was stunned. Even the tour guides at Warner Brothers are pointing it out. Disney has also gotten into a weird habit lately of just buying outside properties instead of licensing them. It bothers me. But I knew that Jaws had passed its time. They either had to revamp it or abandon it. My problem wasn't just that they decided to abandon it. It was that they were abandoning the Universal brand.

**You organized a Jaws skipper reunion just before the ride's closure. Tell me about that.**

Being that I work closely with conventions and pop culture events, I love a good story and a good spectacle. When I heard the ride was closing, I thought we should do something to honor it. I knew a writer at Orlando Weekly who thought there might be a cool story in a farewell reunion with all these former Jaws skippers. It would have been a legacy piece. The goal was to recapture the magic of Jaws and allow all of these former skippers to say goodbye to the attraction together. I reached out to Universal with that idea to see if they could contribute comp passes, which cost them nothing. The idea went through marketing and their stance was that they didn't want to draw attention to Jaws closing because they wanted to create momentum for what was going to replace it. That was incredibly disappointing. This was an important part of their brand even if it was going away. The best thing to do would have been to let it go away respectfully. Universal didn't get the importance of that.

We still did the reunion without Universal. I was proud of what we managed to organize. We had one former skipper who was in the later stages of cancer. One of the last things she got to do in this life was take a final boat tour around Jaws with a bunch of old friends from her twenties. One former skipper is now an actor who works with Tom Hanks. Michael Aiello was there too. I thought it was a nice farewell because it gave us closure and allowed us to say goodbye to both the ride and the overall Amity area. It was disheartening because of the amount of work it took to create the event without any support from the park. That hammered home for me how much Universal didn't understand the importance of its own history and culture. Jaws helped bring Universal to where they are today whether or not the current regime wants to admit it or not. The further you get away from history the less you remember it. Young people today don't even know Jaws anymore. They know the two notes and the shark but they've never seen the movie. They don't understand the impact on our culture. It's sad.

**Were you able to put aside your frustrations with Universal and still enjoy that last tour around the lagoon?**

Not really. I wasn't able to fully enjoy it. The event organizer in me was too busy thinking about everyone else. My mind wasn't really on the boat. At one point, I thought to myself, '*Who the hell are all these old people?!*' That's when I realized just how long it had been since I worked at Jaws. Some of these were friends I hadn't seen in a decade or more. The realization that I wasn't alone in thinking the ride's legacy was a special thing was great to have. People drove down from Virginia and flew out from California just to go on this ride one last time together. There were a ton more former skippers there in spirit if not physically. After we got off the ride, we hung out in Amity telling our stories and reliving our younger days. We told stories of breaking the rules so bad that they had to make new rules because of it! We laughed a lot. That's what the evening was all about. It was just so great to be in that moment and to realize I wasn't alone in being crazy about this movie and this ride.

Skipper Tom posing with Closing Team Skipper Cody. (Photo courtesy TomCroom.com)

# one last time!
## skipper reunion 12/17/11

Organized by Tom Croom, the "One Last Time!" reunion allowed attraction veterans to say goodbye to Captain Jake's Amity Boat Tours together with a final voyage around the lagoon led by Closing Team Skipper Cody.

Photos courtesy of
**TomCroom.com**

# FROM SPIELER TO SPIELBERG

an interview with

## JON DONAHUE

### Skipper (1993 to 1997)

Old friends. (Photo courtesy Jon Donahue)

**What led you to want to become a skipper?**

It wasn't because of the movie. I didn't grow up with the movie because I was always afraid of it. I had visited Universal Studios Florida as a guest the year it first opened. The Jaws ride had already closed by that time so I didn't get to ride the original version. I knew from that first trip that I wanted to work in the park. I moved to Orlando in 1993 and managed to get hired on as a spieler at Kongfrontation before I moved over to Jaws. I did eventually re-watch the original movie and fell in love with it. Jaws has become my number two favorite film of all time right behind Raiders of the Lost Ark, both directed by Steven Spielberg. I was excited to work at rides like Kong and Jaws because I've always wanted to entertain and act. That's been my passion.

**What was it like working first at Kongfrontation and then at Jaws?**

Kong was incredible. I loved it. The park was still new then and this was back when they had mostly actual rides, not video screen motion simulators. You can go to the movies and get that nowadays! I love the physical rides where you come face to face with a giant thirty-foot tall animatronic monkey. That's just impressive. I don't think people even to this day appreciate Kong as much as they should have. It was a huge feat to have giant robots that big in a theme park attraction. Kong was a great ride to work at but going over to Jaws was the best. Jaws was a very hard attraction to get hired onto because it was the elite of the ride and show department. Jaws skippers were the cool kids of the park and I wanted to be one of the cool kids…and work with a giant shark!

I always put so much into my shows at Jaws. I would be jumping all around the front of the boat where the skipper did their spiel. I loved making people scream whenever we went into the boathouse. It was pitch black except for the searchlight which the skipper was in control of. I would always scream and panic when the boat wouldn't drop into gear which would make the guests do the same - it was great! I loved seeing how many kids in particular I could make scream in those moments. You could never, ever do something like that at Disney. After Jaws I became a "Gakmeister" at Nickelodeon Studios where I still worked with kids but without the goal of making them scream. At least I hope I didn't make them scream at Nickelodeon?!

Jaws was an absolute dream to work at even though I was broke as all hell working there. I would eat ramen noodles every single day and they weren't even my noodles. They were my roommate's noodles. I was young and full of energy. I think my time at Jaws was proof that you can still be happy being broke, though it's occasionally nice to have money to eat on. I eventually became a trainer on the ride so I could teach new skippers how to act out the spiel and learn the blocking. Jaws was my world while I was there. It wasn't just a job I made money at because I didn't make much money at it. Honestly, I would go back today if it was still open. I miss it that much. For the record, I haven't eaten ramen noodles since 1997.

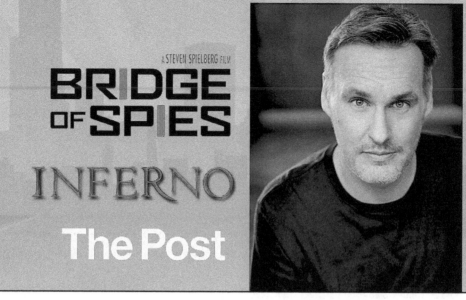

Skipper Jon has appeared in three movies with pal Tom Hanks, two of which were directed by Steven Spielberg.

**The amazing thing about your life after Jaws is that you kind of came full circle, right?**

I did! Years later I got into film acting and was eventually cast in two Steven Spielberg movies - Bridge of Spies and The Post. He actually personally asked me to be in the second one. His exact words were, '*Jon, would you mind if I cast you in the movie?*' And I answered, '*Are you serious? I would be honored.*' They're not large parts, but they're in Steven Spielberg movies. I'm very proud of them. We've talked about both Jaws and the Jaws ride during our time on set together. When I first told him that I used to be a skipper on the Jaws attraction, he replied, '*We're working together again, this time on dry land!*' He also knows that I collect original movie posters and signed my Jaws for me. He's a wonderful human being to work with.

**What was your favorite scene of the ride?**

I always loved the boathouse for the reason I already mentioned – I got to scare the damn kids! It doesn't get any better than that. Plus I always thought the boathouse shark looked fantastic. He was in the dark under these blue lights that made him look a little scarier. I also thought all the show effects came together nicely in that scene. You've got the sound of him breaking through the boathouse wall plus the plumers, the sparkers, and the water mortars. When everything worked like it was supposed to it was a great scene. The shark came up so close to the side of the boat too. I would reach over the side of the boat with my grenade launcher, which is a big no-no, and found that I could almost touch him as he went past. My favorite time of the year to do Jaws was Halloween Horror Nights because that's when we did what we called "shark in the dark" late into the night. The guests were also a ton of fun because they were mostly drunk and just out for a good time. It never happened on my boats but I know there are stories from Horror Nights of guests who jumped overboard to go swimming in the lagoon, which was not safe at all. I would never, ever go in that dirty water.

**As an actor and a trainer, what was your take on spieling improv? Did you ever go off script?**

It wasn't encouraged, but sometimes if it was called for. If a tourist reacted in a certain way and you could sneak something in that worked, sure. I had one thing I would stick in when the gas dock exploded. People would always go, '*Oh God, it's hot!*' And I would say, '*Of course it's hot. It's fire!*' And I'd get my laugh and move on. For me, the best time to improv was when the ride broke down which was somewhat frequent. Breakdowns were inevitable when you've got an attraction with complex animatronics in water and huge fire effects and such. I'm kind of impressed it performed as well as it did being operated every single day in the hot Florida sun. I think people came to take Jaws for granted considering how much of a technical achievement it was. Kong was the same way. Remember "Ride the movies?" You literally rode a movie on those attractions. Now with motion simulators, you're just watching a movie while your seat moves. It definitely was different back then.

**Speaking of breakdowns, what would a bad day at Jaws look like?**

There was one day I nicknamed it "The Great Bubble Ride." It was a busy peak day of summer. I always told friends, '*If you want to ride Jaws, come to the park right when it opens and do it early in the morning.*' That's when everything on the ride was most likely to be working. Things would start to give out by midday. On this particular day, all we had were some plumers and a couple of shark fins. We had fin number one and the dead shark. Hence "The Great Bubble Ride." It was ridiculous that we even kept it open that day. Sometimes you'd go into the boathouse and the shark would be sticking up out of the water and you'd have to go, '*Whoa, it looks like Quint stuffed one of the sharks to scare us!*' Like I said before, the best time to improv was when the ride broke or stopped altogether. That's when you really had to be an entertainer in order to hold the attention of your guests in the middle of the lagoon. I loved those moments because that's when I got to do my own show. Actors, you know, we're very into ourselves! (laughs)

**As spieling attractions, were Kongfrontation and Jaws more alike or more different?**

I would say more different. The thing about Kong is that he was always just there. You could set yourself on fire and no one would notice. Okay, maybe a few people would notice but most guests would be staring at the thirty-foot tall animatronic monkey. No one cared what the tram driver was doing. On Jaws, the shark wasn't always there so the skipper got to be the center of attention in the moments before and after the shark appeared. The story played out largely through the skipper. I thought the ride script was really well written on Jaws. It was written in such a way that you could create a character within the dialogue they gave you. My skipper character was this kind of cocky young guy who'd done this boat tour a thousand times. Then the shark appeared and I had to go from scared shitless to becoming this tough hero guy. The skipper actually changes throughout the ride if you pay attention. It's one of the only spieling attractions I can think of where there's a character arc. Like I said, it was a good script.

**What was it like being a trainer on the attraction?**

It was great but not for the reasons you might think. Universal would periodically close the ride for maintenance which involved draining the entire lagoon. If you were a Jaws skipper, you would still need hours which you could get one of two ways. You could fill in at various other attractions or you could stay at Jaws to clean out the shark pits. That involved putting on these huge rubber waders and literally shoveling sludge and dirt from the dry lagoon. As a trainer, I didn't have to do either of those. I got to train the new bunch of recruits for the ride during that down time. I used to love looking out over the bridge at my pals who were shoveling sludge out of the kill shark pit. I'd go by with a group of six cute girl trainees and I'd yell, '*Hey guys, we're going to go run through the script in the boathouse! See you later!*' (laughs) That was a huge perk of being a trainer, not having to shovel the sludge. Of course I also loved teaching acting and seeing what each new skipper could do with the script. I saw it as my job to instill a certain enthusiasm into them so that they didn't see their job as just a job. You could actually have fun doing this position.

**Do you remember your last day at Jaws? And did you leave your shoes behind?**

No, I didn't leave my shoes behind. I was too broke to leave my shoes. I was much more likely to take someone else's shoes because I couldn't afford new shoes. I don't much remember my last day at the attraction. I landed a position in the Entertainment Department at Nickelodeon Studios. The tradition at Jaws was to throw whoever was leaving into the lagoon on their last day. Interestingly, they did something similar at Nickelodeon. Over there you would get slimed on your last day. Of course, the water at Jaws was so filthy that it was kind of like being slimed. Getting thrown into the lagoon wasn't so bad back then because we didn't have cell phones in our pockets. We didn't have them because they didn't exist!

I did briefly go back to Jaws a year or two later. They were desperate for skippers and had me go over to work the ride while still making my Nickelodeon pay rate for a day. That was cool, kind of like going home in a way. I'll tell you this. It's now more than twenty years later and I still remember every word of the Jaws ride script. I could spiel the entire thing right now. I don't remember Kong or Nickelodeon, but I remember Jaws word for word.

**When was the last time you rode Jaws?**

I visited several times right at the end. I got together with some other former skippers about a week before the ride closed, which was a lot of fun. God, how many years ago was that? Six? It's sad because some of us from that reunion aren't around anymore. We've lost some people. It was like a family reunion. We had such a good time yelling out lines of dialogue with the young skipper on our boat. We're all so old now. I felt like Father Time riding with these young twenty-something skippers. I was also there the night Jaws closed. It was a very sad evening. Everyone gathered around unload as the final boats came in and sang, 'Show me the way to go home' from the movie. Those young skippers took me in and made me a part of their group that night. People were holding lighters up in the air and even crying. It felt like a part of me was closing down with the ride. It may sound silly to some but I've never been a part of something like that before or after. It was a special thing. Sometimes I go back to the park just as I'm doing today to walk around and try to feel that nostalgia. It's bittersweet.

Top: The Jaws skipper shoots with the accuracy of an empirical stormtrooper - and ultimately misses. (Photo courtesy Colin Peterson)

Right: Skipper Jon locked and loaded on the ride's final night of operation. (Photo courtesy Jon Donahue)

# SKIPPER FROM THE HOUSE OF MOUSE

❖

an interview with

## BILL MOORE

### Skipper (1994 to 1995)

Skipper Bill still rocking an Amity Boat Tours tee. (Photo courtesy Bill Moore)

**How did you come to join the ranks of Captain Jake's?**

I was already working full time at Disney doing the monorails and wanted to pick up a few extra dollars. I figured the best way to do that was to try out another theme park. I wasn't sure at first if that was going to work since they were competitors. I showed up to Universal's open interviews anyway to find out. They were not just okay with my job at Disney - they were thrilled that I had experience in the industry. They asked if I was interested in working at Jaws and, of course, I told them I would be very interested in that. I interviewed for that position, got the job, and began training the following week. It happened very quickly. I should also mention that no one at Disney seemed to care that I'd started working at Universal. I was kind of expecting someone to say something but no one ever did. Everyone knew about it and the managers at both parks were good about working around my schedules.

**That's great they were so accepting of your dual allegiance. Do you think that would still be the case today?**

From what I've heard it's still somewhat the case. I think it's almost like a '*don't ask, don't tell*' kind of thing. As long as it's not interfering with your job and you're not actively sharing confidential secrets, it's not all that frowned upon to work for both parks.

**Which did you experience first – Jaws the movie or Jaws the ride?**

Oh definitely the movie. My first experience with Jaws was when it originally premiered in theaters. I saw it within the first week and fell in love with it. It was both scary and fascinating at the same time. I've been crazy about it ever since. Growing up we basically lived across from the beach, which became pretty unnerving to me after I'd seen Jaws. I'd never before cared about what might be lurking under the water that I couldn't see. Jaws changed that.

**I take it you'd ridden Jaws before becoming a skipper?**

Yes, I had. I had even ridden the original 1990 version but only once. I don't remember all that much about it except that the lines were long and the guests were complaining. The ride was up and down that day as I recall. It would run for a little while and then go 11-1. That wasn't a great time to be at the park, just after it opened, because you'd have multiple big ticket attractions go down at the same time. I remember being fascinated with the exploding shark effect that originally ended the ride. I wasn't entirely sure how they managed to pull that effect off but I had an idea.

**How was skipper training? I assume it was nothing like working the monorails.**

Skipper training was definitely interesting. I did an initial Universal training where you got to know the company a little bit. Training for the Jaws ride itself happened in three parts. The first part was water safety training like you might get as a lifeguard. We went to an area pool and did extensive swimming exercises. I think most people were probably aware that the water wasn't all that deep on Jaws except where the sharks were. In those places the water was quite deep! Fortunately, I never had to use my water safety training.

Top: This would have been a good day for an Express pass! (Photo courtesy Colin Peterson)

Bottom: The entrance stairway to the crow's nest. (Photo courtesy TomCroom.com)

The second part of Jaws training was similar to an acting class. We had to learn the spiel script and master the timing of it. It took some time to learn how and when to react to everything happening around you. The third part of Jaws training saw you getting on a boat with your fellow trainees. You would just circle the lagoon over and over for hours at a time doing your spiel until you had it perfect or near perfect. The trainer on boat would give you feedback on how to make your performance feel more natural. Once you were signed off on all that you would go train on the other positions at Jaws like greeter, load, unload, and so on. It was a lot of information to remember.

**What was your favorite scene from the attraction?**

Definitely the boathouse. That scene played out mostly in the dark except for some cool lighting effects which I thought made it a little scarier for the guests. It was so much fun to watch the people who hadn't been on Jaws before because they had no idea what to expect in there. That scene was also a lot of fun to spiel because the skipper reacts to everything happening with increasing terror. That never got old for me. Of course, the boathouse was also a great reprieve from the summer heat so I may've liked it best for that reason as well!

**What do you think set the Jaws ride apart from other opening day attractions?**

I think it was the complexity of it all that made Jaws special. Not everyone is aware of how much had to come together for that ride to work perfectly. Hopefully your book will enlighten them on that. You had these incredibly complex shark animatronics operating underwater and interacting with other fire and water effects. It all came together to make a really good ride experience. I also think the skippers were a big part of the ride's success. The crew I worked with at Jaws were so passionate about the attraction and really threw themselves into it. I think the spiel script for the Jaws ride was also a little more energetic and physically involved than other spieling attractions. Take Kongfrontation for example. Kong had some really cool effects but the spieling just wasn't all that exciting. On Jaws, the skippers are steering the boat and firing a grenade launcher. On Kong, the spielers had a much less active role to play. They were just basically reacting to what was happening.

One thing I loved about Jaws was that you couldn't tell anything about it from standing outside of it. Walking up to the entrance and going through the queue did nothing to prepare you for it. Even the first ride scene didn't indicate what was about to happen when you rounded the lighthouse. Most every part of the Jaws ride was blocked off from view. It wasn't like a rollercoaster where you could see part or all of the ride from another part of the park. With Jaws, all you could see were the boats pulling into unload and people getting off the ride looking like they just had a great time. It made you want to ride it and see what all the mystery was about. As a skipper, I got to experience the ride over and over again through the guests who were having so much fun. I loved that about Jaws.

**Did you ever improvise or go off script with your spieling?**

A little but not much at all. I know my comrades would throw different things in there, an extra joke or some physical comedy. I know I thought about improvising way more than I actually did. I was probably afraid of getting pulled off the ride. Other skippers were far bolder than I was.

**You started at Jaws in 1994 just after the re-opening. What were those early crowds like?**

They were very into the ride. As a loader for the attraction you could easily tell who had ridden it before. Repeat riders would often ask to sit on the left side since most of the action happens on the that side of the boat. That's where you see Amity Three sinking, the first fin, the dock explosion, and the final kill shark. It seemed like most guests were terrified of getting wet, which I felt didn't happen all that much. It was a real possibility and we had to warn people as if everyone was going to get soaked. On some days the queue lines got really, really long and we had to open up the extended queues. That's when you felt the pressure to deliver a good show because you realize that people have been standing in line for an hour or even two hours just to experience a five minute ride. I think most people thought Jaws was worth waiting that long for. There was nowhere else on the planet you could see something like this.

**What was the Jaws ride like when it didn't work as intended?**

That depended on what exactly wasn't working. Sometimes it wasn't that big of a deal. Other times it was a *huge* deal. The easiest effects to lose were the fin sharks in Scene Two. It wasn't that hard to pretend there was a shark in the water as you cruised past the sinking boat. It helped a lot that your boat rolled back and forth so that you could go, '*Did you feel that?! The shark must be under us!*' They also gave you suggested cover material for those moments. The hardest sharks to lose were the final two, the shark that bit the cable and the dead shark. The worst part of the ride to malfunction was the finale because that was the big moment you've been building towards the whole time.

The worst covering for missing effects I ever had to do was one morning when it seemed like nearly all of the sharks were acting up. They were all out of the water on their platforms when we arrived to work. We were told that six out of the seven sharks were either malfunctioning or unreliable but that we were still going to open up for guests. There was only one shark we knew for sure was going to appear, the one by the exploding gas dock. The fins weren't even working! The entire opening team had a meeting shortly after that and decided that we weren't going to operate the ride that way. It wasn't fair to the guests or to us for that matter. A couple of managers came over soon after to try and smooth things over. They said, '*It's not going to be that bad. We're going to go ahead with the opening and hopefully the other sharks will start working soon.*' They came up with a plan to stand at unload and personally take care of any complaints. That only lasted maybe two or three boats before they disappeared completely. We were stuck operating the ride that way, which was embarrassing. The surprising thing was that we didn't get as many people complaining as you might think. It helped that the boats weren't full loads yet because it was so early in the morning. But it was still so awkward doing the show like that. After a couple of hours they finally took the ride down for maintenance, which lasted the rest of the day.

The most commonly missing effect during my time at Jaws seemed to be the fog effect in the boathouse. The gas dock fire effects didn't go down too often, though I believe they eventually added more safety features to it after I left which resulted in a little more downtime. The cover material wasn't too bad for most of the missing effects. The pace and stall material was a little harder because it became your job to hold people's attention while the ride was stopped. Universal wanted you to stay in character as the skipper for as long as possible, which is a lot harder than you might think. You'd have all of this trivia and knowledge about Amity Island and the making of the movie but you had to tell it in an engaging way or else guests would mentally check out after about thirty seconds. Keeping people's attention when the ride was stopped was a definite challenge.

**What's your fondest memory from working at Jaws?**

I don't know if this is my fondest but it's definitely my most amusing memory. One day I was on boat doing my usual spiel and the tower person came over the radio and said, '*Bill, we've got the Hawaiian Tropic girls coming over and they're going to be videotaped riding Jaws for a television special.*' Sure enough they got on my boat with their camera crew. It seemed like every skipper working that day came over to make sure I didn't need a break. Everyone wanted to be the skipper that took these beautiful Hawaiian Tropic models around the ride! They'd go, '*Hey Bill, are you sure you don't need to stretch your legs for a bit? How about an extra lunch break today?*' I stayed on boat and we did several tours around the lagoon with the girls and their crew. It was very relaxing on my part because they were going to enjoy the ride no matter what since they were on camera and none of the cameramen ever panned over to me. Each time we passed the load dock to go around again there would be a gathering of skippers and managers asking, '*You sure you don't need a break yet?!*' Unfortunately, I've never been able to find that special.

# SWIMMING
## WITH JAWS

Ever wonder what it would be like to take a swim in the Jaws Ride lagoon? This 2005 crew did and found out together one night after closing! By all accounts, the lagoon was a filthy brew of hydraulic fluid and God-knows-what-else. In addition, the lagoon made for an incredibly dangerous swim due to the deep shark pits and assorted machinery contained within. Such antics were increasingly frowned upon in the ride's later years and eventually banned altogether by management. Here's to swimmin' with bow-legged women!

(Photos courtesy Colin Peterson)

# EIGHT YEARS AT CAPTAIN JAKE'S

an interview with

## LEVI TINKER
### Skipper (2000 - 2008)

Skipper Levi about to deliver the *best* and only scenic cruise on Amity Island.
(Photo courtesy Levi Tinker)

**How did you come to work for Universal Studios Florida?**

I started in 2000 not at Jaws but as part of Halloween Horror Nights. I was just beginning to move out to Los Angeles during this time but still spent much of the year in Florida. I auditioned for Halloween Horror Nights 10 and was hired as a scare-actor in the Amity section of the park. That year they gave several of the big attractions makeovers to be a little scarier for the event. The Jaws ride became Jaws: Bloody Waters. The big difference was that they added Jack the Clown to Scene Three. As you entered the boathouse, you would see Jack killing a victim on the walkway to your left. The victim would drop dead and he would walk over to the boat holding a gas hose that sprays everyone. Then the skipper would kick the boat into gear and leave the boathouse just as the shark attacked.

For whatever reason, one of the two alternating Jack actors had to leave suddenly and they needed a replacement Jack for the boathouse. They asked me and I agreed to do it. I enjoyed that role quite a bit. When Halloween Horror Nights was over, I went to see where else I could work in the park. I originally applied to be at the Alfred Hitchcock: The Art of Making Movies but ended up getting picked for Amity Boat Tours instead. I was already a fan of the Jaws ride but I'd never given any thought to working there before.

**How was training for the ride?**

My training lasted two weeks. The weird thing was that they drained the Jaws lagoon for its yearly maintenance following Halloween Horror Nights, so all my training happened with the lagoon completely dry. That's different than how training would normally go because you can't actually do the ride without water. I just remember going through the motions and learning the dialogue as best I could. I also became very familiar with the pace and stall material, which I kind of enjoyed. I was eventually signed off as a spieler after performing the entire show on a boat in the dry lagoon. I did all of the lines without actually going through any of the show scenes.

**What was it like when you finally got on a boat with water in the lagoon?**

It was so much fun. It was *always* so much fun. Some people thought being a skipper was a difficult job but I never did. I preferred being on boat over any other position at the attraction. I would actually freeze myself on boat and let whoever bump over me and keep going. I loved the attraction that much. I literally drove three hours to work every day from New Port Richey and then three hours home. I knew if I ever moved to Orlando I would never be able to get out to Los Angeles where I am now.

In 2002, I did something I had been wanting to do for a while but had been unable to; I froze myself on boat all day long. I was wanting to do more shows in a single day than anyone else had previously. This was right around the Christmas season. We were open that day from about 9am to midnight. I did show after show after show without taking any meal breaks. I ended up doing one-hundred-and-twelve shows in a row. I've yet to hear of anyone that broke that record.

**What's the craziest thing you ever had a guest do? Ever have someone fall overboard?**

I never had a guest fall in but I fell in once! This was back when I was playing Jack in the boathouse for Halloween Horror Nights. I think we were performing in thirty minute sets, so I'd be Jack for thirty minutes and then get a break. The alternate Jack actor had adjusted his safety harness while I was on break so that he could do flips inside the boathouse, which he wasn't supposed to do. Then he went on break and I put on this harness that no longer fit me correctly. I lean over to spray the guests like I've been doing all night and I fall right into the water. It was so dark in there that the skipper didn't even see me at first. They hadn't gotten to the part where they use the spotlight. He hit the e-stop as soon as he saw me in front of the boat. The person playing Jack's victim eventually had to help pull me out. Falling into the water didn't really scare me at the time. I just thought it was funny. Had this happened after I became a Jaws skipper I would have been much more freaked out because those pits get quite deep. They were most insistent that I get a tetanus shot after that but I had just gotten one and wasn't eager to get another.

**You mentioned memorizing the pace and stall material. What was it like to have to spiel that?**

It wasn't too hard for me but then again I memorized all of it early on. Depending on the situation, you could very easily run through all the official pace and stall material and be left with nothing else to say to your guests, which was not good. I came to know so much about Jaws the movie that I would transition into stories about the making of the film to fill the silence. The longest I ever had to stall and pace happened out in Scene Five. We were stuck out there for about an hour and I was fortunately able to keep it going. I think part of the track had blown so they weren't able to get the boats running again very easily.

Similar to pace and stall, you'd sometimes have to cover for a missing or malfunctioning show element. I thought most skippers did a great job of doing that. A good skipper could cover for a missing shark without impacting your experience on the ride. They might even have been able to cover for two missing sharks without ruining the experience. Any more than two missing sharks and guests are probably going to know something has gone wrong. It was kind of cheesy sometimes to exit the boathouse and find the gas dock shark frozen above the water. A missing shark is one thing but a shark frozen above the water is probably when you should go ahead and shut down the ride until maintenance can address it.

**Did you ever improvise or go off script?**

*Never!* First of all, I'm horrible at improv so I'm the guy who is going to stick by what's written on the page. Secondly, I would never want to do anything that would get me in trouble or negatively impact a guest experience. There were some interesting improvs and also some not so interesting ones. There was one skipper who on his break ran out onto the beach near the church cemetery and laid there like a dead body. He got away with that for a good thirty minutes before someone caught on and they pulled him out. Another skipper decided to faint once they found Gordon's boat sinking by the lighthouse in Scene Two. This skipper would lay on the floor of the boat for most of the ride and only jump back up after Scene Five as they pulled into unload. It would be like he missed every appearance of the shark. Someone eventually found out about that and he got in trouble for it.

**Why do you think so many people look back so fondly on the Jaws ride?**

One of the big reasons is that Jaws is just such an iconic and beloved film. Jaws is over forty years old now but it still holds up incredibly well. The ride is still beloved because of the care and quality that went into designing the attraction itself. There was also something special in the way that the skippers engaged the audience. Some thought the spieling was cheesy or funny but I thought it worked. You could tell in the later years especially that people just fell in love with that attraction. There were often long waits in the queue line even though it was such an old ride.

**I've seen a picture of you standing outside the ride with a shark puppet. What was that about?**

Around 2001 or so, Universal gave us this shark puppet to use in the greeter position outside the ride. They said his name was Chompy like in the queue video. They wanted us to use the puppet to answer questions from guests, so you'd talk to them in what you thought was the voice of this little puppet shark. That didn't last very long.

**What did you and the other skippers hear about the original 1990 version of the ride?**

Not much! We knew that the original ride was different but we didn't know how different. The one story I remember hearing involved the celebrities who rode Jaws on opening day back in 1990. Apparently, Jimmy Stewart's boat stalled out in the the lagoon and was stuck there for an extended period of time. That's a really strange thing to imagine - eighty-two-year-old Jimmy Stewart stuck on the Jaws ride. Otherwise the original version sounded like a cool experience. I would love to have experienced the attraction in its original version.

Skipper Levi using the fortunately short-lived Chompy puppet to interact with guests.
(Photo courtesy Levi Tinker)

Skipper Levi keeping Amity safe while wearing the *actual* Chief Brody jacket! (Photo courtesy Levi Tinker)

**Do you remember your last tour spieling around the lagoon?**

No because I didn't realize my last tour was going to be my last tour. I worked full time at Jaws from 2000 to 2002 and was seasonal from 2002 to 2008 when they decided to get rid of all seasonal positions. I received a letter one day thanking me for my time working there because they were eliminating those positions. I was honestly devastated because that was always one of the highlights of coming back to Orlando for me. The previous standing agreement was that if you worked at least one shift quarterly you could stay on as a seasonal employee. My more memorable farewell tour was in 2002 when I stopped working there full time. There was one thing I was able to do then that I'd always wanted to do. Remember in the queue line how they had Chief Brody's actual police jacket from the film in one of the display cases? I just knew that jacket was the perfect size for me and I wanted to get a picture of me wearing it. I managed to get someone to open the case for me and I snapped a few pictures while wearing it out by the hanging shark. I also took some pictures out by Neptune's Folly. That was an incredible memory for me. I'm sure there aren't too many skippers who can claim to have done that.

**Did you participate in the skipper tradition of leaving your shoes behind at the ride?**

Yes, I did! That was a big thing that many skippers did. I left a pair of my shoes in the boathouse. I threw them and they landed on the walkway on the opposite side. So coming into the boathouse, my shoes were on the right.

Top: Skipper Levi reuniting with Skipper Jon Donahue by the hanging shark in 2018.

Bottom: Since 2000, Levi has been the general manager of LA's iconic Chinese Theatre. Here he is with Dwayne Johnson, star of Frank Kincaid's upcoming *disaster* epic "Mutha Nature." (Photos courtesy Levi Tinker)

# WE'RE NOT REALLY DRIVING THE BOAT & OTHER REVELATIONS

an interview with

## NATHAN KEY

### Skipper (2000 to 2002)

Skipper Nathan welcoming guests aboard Amity Six.

(Photo courtesy Nathan Key)

**How did you wind up at Captain Jake's Amity Boat Tours?**

I applied to work at Universal Orlando about a year-and-a-half after Islands of Adventure opened in 1999. As an annual passholder, I had fallen in love with the whole Islands of Adventure park. I originally applied to be a boat captain over at Island Skipper Tours thinking that would be pretty cool but my interview took me in a different direction. They said, '*Given your interest in the nautical, would you consider working at the Jaws ride?*' And I said, '*Absolutely!*' I didn't even think that was an option at the time. I didn't go in hoping to work at Jaws. I got there by pure happenstance, but it was ultimately a great opportunity.

**What was your impression of the Jaws ride heading into that position?**

I hadn't even seen the movie at that time. Although I was a child of the late '70s, I didn't really have the full cultural understanding of it all. I had been on the ride, which I thought was somewhat similar to Disney's Jungle Cruise. They both have a couple of laughs and a couple of scares. I found Jaws to be something completely different once I started working there. It was an entire sub-culture at Universal. There was something so tangible about the experience of being a part of that attraction. You can still see it on blogs and social media posts. There are people who worked there twenty years ago who still can't get it out of their head. I still dream about the ride!

**What do you think set Jaws apart from other Universal attractions?**

I think it had to do with the fact that it was simply better than the other rides. There are a lot of things that set Jaws apart, though. It was an open air ride instead of being set inside a building, which gave you the ability to have an atmosphere that was a little truer to life. You also had the natural element of weather. In the spring it felt like a spring boat tour and in the fall it felt like a fall boat tour and so on. Another unique aspect to Jaws is that the skipper really drove the story forward.

I would often compare Jaws to Kongfrontation to see what really set it apart. Kong was a good attraction but it was really, really loud inside an enclosed space. The trams didn't move all that fast and Kong himself didn't move anywhere near as fast as the shark did. Jaws was hidden almost the entire time you were on that boat, so most of the ride is about the skipper and not the shark. I think that's what made it work. When you came around the corner on Kong, you could see the monkey from a mile away. He was right there. It wasn't like he was hiding or about to jump out at you. And again, you're moving very slowly. Even his arm comes down slowly on top of the tram. It's just not as exciting or scary as when you're out on the open water and the shark bursts up and goes right back down. Kong didn't have that kind of energy to it.

Here we see Skipper Nathan driving too close to the flames *again*. Steer clear, Nathan!!!

**What was your favorite scene in the attraction?**

The boathouse for sure. You had this wonderful moment in the ride right before you go into the boathouse where the skipper considers how to best escape the shark. Should he go out to sea or should he go hide in the boathouse? The shark has already destroyed a tour boat just like the one you're on, so he figures going into the boathouse is the best option. Inside it's dark and creepy and you've got all these dripping sounds. The chum barrels just explode when the shark rams into the the outside wall. At that moment it feels like you're in a horror movie. There's nothing much to see but you're listening so intently to all these terrifying sounds. It was intense.

**What's something most guests never realized about your job as skipper?**

I don't think most guests realized we weren't actually driving the boats. I was in high school when I first rode Jaws as a guest and I never realized that the boats were on tracks. This relates to the best compliment and complaint I ever received on the ride. A woman once complained to guest services that I was driving the boat too close to the fire. She actually thought I was in control of the boat and was putting everyone in danger! (laughs) That's the best compliment I've ever gotten! It's all automated, you know. And it's not all that easy to fake like you're driving a boat when you're not. That took practice.

**Did you ever have any VIPs come onto your boat while at Jaws?**

I did! I had several encounters with celebrities but my favorite was probably Robin Williams. I have to give you a little context first. At Jaws, there was this little boardwalk bridge that skippers used to go between the load and unload areas. If someone in a wheelchair got on the ride, I would take their wheelchair down this path to unload so that it would be there when they got off the ride. Sometimes in the summer, the wheelchairs could get backed up. So I developed this weird technique where I would line two of them up and sit in the second wheelchair. I would then propel myself forward using my feet. It looked strange, I'm sure, but it helped me make less trips. One day as I'm doing this, I look over and see Robin Williams standing alone over by this walkway just watching the boats go by. On my fourth or fifth trip doing this, he stops me and goes, '*Is this really your job here? You just... ride wheelchairs back and forth all day? What a great thing to get paid to do! You look like Fred Flintstone taking these things back and forth!*' And he did this whole two-minute monologue making fun of this weird task I had to do. We both had a really good laugh about it. I thought it was cool. He didn't have to engage with me at all, but he did.

I also had Dwayne "The Rock" Johnson one time. No one is going to top Robin Williams, but he came pretty close. The celebrity liaisons liked to put the more famous guests in the last row of the boat to avoid being noticed. Celebrities often need to be discreet when visiting a theme park so they don't wind up having to take pictures and sign autographs all day. That's what the liaisons are there for. The Rock was there with his family and insisted upon sitting in the first row. He was so into it! He was doing the people's eyebrow at the shark and freaking out when it attacked. He shook my hand afterward and thanked me for taking him around. He was a very nice guy.

**You had run-ins with the stars of both Jumanji movies while at Jaws. That's a unique claim!**

Oh yeah! I didn't even think about that until you just said it. I'm going to have to tell my kids that.

**What was your impression of the attraction when you arrived in 2000?**

The Jaws ride was no longer brand new when I got there as it had been six or seven years since it re-opened. Men In Black: Alien Attack was the hot new ride at the time. It opened three weeks after I started working at Universal. It was interesting seeing the competition between Jaws and Men in Black. We were still packed with crowds every single day due in part to the enthusiasm of the crew that was there. It remained a popular and loved attraction right up until the day it closed.

**Were there ever any pranks or running gags amongst the skippers?**

When I was there the pranks were mostly between Jaws and the other attractions. One time someone stole the couch from our breakroom and stuck it on one of the boardwalks in the park. That was pretty good. Another time we stole the Speak-n-Spell from the E.T. Adventure and stashed it in the boathouse for a couple of days. Little things like that made the job more fun for us. Every once in a while the leads would go see who had the most people through their attraction on a given day. Men in Black was almost always the most popular. I loved to rub it in their face at the end of the night when we could say we had more guests come through than they did, even though they were at full capacity the entire day. I'd say, '*Well, I guess not everyone cares about the new bright shiny thing. They just want to come ride Jaws!*' That obviously had more to do with ride capacity than popularity, but that didn't matter. Then the Terminator lead would come in and say, '*We had ninety-thousand people come through!*' and I'd go, '*There weren't even that many people in the park today!*'

**It seems every skipper eventually encountered temperamental sharks or effects. What was that like?**

If you knew something wasn't working in advance, you could sort of prepare for it. It wasn't as exciting when you knew something was out, but it was even worse when you didn't know something was out. It could be really jarring to your spiel performance when you spin around fast expecting the shark to be there and he doesn't appear. Then you're like, '*Oh great. I just spun around really quickly for no apparent reason at all,*' and you're stuck trying to play it off. The ride is so focused on the skipper's performance that I think the shark is almost secondary to that. It was still an exciting experience if you were missing a fin or shark. There were enough left in the attraction that it still worked.

Far worse than a shark not working was the fire dock not exploding because the sound still went off no matter what. So you turn around to the sound of an explosion... only there's no explosion. That was a bummer. Everyone could tell what was supposed to happen even if they hadn't ridden before. They could figure it out. It was a bummer because there wasn't much you could do to cover it. '*Oh no! I guess there was some kind of propane explosion of hot air. Hot air exploded!*'

**Did you ever deviate from the spiel script?**

Now that the ride is no longer there and I don't have to answer to any supervisors.... yes, I absolutely did. I had a couple different spiels I would do. I had one where I just happened to be looking the other way every time the shark appeared. I think I got it from Mike Brown or Elliot Hansen. So everyone is yelling '*Shark! Shark!*' and I'd be like, '*Oh man. My shoe's untied!*' and bend down and miss the shark. That was probably my favorite variation, to do the entire show and not see the shark once.

The funniest thing I ever did was to give the grenade launcher to someone in the front row after I'd missed the shark with it twice. I'd be like, '*I can't hit anything with this. Here, you hold it.*' They'd have it through the next scene and then we'd go out to the gas dock. I'm looking the other way as the shark pops up and the gas tanks suddenly explode behind me. I look at the explosion, then at the person holding the grenade launcher, then at the explosion, and I go, '*What did you do!?!? I gave you the gun for like a minute and you blew up the gas dock!*' And they never changed the prices on the gas pumps from the early '90s, so I'd go, '*That was the cheapest gas in Amity, you fool!*' Those were my biggest deviations. Everyone on the boat would just be howling by the end of it.

**Did you ever have anyone fall overboard?**

I don't know of anyone falling into the water while I was there. Levi Tinker fell in one time during Halloween Horror Nights as Jack the Clown. Have you heard that story? He was in the boathouse trying to scare the guests and fell right into the water. You probably already know this, but Levi became a skipper after that and worked at Jaws for many

| Skipper trio - Levi Tinker, Nathan Key, and Chris Hecht. (Photo courtesy Levi Tinker)

years. I saw lots of skippers do that ride, but Levi was unquestionably the most dedicated Jaws skipper in the history of the ride. He embodied that role every single day and never, ever went off script. I don't know how he maintained that level of intensity throughout all his years there, but he did. Levi lived for that ride.

**What was your least favorite role in the staffing rotation at Jaws?**

Definitely pre-board. It may have been because I didn't want to work that hard, but it was a tough position. Time is of the essence when you're trying to get people onto those boats. You've got to have six guests per row to get maximum capacity and people never wanted to split up their parties. It was always a negotiation to get the most people possible on the boat and then also line up guests for the next boat as fast as you could. I was always hoarse by the end of the day. It was a fast-paced position to be in. People would be mad having been in line for forty minutes watching people go right through the Express line. Apparently I am in the minority on this opinion as I brought it up in an online discussion recently and a lot of skippers disagreed with me.

**How long was too long to be on boat? And what exactly did it mean to be "frozen on boat?"**

At Jaws, you could spiel a few shows with the same energy but eventually you'd need a break like with anything else. If you just kept doing it, your show would start to suffer. So we'd put together rotations where you would do fifteen or thirty minutes on boat, which was three or four shows, and then you'd change to a land position like pre-board or greeter or tower. That would give you a chance to rest up. Then you'd get back on boat or if we had enough staff you could take a fifteen-minute break. It kept the day moving to do a few shows, switch to a land position, then do a few more shows. Being frozen on boat meant that was all you were doing. Show after show after show. I think a lot of skippers first starting out thought being frozen on boat was cool because they were just so excited to be doing it. Then they realize that it's actually a lot of work and you can't do it for more than maybe forty-five minutes before you need a breather from it. That was like nine or ten shows. It would seriously drain your energy and your show would start to go downhill. Some people could do it a lot longer, Levi Tinker being one of them.

**You became friends with Universal legend Mimi Lipka, didn't you?**

Yes, I did! She was really wonderful. Mimi was the spiel coach for all of Universal Studios Florida and helped us all learn the ride script. You couldn't get on a boat by yourself unless she personally signed you off on it. She would also come around periodically to do evaluations on everyone. I really loved working with her in that capacity. I got to spend a lot more time with her once I became a lead as she coached me on how to coach other people. Based on that working relationship, she invited me to apply to be a service coach, which was a new position in human resources. In that role I worked closely with Food/Beverage and Merchandising to help them with their service interactions. It was really cool to be training others alongside Mimi in that position since she was the one who first trained me. She was at my wedding and even made my groom's cake. The whole sheet cake was blue and had Jaws popping up like the last scene of the ride where he bites the cable. She made the shark out of red velvet, so it looked like it was bleeding when you cut into it. It was the best!

**Do you remember your last day at Jaws?**

I remember that the techs were threatening to throw me into the lagoon. They were thwarted, however. Not that I didn't want them to. I thought it sounded like fun. The supervisor that day came down to wish me farewell and also to make sure that I didn't go into the water because it had been deemed an extreme safety hazard. I did try to leave my shoes behind, though. I was closing lead my last night. This was near the end of December, so it got dark early in the evening. One of the other leads and I used to conduct our meetings out at Glenn's Bait and Tackle. We would grab some poles and pretend to be fishing. I tried to get onto the main island that night but it was so dark that I tripped and wound up dropping my shoes into the lagoon. They're probably buried deep under Harry Potter by this point.

**Did Kongfrontation's closure make you worry at all about the Jaws ride?**

Not really. Kong's lines were non-existent in the months before they closed it. It was just not a well-attended attraction by that point. Our ride still had people standing in line for an hour or more. That might have been because of our close proximity to Men in Black – I don't know. No one was lining up for Kong like that, which I figure is why they shut it down to make room for a more popular ride. It made sense. I never worried for Jaws because our lines never became like Kong's lines. It completely blindsided me in 2012 when they took it out. It had been a staple of that park. There's no way Jaws had the same kind of walk-on status that Kong did in its final days. No way.

Quite frankly, I was devastated when I first heard they were closing it. I had always wanted to take my son to Universal to show him what his dad did at the Jaws ride. It's really sad to me that I'll never be able to show my kids that beyond videos on YouTube. I will go back to the park eventually, though. My kids are loving Harry Potter. I missed out on the Potter craze and I haven't read the books. I've heard that they're remarkable areas in the park. Still, it won't feel entirely right walking those streets knowing that it's no longer the attraction I loved. Most people will probably think it's way better than the Jaws ride ever was.

**I beg to differ.**

So do I.

# IT'S A HARD DOCK LIFE

an interview with

## COLIN PETERSON

### Skipper (2004 - 2009)
### Director - "Jaws the Musical: How To Tune a Fish"

Skipper Colin captures the "Don't Cry For Us, Universal" scene from Jaws the Musical. (Photo courtesy Colin Peterson)

**How did you come to work for Universal Studios Florida?**

I had known about the Jaws ride from growing up in Florida and visiting Universal Studios in the mid-nineties. Years later, I needed a job when I was in college at the University of Central Florida. Working at Jaws seemed like a good idea at the time. This was around 2004. They were having a casting call for both Earthquake and Jaws. I went in to interview and they had me read some lines from the script. It was the opening load spiel to get people on the boat.

**Why Jaws and not Earthquake? Did you have a choice?**

I did have a choice but they were definitely pushing the more energetic folks toward the Jaws ride. I think that's why all the attendants got along so well. All of us were kind of cut from the same cloth. Many of the skippers were theatre kids. I thought we had an excellent team. Nothing against the Earthquake folks, but that was more of a low key position. You weren't outside killing sharks every five minutes at Earthquake.

I was at Jaws from about 2004 to 2009, so roughly five years. I personally felt I had the best trainer, a guy named Ted Messimer. One thing I learned a lot about was pace and stall, which covered all the ins and outs of Amity. The pace and stall material allowed you to continue spieling if the ride ever broke down and you still had guests on your boat. Universal insisted you stay in character during those situations and keep the conversation going. So I would tell stories about how Gordon and I used to go fishing or how I had a run-in with Mayor Vaughn in high school. We had to memorize this huge backlog of Jaws story information.

**Your Amity Boat Tours experience was a little different than most others, wasn't it?**

It was! I actually met my wife Alicia while working at Jaws. We were both skippers. It was a great place to find likeminded people who were interested in many of the same things. A lot of the skippers dated each other too. The Jaws skipper parties were... um... you know Caligula? Not quite that, but sort of that general vibe. Neither I nor my wife were into that, though. We've been together for thirteen years and now have a son. That means there are people currently on the planet who would not exist were it not for the Jaws ride. How crazy is that?

**What was it like finding love at Captain Jake's of all places?**

Dating and working together at Jaws was interesting. We couldn't outright act like a couple on the boats or in front of guests, so we would try to add code words into our spiel at either load or unload. These were words that let the other person know we were thinking of them. The word "lobster" still holds a pretty significant place in our relationship. If she was in tower, I might tell guests getting onto my boat, '*I went out fishing with Captain Jake last week and we caught a forty-pound lobster!*' That would be my way of telling her that I was thinking about her. Believe it or not, Jaws turned out to be a great environment in which to foster a long lasting relationship.

Skippers Colin and Alicia from Amity Isle to the Wedding Aisle
(Photo courtesy Colin Peterson)

**How important were the skippers to the Jaws ride?**

They were integral to the experience. Without the skippers, the ride would have been nothing. They added a very important human element to that attraction. Jaws by itself might have been exciting on a base level with just the sharks popping up every few seconds, but the skippers truly made it something special. That's why it became an experience that many who rode it never forgot. There was a unique shared energy between the skippers and the guests. That human connection, I think, is why Jaws stayed around so long even as Universal was going through a massive transition as a company. Without the skippers, I think Jaws would've closed much sooner than it did.

**What were the challenges of being a skipper at Jaws?**

Obviously it was challenging when things didn't work as planned. If one or more of the sharks weren't working but the ride was still operational you would have to spiel with everything you've got. You might hear over your headset, *'The kill shark is not working. Repeat, the kill shark is not working!'* You would then have to somehow convince your guests that the shark was, in fact, underneath you because the boat would still rock back and forth. All the other effects would still trigger regardless of the shark. That's when you hit it with the grenade launcher and sell it as best you can. Even worse was when Jaws was closed entirely and they put you out front to tell people that the ride was closed. Sometimes the ride would shut down with a queue full of people and you'd have to flush out guests who had already been waiting an hour or more to experience it. That was bad.

For me, the hardest part of Jaws would happen as you came around the bend after you've killed the shark. You know when you do the whole '*Call off the marines, we're coming home!*' Sometimes you would turn around and the audience would have no response whatsoever. No smiles, no cheers. They would just stare at you like you're an animatronic at Disney. To not get any response in that moment is heartbreaking, especially when you've worked so hard to deliver an excellent experience. That could make you jaded and for some it did. You are truly wanting to give guests a great time because they've come to Universal from all over the world and waited in a long line for this one attraction. The best times were when you turned around and the guests cheered along with you.

**You joined Jaws just prior to the infamous 2005 closure due to rising fuel costs. Did that seem like the end?**
We thought it was the end. We were terrified that we were losing this thing we loved so much. We considered ourselves a family and suddenly we were spread out all across the park. Some went to Mummy, some went to Back to the Future, some to E.T.. These were rides that had no spieling whatsoever. We wound up losing a lot of good people to those other attractions because they quickly recognized how hard working the Jaws team members were. Skippers were offered lead positions at those attractions and remained there even when Jaws opened back up. At the time, I think most of us felt like we were being kicked out of our home. It was a big deal to us. We mourned the loss of Jaws. I have to say that our supervisor, Dan Gurwitz, was unbelievably positive during the whole thing. He was a great leader and made everyone continue to feel connected even though we were spread throughout the park.

**Did the subsequent backlash from guests over the 2005 closure surprise you?**
Not at all. I think it's important to remember why they eventually brought the attraction back. They didn't re-open Jaws because the cost of fuel went down. It didn't. They brought Jaws back because they were getting very poor customer service feedback at the front of the park. People were still coming to Universal specifically to ride Jaws and leaving extremely disappointed when they couldn't. Guests would write angry letters demanding to know when they could ride it again. I know more than a few skippers also wrote letters to the powers that be explaining why the ride still needed to exist. Guests soon came to learn that Jaws wasn't closed for maintenance or bad weather but because Universal considered it too costly. People found that to be an unacceptable reason to close it. And so when Universal brought Jaws back, we considered it an unbelievable triumph.

**Tell me all about your now infamous production of Jaws the Musical: How to Tune a Fish.**
Each year Universal's Ride & Show Division would hold a contest called the Golden Clicker Awards where they screen video skits made by the various ride teams. The employees would get together before and after their shifts to make these videos. The great part is that they were allowed by management to tape these skits at their own attractions. Basically if you had a camera and an idea you could submit a video to the Golden Clickers. These short films were often designed to be completely ridiculous. Universal would then organize a night where all the Ride & Show people could get together to screen these videos and pick the winner. This was strictly a behind-closed-doors contest never intended for the public to even know about.

So one year I directed a video for the Jaws ride called Jaws the Musical: How to Tune a Fish, which told the story of the ride's closure and eventual re-opening through parodies of then popular Broadway musicals. It was a huge undertaking that required around a thousand hours from everyone involved. The script was written by skipper Kristy Foster, who later married another skipper named Phil Whigham. The music was handled by Rick Percoco. My personal favorite parody in the video is where we spoofed "Seasons of Love" from RENT, only ours is "Where is my Bump?" and it's about trying to get a break. We would arrive at five in the morning to set up for shots that we would capture as soon as the sun came up. We didn't have long to film because folks would have to start their regular jobs at seven. The folks who weren't on shift would try to get as much footage as possible whenever possible. We did a lot of guerrilla filmmaking around the park and at other attractions.

The final scene of the video has the skippers singing "All That Jaws" on the dock beside the kill shark, which then makes an appearance. We grabbed that shot just as the first boat of the day was rounding the lighthouse in Scene One. We worked as fast as humanly possible to get the shot and then get out of view of the guests. There was a lot of staunch competition that year, but "How to Tune a Fish" definitely won. The award went to the ride, though I'm not sure who actually ended up with it. I was so proud of our team who had worked exceptionally hard to make it happen. Wrangling that many people for that many scenes was a challenge.

**So how did your video wind up on YouTube?**

It wasn't me, at least not originally. Somebody else uploaded it. The public was never supposed to see it and I got in big trouble over it. It very quickly amassed many thousands of views. Theme park websites were asking to interview me and the Orlando Sentinel even ran a piece on it. John Landis saw it and loved it. It was crazy how many people were liking our video. Then I got a call from Universal's Human Resources. This wasn't some middle manager but the tip top of the department. She called and was like, '*We love your video. We want you to come in for a meeting so that we can discuss your future at the company.*' And I was like, '*Oh wow. This is great! Sure, I'll come to this meeting.*' I thought I was about to be praised for the video.

**(laughing) Oh my God, that cannot be how they invited you. Seriously!?**

They played it perfectly. I thought I was walking into a meeting to jumpstart my filmmaking career. That's the naivety of a twenty something year old. Needless to say, that was *not* the meeting I walked into! (laughs) It was *so* not that meeting. They were pissed! They were so incredibly angry at me, all except for the guy from marketing. He actually loved it. So did the head of Universal Creative who met with me afterwards. The HR lady was like, '*You did this video in front of guests! There are guests in the background of your video! There are safety issues! I can see skippers on top of the boats!*' She listed off all these things that we had done wrong with the video. '*You put images of backstage areas onto the internet! This is not something that Universal as a company is happy about!*'

By this time, the original upload had been taken down but I had re-uploaded it from my own account. And because of that, the HR lady was like, '*We can't force you to take the video down, but we can fire you.*' And while I still wanted to work at Jaws... at the end of the day this was a job that paid $8.25 with a fifty cent spiel rate. It was

"Amity, as you know, means friendship." (Photo courtesy Colin Peterson)

not something I was going to do for the rest of my life. And Universal knew that I was not opposed to leaving over the video so they offered me a deal. If I took the video down, they would give me an entry level job in the production department. I accepted their offer and took the video down. But then I put it back online six months later after everyone had moved on. You know how the internet is. No one cared by then. Still, that meeting was harrowing for me. These were some serious high level people that had taken time out of their day to come tell me how pissed they were at what I had done. I did take the production assistant position and also kept my position at Jaws. I worked mostly as a gopher on iVillage Live, which was this now defunct, extremely ill-conceived morning talk show that they did in the Toon Lagoon Amphitheater at Islands of Adventure.

**That has got to be the weirdest use of that space ever.**

Yeah, it really was. They had set it up like a regular talk show but you would constantly hear the Hulk Coaster going off in the background. It was not a good idea and didn't last all that long.

**When did you wind up leaving Jaws?**

I left Jaws when I left Universal, which was probably around 2009. The last time I ever rode Jaws was with my buddies for my bachelor party. It was one of those bachelor parties where I didn't know what was happening next and that's how it began. They wanted me to go up front and spiel but I wasn't working there anymore at that time. John Bernard was our skipper on that one, the last skipper I ever saw do the ride.

# JAWS
## THE MUSICAL
## HOW TO TUNE A FISH

Skipper Colin Peterson's JAWS: THE MUSICAL spoofs popular Broadway showtunes to tell the story of the Jaws ride's temporary closure in 2005 due to rising fuel costs and decreasing park attendance. The subsequent outcry from guests over the attraction's seasonal nature ultimately led Universal to re-open Jaws and restore it to full-time status. The video itself was made for an internal contest and never intended for public release. Despite that, it eventually leaked online and became an instant hit with theme park enthusiasts.

(All photos courtesy Colin Peterson)

# "This is just brilliant.

If Universal's PR department wasn't at least tangentially involved with this, it should have been, because this is the most convincing piece of video marketing for a theme park attraction I have ever seen. Forget Disney's made-for-cable Everest special. This piece made me want to get on a plane for Orlando to go ride Jaws with this crew before they find other gigs or Universal foolishly closes it again."

— Robert Niles 6/3/06

**THEME PARK INSIDER**

## WATCH IT ON YOUTUBE!

**Jaws the Musical: How to Tune a Fish**

http://youtube.com/BigJawsFan

The infamous Golden Clicker Award-Winning video that recounts the story of the Jaws ride's devastating closure and triumphant re-opening.

205

# I LEFT MY HEART IN AMITY

an interview with

## DAN GURWITZ

**Skipper (1996 - 1998)**
**Supervisor (2004 - 2006)**

Dan addressing skippers from the Crow's Nest balcony.

(Photo courtesy Colin Peterson)

**How did you wind up at Amity Boat Tours?**

My wife and I moved to Orlando in 1993 because the company I worked for was supposed to be opening a store there. That never happened and I went over to Universal because I needed a job. They asked where in the park I would like to work and I told them Jaws. I knew it wasn't back open yet but it was about to be. They told me, '*We're not hiring for Jaws yet so we'll have to put you elsewhere. You can audition once they do start hiring.*' Unfortunately, they started hiring for Jaws several weeks later at which time they told me I hadn't been with the company long enough yet to audition. So I kind of got shafted there. I did ride the new Jaws when it re-opened and immediately loved it. I knew I wanted to work on this attraction as soon as I possibly could. I initially went to work at Back to the Future, which I also loved, but I wound up leaving because I had another job that was bumping me up to management. Then in 1996 I went back to Universal because I really missed working there and this time they did start me out at Jaws. I was there from 1996 to 1998 when I left to go help with the opening of Islands of Adventure.

**You remained a boat skipper over at Islands of Adventure, didn't you?**

Yes, I did. When I first went over to Islands I was just helping cycle ride vehicles through the attractions. As we got closer to opening they had us put down our first, second, and third choices for what ride we'd like to work at. I definitely did not put down Island Skipper Tours as any of my choices but that's where they wanted to place me. I told them I'd rather work at one of the bigger attractions and they came back with, '*We'd really like someone with some spieling experience to work at Island Skipper Tours.*' So I took that position and wound up falling in love with it. I went from pretending to drive a boat on Jaws to actually driving a boat on Island Skipper Tours.

The guy who designed the boats at Islands trained me and one other person to be the opening leads. We then trained everyone else. I later wound up training all of the boat skippers that drove guests to and from the hotels throughout the resort, who then trained everyone that came after them. So I like to think I'm the great, great, great grandfather of everyone who drives a boat at Universal Orlando because I trained whoever trained them.

**What was it like finally getting to work at Jaws?**

Being a skipper at Amity Boat Tours was the best job I ever had. I've had positions higher and lower but Jaws was the best. It was an actor's dream with a new show every five to six minutes. You had a captive audience who had to watch your show. I guess they could've jumped overboard but they didn't. You also had some incredible show effects to work with. At the time we had the famous rocketing barrel in the Scene Four explosion, which became a thing of legend because at some point it mysteriously disappeared and never came back.

Jaws was an amazing attraction and had the most close-knit team I've ever worked with. The spieling attractions are special because anyone can push a button. Spieling attractions were so much more than that and Jaws was arguably the best. I enjoyed all of them, though I did used to openly mock the Earthquake supervisors whenever I could. I'd make fun of their merchandise or lack thereof. '*You guys don't have t-shirts. You don't even have a pin!*' People would come from all over the world to ride Jaws. When they thought of Universal, this is what they thought of. It was as linked to the studio's legacy as any other property they've had. I absolutely adored it.

I'm sure everyone you interview for this book will tell you they had the best show ever but I can attest that mine was the very best. I would put every single cell in my body into my spiel performance. I could still do it right this moment without looking at a script. The lines are embedded in my brain. I would freeze myself on boat for hours and hours. When I later went back to Jaws as a supervisor, I would freeze myself on boat on Thanksgiving as my little gift to the skippers. I would do shows all day long.

### What's something most guests don't realize about being a Jaws skipper?

There are so many things you had to pay attention to. You weren't actually driving the boat but you had to make it appear as though you were, which was in some ways more difficult. You knew where the turns were but you had to make it look as though you didn't. You had to deliver your performance with perfect timing or else the show was going to be lost. You also had to be ready at any moment for something not to work and then be able to recover from it and move on with the spiel. Even if something was out, it was your job to maintain the integrity and intensity of the show. I remember one time I was on boat and the ride stopped for over forty minutes. We ended up having to get another boat to push us back to unload. I stayed in character the entire time and just said, '*Well folks, it looks like the shark is finally gone. Unfortunately it also looks like he damaged our engine. Captain Jake is on his way out here to help us out.*' And then I'd go into some of the history of Amity to fill the time. That was the mark of a good skipper, being able to keep the entertainment going in moments like those. We had a lot of pride in our show. We wanted every guest to leave satisfied with what they got.

Being on boat was only one part of working at Jaws. You also had tower, load, unload, preboard, greeter, and so on. The Jaws ride was a well operated machine when everyone did their part. It was a fairly difficult job to learn but it was fine once you had it down. Brain surgery is also a difficult job but I assume any brain surgeon will tell you it gets easier the more they do it and the more know what they're doing. It was the same with Jaws.

### You left Jaws for Island Skipper Tours. How did you wind up back at Jaws?

I was a skipper at Jaws from '96 to '98. I actually trained as a lead right at the end of my tenure at the ride but I never did a full shift in that position before leaving. They did call me one day and said, '*Hey, the closing lead called in. We need you to close up. Don't worry, the opening lead is here until 5:15 and you close at 6. You only have to cover the attraction for forty-five minutes.*' After the opener left we cycled the boats and did a bit of cleaning. I went up to turn in my paperwork and that was it. Then I transferred over to Islands of Adventure as a lead on Island Skipper Tours. I guess having been a fill-in lead for forty-five minutes at Jaws qualified me to be a lead at Islands, which I thought was cool. In 2001 I became supervisor over at Triceratops Encounter and went on to cover pretty much the entire island of Jurassic Park. After that I went to Ripsaw Falls and finally transferred back to Jaws as a lead. Going back to Amity Boat Tours kind of felt like I was coming home.

Left: Locked and loaded for one final tour before the ride closes.
Right: Reuniting with Bruce in San Francisco. (Photos courtesy Dan Gurwitz)

**I'm noticing a trend with you and water attractions.**

I definitely gained a reputation for working at water attractions. I also gained a reputation for closing down attractions! I was with Island Skipper Tours when that closed. Then I went over to Triceratops Encounter and that closed as well. I very nearly closed Jaws when it went seasonal in 2005 due to rising fuel costs. I told management, *'I'm really hoping there's nothing to this 'attraction killer' reputation I'm getting. If there is any truth to it, you need to transfer me out of Jaws right away. I cannot be the supervisor that shuts down Jaws!'* That would have been one of the worst legacies of all time. It was my favorite attraction in either park. I didn't want to close it!

**If you're truly an attraction killer, I'm going to need you to go work a few shifts at Fear Factor, please. Speaking of closures, Kongfrontation bit the dust in 2002. Did that surprise you and did it raise any concerns for Jaws?**

I was very surprised when Kong closed down but I recognized there was only so much space around the park they could expand into. I also recognized that Revenge of the Mummy was supposed to be a pretty amazing ride and certainly it was. I still think Mummy would have been better if you had someone up front spieling a show! (laughs) I wasn't nervous about the future of Jaws at the time because I didn't think they would ever actually close it. It was just such an iconic thing. I guess I should have seen it coming since so many opening day attractions were closing around that time including Hitchcock and Hanna-Barbera.

# JAWS

**APPROXIMATE WAIT TIME**

**minutes .**

**E N T R A N C E**

PERSONS WITH HEART, NECK OR BACK CONDITIONS,
SUSCEPTIBLE TO MOTION SICKNESS, EXPECTANT
MOTHERS AND CHILDREN UNABLE TO SIT UPRIGHT
IN THEIR OWN SEAT SHOULD NOT RIDE.
THIS ATTRACTION UTILIZES SPECIAL FOG EFFECTS
THAT CAN AGGRAVATE ASTHMATIC CONDITIONS.
PLEASE NOTIFY ATTENDANT FOR ASSISTANCE.

PLEASE REFRAIN FROM SMOKING, EATING, DRINKING
AND FLASH PHOTOGRAPHY WHILE EXPERIENCING
THIS ATTRACTION.

## <u>YOU WILL GET WET</u>

THANK YOU.

A relic from the past. (Photo courtesy Jim Beller - JawsCollector.com)

**Tell me about the infamous 2005 closure of the ride. Was there any concern it might turn out to be permanent?**

Being a supervisor, I definitely had the assurances of everyone in management that this was a seasonal thing because they also closed Ripsaw Falls during this time. Everyone knows that the years between 9/11 and the opening of the Wizarding World were dark times for the company. Theme parks across the board were hurting because people just weren't visiting. We needed to do what we could to keep the parks running and keep some kind of profit going. At the end of the day Universal is a business, not a charity. I recognized that they had to take certain measures to do that. I wasn't happy about it but I understood it. So Universal took two of the more expensive attractions to operate and made them seasonal. Jaws was certainly expensive between the spiel pay and the fuel costs. Same with Ripsaw. The plan was to open back up for the holidays and remain open from then on. It was pitched as a very temporary thing. I tried to reassure all the skippers but they were understandably nervous.

Flash forward to the end of the year as we're having our manager meeting with Bob Gault, the CEO at the time, and he's going over the year end recap. He brings up some of the things we did to save money and mentions how Jaws and Ripsaw have been closed these past months but would re-open for the holidays. Then he says Jaws will continue as a seasonal attraction going forward. He said that and my heart stopped. I said, '*Oh my God. That's not what the original plan was.*' And I tried to accept that the plan had changed. I tried to be positive about it. At least it wasn't closing permanently. I was hopeful that once attendance started to build again they would change their minds. And eventually they did and Jaws re-opened and remained in regular operation until it closed years later. Improved attendance certainly helped that happen but so did the many phone calls and letters that the park received. The public made it very clear that they expected to be able to ride Jaws when they visited Universal Studios Florida.

**Would it have been better to cut the fire effects to keep the ride open? Or should it have been all or nothing?**

At the end of the day, if I could just push a boat around that area of the park and act out the spiel, I would do that. Some Jaws is better than no Jaws. Certainly the fire effects were an important part of the ride. Sometimes we didn't have those effects for different reasons. Of all the scenes in the ride, Scene Four with the fire was the scene most dependent on having an effect. You would have to dramatically change that scene if the ride were to operate without fire effects. But given a choice between shutting down those effects or shutting down the ride, I would say shut down the fire and keep the ride. I don't know that it was a decision I would've wanted to make, though.

**Do you remember your last day at Jaws before you went to Islands? Were the regular skipper traditions observed?**

I assume you mean the tradition of throwing a skipper on their last day into the lagoon or hosing them down. Yes, I got hosed in the boathouse. They came at me from all directions with like four different hoses. Those traditions eventually went away due to safety concerns. They later changed it to having a giant container of Gatorade dumped on you like at football games. That's what they did to me when I left Jaws the second time as a supervisor. And yes, I also left my shoes. Two pairs, actually. One was out in the actual ride, which didn't last very long. I left another pair in the queue, which stayed a bit longer. You had to be kind of sneaky with where you left your shoes because they

Dan Gurwitz in Jaws: The Musical backed by voice double Rick Percoco.
(Photo courtesy Colin Peterson)

would occasionally come through on search and destroy missions to remove them. Someone once left their shoes right on top of the lawnmower outside Chief Brody's house and they stayed there forever. I guess they looked like they belonged, like Brody had finished mowing his yard, taken his shoes off, and gone into the house.

**As a former skipper, tell me about any improvisations**

I tended not to go too far off script in front of guests. I might do certain voices or characters. It was important that whatever I did not detract from the integrity of the show. I had one character where I would act like it was my first day at Captain Jake's and I had no confidence in what I was doing. I would be nervously doing the spiel, constantly checking my hand for notes I'd written there to help me remember what I was supposed to say. Then as we rounded the lighthouse, I would kick it up a notch and be that much more scared since this was supposed to be my first day on the job. I actually thought this somewhat helped with the integrity of the show.

I would also do an overconfident southern redneck skipper. I'd go, '*Welcome 'board ever'body. Go on 'head take yer seats we're goin' git ready to go!*' With that I was technically still mostly on script but doing it as a unique character. The southern skipper wasn't anything like the nervous skipper. He was kind of the complete opposite. He'd be really excited about the possibility of finally bagging a shark. That one I was more likely to do for special events or after hours when we would do tours just to make each other laugh. There were definitely people who went off script more than others. There was one skipper who was supposed to pick up the grenade launcher to shoot the shark but grabbed an umbrella instead. That was too far out there. They wound up getting pulled from boat for that stunt. And sure it's funny to an extent but you have to remember that you always have guests on your boat riding Jaws for the first time. You might have someone who came all the way from Sweden to experience this and here you are ruining it for a laugh. One improv that was more popular than I realized at the time involved the skipper doing an entire show where they never saw the shark. They were either facing the wrong direction or bending down to pick up a quarter whenever it appeared. And they would only see the shark when it came up at the electric dock because there's no way you miss that one.

We did have spiel coaches that would ride the attraction from time to time to watch for these kinds of things. And it was always obvious when they rode. It was either Mimi or Margaret. It's not like they came wearing trench coats and Groucho glasses. You knew when they were riding. And if you were wildly off script knowing they were there then you deserved to get pulled from boat.

**Did you ever have any celebrity VIP guests come through the ride?**

Oh definitely. I did a show for Bridget Fonda once. Sylvester Stallone and Arnold Schwarzenegger both rode on my boat together. Universal did a Fox Night during Halloween Horror Nights where the casts of the popular Fox shows at the time came through. I had pretty much everyone from Beverly Hills 90210 and Melrose Place. Tiffani Amber Theissen and Jennie Garth both did the ride twice with a different skipper each time. Afterward the other skipper came up to me like, '*You just know they liked my show better. They couldn't take their eyes off me the entire time!*' (laughs) I was like, '*Okay, buddy. Whatever gets you through the night.*' Brian Austin Green rode my boat as well and laughed hysterically through the entire ride. When he got off he shook my hand and said, '*Dan, you are the shit!*'

**What was it like learning of the ride's final closure in late 2011?**

It was very hard. Fortunately or unfortunately, I was one of the first people to know about Jaws closing in advance of the announcement. I was at a birthday party for a friend of mine and someone came up to me saying, '*Look, I know something that I shouldn't tell you but I'll tell you if you swear you won't talk about it.*' And they told me everything, that Jaws would be closing in order to become the London side of Harry Potter. I thought it was the most ridiculous thing I'd ever heard. He might as well have told me he had the ability to fly or something. But he assured me, '*It's already happening and it's a done deal.*' This was probably two months before the official announcement.

The next day I went to work at Guest Services and I pulled my senior manager aside. I said, '*I need to ask you about something because I need to know if it's even remotely true or just some crazy story.*' And I told him and he said, '*I've not heard anything about that. If it was happening, I would tell you I couldn't talk about it but I've literally heard nothing. It sounds like a fairy tale.*' Several hours later, we're in a staff meeting and he comes in and waves at me from across the room with a half-smile on his face. I knew then that the information I'd been given was true. After the meeting he came up to me and said, '*I like to pride myself on being someone that knows what's going on, but I had to ask four people before someone would tell me it was true.*' So for those two months, I had to sit on the saddest, most confidential information I've ever been told.

I was working my Guest Services job on December 2nd running the Guest Communication team that handles phone calls and e-mails. I had to pull the team together that morning and say, '*In a couple of hours they're going to announce the closure of Jaws.*' And I literally began to choke up as I said it. It wasn't until I said it out loud that it really hit me. I was emotional about it. We got many, many calls and e-mails about it, some from former skippers but many more from guests who were none too pleased. By the time Jaws closed a month later, it had accrued more guest complaints about its closure than any other ride or attraction before it. Previous to that the record holder for closure complaints had been for Back to the Future. Looking back on it now, it is what it is. Yes, we do have the amazing Diagon Alley out of it. If I've learned one thing at Universal, it's that you can't improve the resort without taking some stuff down. It's just that Jaws should've been the last thing we ever closed.

**What a crummy position to be in, fielding complaints about the closure when you're broken up over it.**
Right? I definitely saw both sides to it, though. I also recognized that Jaws closing was a big deal to a lot of people. There were a ton of calls that went, '*Can I talk to your manager about this?*' and some of those turned out to be people I used to work with at the attraction. Jaws closing was not something that a petition or writing campaign was ever going to change. It was way beyond a done deal by the time they announced it. Nothing was going to stop it by then. Maybe we should've shot another musical?

**Do you consider Diagon Alley a worthy successor?**
Honestly, I love and adore Diagon Alley. Somehow they took the spirit of Hogsmeade, which was already one of the most amazing theme park areas ever, and made it even more amazing. I wouldn't want to put anything in place of Jaws, but if something was going to go there, Diagon Alley is about as good as it gets. It's not like I walk by where Amity used to be and grimace or anything. I love that area.

**It sounds like you weren't alone at Universal in your appreciation for the Jaws ride.**
Oh I definitely wasn't alone. I think everyone at Universal either worked at Jaws at some point or wished they did. The head of attraction operations started as a Jaws skipper. Half the management team worked at Jaws at one point or another. As a former skipper, I come down kind of hard on the ride's closure but I don't think it's a decision anyone at Universal took lightly. I know at Universal Creative they love Jaws as much or more than everyone else does. That's why we have all the tributes in Diagon Alley. That's why the hanging shark is still around in San Francisco. Those all exist out of respect for the Jaws ride. I also think Universal as a company knew how special the ride was to people. They made these wonderful closing team t-shirts for the last night. They took props from the actual attraction and gave them as gifts to the skippers. They have a prop shop in the park now and you don't see too much from Jaws in there because everything from Jaws was given away as gifts.

But again, working at Jaws was the best job I've ever had. I know it's a cliché to say our attraction team was more than that just a team, that we were a family, but if that was ever true it was true for Jaws. I've worked in a million locations at Universal and I've never had a team get along so well during work and after hours. It was pure fun every single day. Remember in the movie when Mayor Vaughn says, '*Amity means friendship?*' That was something we took to heart.

**What kind of mementos did you keep from Jaws?**

I have a closing team shirt and three or four skipper shirts. I have one of the displays saying, '*We apologize but Amity Boat Tours will not be operating today*' as well as a '*Jaws This Way*' directional sign. I was angling for something that wasn't given away that hung by the entrance for many years. It was an animated sign with Captain Jake and Sharkey. I've always wanted that sign. I've seen it hanging up in prop storage. The other prop I wish I could've snagged was a grenade launcher, but then everyone wanted one of those.

The sign that greeted guests at the queue entrance for many years.

# HOW I BROKE THE RIDE
# AND BECAME A LEAD

an interview with
## MICHAEL GRAY
### Skipper (2004 - 2006)
### Lead (2006 - 2008)

Shark? What shark? (Photo courtesy Michael Gray)

**How did you wind up at Captain Jake's Amity Boat Tours?**

Growing up in central Florida, my family often went to Universal Studios Florida. My mom actually worked there as a spieler on the back of the parking lot trams, back when they had a parking lot. At the time, she had a friend who worked at Kongfrontation and they invited us to come ride with them one day. The Kong trams had a half seat up front where the attendant was and we got to sit there and watch them spiel. I was so enamored watching them that I held onto that vision for many years. I knew one day I wanted to do what they did. Unfortunately, Kongfrontation closed before I got the opportunity, so that was no longer an option.

A couple years later I went to Rock the Universe, the Christian youth event they hold annually. I'll never forget going on Jaws that night. There were two spielers on our boat instead of one, both of whom were way off script. One skipper rode on the back of the boat and shimmied up to the front during the boathouse scene to help his fellow skipper who was somehow stricken. It was all so awesome. I figured if I couldn't work at Kong I at least wanted to work at Jaws. I spent the next couple weeks checking for open positions on Universal's website. I applied to be a Jaws skipper as soon as a position became available. That was where I wanted to work. I had no interest in doing anything else at the park. I definitely didn't want to be a regular button pusher. It was Jaws or nothing.

I went in to interview for the job a short while later. Interviewing for a spieling position is a bit different due to the added step of having to audition. I did my audition with Mimi Lipka, who was the acting coach in charge of all of the spielers throughout the park. I don't remember much about my audition except that I felt like I completely bombed it. My assumption is that Mimi hired me based on my enthusiasm and not my acting skill. I like to think I eventually came to have a pretty solid show at Jaws. I certainly worked hard to improve it over time.

**What was it like coming onto the Jaws team?**

It was fantastic. From the outside looking in, Jaws seemed like an awesome place to work and it was. There was a great sense of camaraderie amongst all the people who worked there. I also really liked the job itself. I came to enjoy the make believe of it all and tried to put everything I possibly could into my show. I also took interest in the technical side of the ride. There was so much more to it than most guests realized. I found all of those details to be fascinating.

**You eventually became a lead on the attraction. What was that like?**

As a lead I was a huge stickler for show quality. It cost about fifty bucks to get into the park back then, far more than that now. I knew I couldn't control anyone's day at Universal beyond their time at Jaws, so I made sure they got their money's worth on our ride. That was something instilled in me by Mimi during my training. As part of that, I was big on not deviating too far from the ride spiel. I thought most skippers stayed pretty close to the written material. I would occasionally overhear someone going wildly off script and have to pull them from boat as a result.

One person I sometimes struggled with was the infamous John Bernard. I don't think John was ever once word for word on script because he liked to add in his own flair. I imagine he was probably talked to by supervisors a few times, but more often than not we cut him slack with it. Everyone knew he had the utmost respect for the attraction and put on a great, great show. Sometimes I'll watch one of his YouTube videos and go, '*Oh man! You are SO off script!*' But you can't not respect a guy like that. He had such an immense love for the attraction. Quite honestly, it was a great day for Jaws when he became a skipper.

**You also became a trainer on Jaws. What was your approach to training new skipper recruits?**
I felt it was best to spend most of training on the ride portion of the attraction. The land positions were important but they weren't as important. Speaking of which, I always thought pre-board was kind of like playing human Tetris. But with regard to training on the boats, there was this one method I liked where I would sit in the second row with a water gun and squirt the trainee every time they got something wrong. It was kind of like puppy training. One of the supervisors later came to me and said, '*Wow, that's really demeaning.*' And I was like, '*Hey, it's a water ride. You're supposed to get a little wet.*' And they said, '*These people are new. You've got to be gentle with them.*' I've had people come back and tell me how helpful that method was because it let them know they needed to correct something without stopping their show. If you interrupt someone's spiel to have a conversation every time they mess up, they'll never be able to get back the rhythm of it and finish the show. I thought it was a fun and effective technique!

I also thought it was important to let new skippers know they could have a lot of fun with this job. So on their fourth or fifth day, I would take my trainees out to the firehouse, which was a building adjacent to Bridewell's Gas Dock on the island. This is where all the controls for Scene Four were kept. Here I would allow the new skippers to engage in what I called reverse hazing. There was a way to flood the skipper compartment on any given boat by triggering a certain effect at exactly the right time and we did just that. It was so much fun. The goal was to make new skippers feel like they were part of the team and to help give them the confidence to go spiel in front of fifty people and do a good job at it. That could be a difficult thing if you didn't have a background in theater. I also wanted the new people to know that it was all in good fun when we eventually pranked them back.

When I started at Jaws, I did so with the benefit of this huge reservoir of skipper wisdom and talent to train from. So much knowledge and lore got passed down to me from skippers who had it passed to them from previous years. The 2005 closure disrupted that continuity because not all the skippers who left the ride came back after it re-opened. There was this huge influx of new blood into the attraction. I took a year's break from Jaws and came back after the re-opening. They wanted me to re-train on the ride and I kind of wound up training my trainer. There were so many details about the ride he had no clue about.

**In your opinion, what was the worst shark or effect to have to cover for when it was missing in action?**
This may surprise you, but it wasn't a fin or a shark. It was the gas dock explosion in Scene Four. There was just no good way to cover if it didn't happen. The sound of the explosion still played and the pumps still fell over into the

water. Without the flames, Scene Four just fell flat. Sometimes those effects wouldn't trigger due to the multiple safety mechanisms installed into that part of the ride. If any of those were triggered for any reason the fire would shut off immediately. You came to expect that on particularly windy days. The fire effect might also fail to trigger if your boat was following too closely to the boat ahead of you and the scene couldn't reset itself in time. That was ultimately the skipper's fault since we had the ability to drop out of auto mode and space the boats out a little bit.

On that subject, it was interesting to me that a key concern of many who rode Jaws involved the fire effects going haywire and accidentally burning them. What those people don't understand is that there were so many safety mechanisms in place that it was far more likely they would disable the effect than all malfunction together and something bad happen as a result. There were wind sensors all throughout that scene. There was a pressure sensor on the track so that the effect wouldn't trigger if the boat wasn't in the right spot. There were gas detectors that would measure how much gas was present prior to ignition. If the sensors detected a leak it would cause the entire ride to shut down in order to prevent boats from entering the area. I only ever saw that happen once and it was due to a faulty sensor, not an actual leak. There was even a special fire stop button on the boat console just above the fake throttle. It was right beside the dispatch button and it was accidentally pressed all the time, far more than the emergency stop ever was. Accidentally hitting that meant not only were you not going to get fire effects on your tour, but none of the boats ahead of you would either. The fire would have to be reset by a tech before it triggered again.

The boathouse shark lifted out of the water. (Photo courtesy Michael Gray)

**I know about fire stops and emergency stops, but I need you to explain what a "duck stop" is.**

This story was told to me firsthand by someone who was there. It occurred at a time when I wasn't at the attraction but several others who were have corroborated the account. I have full confidence that this is true Jaws lore. Anyone who has ever been to Universal in the spring knows that ducks make their way into every waterway in the park. Unfortunately, there was a family of ducks who didn't know the difference between the serene central lagoon waters and the far less serene waters around Amity Island. Occasionally these ducks would float very close to the ride effects, which led some skippers to wonder if they should hit the e-stop. Management responded that we were not to stop the ride for duck safety. They reasoned that if the ducks were dumb enough to go near a shark that kept popping up in the exact same spot all day long then they were taking their little ducks lives into their own hands. That quickly changed after an incident in which a duck floated overtop one of the mortars in Scene Five where the shark bites the cable. As I understand it, the duck flew up in the air, bounced off the inside top of the boat canopy, and landed on or near a family with small children. Feathers went everywhere. The children were traumatized, to say the least, by the apparent shooting death of this poor duck. To them, it looked as if the skipper had aimed the grenade launcher right at the duck and killed it. There was substantial compensation given to that family and the term "duck stop" became a thing. From then on, skippers were allowed to hit the e-stop for a duck in the interest of both duck and guest safety.

**John Bernard has joked about having "Post Jaws Ride Disorder." Would you diagnose yourself with PJRD?**

I just might. I still think about it all the time. I did so many shows around that lagoon the spiel is kind of burned into my mind. I estimate that I did anywhere from 18,000 to 20,000 shows during my time at Jaws. It's probably been about ten years now since my last spiel but I can remember every single word of it. I close my eyes and I'm right back there in Amity. It's so vivid I can even smell it. There has been no other place in my entire human existence that I can do that with. I've had numerous jobs before and since Jaws but nothing comes close to it.

I actually have a recurrent Jaws ride dream, which I've learned is kind of a phenomenon with former skippers. In it the ride is back open because I guess my subconscious hasn't acknowledged that it's been closed and demolished. The ride is open but they've made huge changes to it and not told me about them. So I start spieling and turn the first jetty into Scene Two and realize the whole ride is different. I'm not at all prepared for this and my show winds up being terrible because of it. It's the worst possible feeling in that dream. I think psychologically it harkens

back to my fear of change and not being prepare for things, which is something I tried to avoid while working there. As either skipper or lead I always tried to be prepared for any eventuality. I like a good crisis but not the ones I personally cause or can't immediately solve. In my dream, I can't solve the problem.

**What did a bad day at the Jaws ride look like for you personally? Missing effects? Angry tourists? Bad weather?**
There were only a handful of days I didn't enjoy working there. Some of those were consecutive rainy days like when we had a tropical depression blow in. There was no lightning to close the ride but just enough wind to kill the fire effects. And nobody came to the park on those days either, so you're outside getting drenched for nothing. That's the least amount of fun you can have at Jaws except for maybe causing a ride vehicle to go off the track, which I did.

**I'm going to need to hear about that. How did you cause a boat to go off the track?**
I'll need to give you a little technical background before I tell that story. When I started at Jaws in 2004, the skippers were very involved in the mechanical operation of the ride vehicles. They gassed up their own boats and brought them on and off the tracks by themselves. When I came back after the 2005 closure, the skippers were no longer doing any of these things. When I asked about this, I was told there was an incident that resulted in the skippers having lost the privilege to bring boats on and offline.

There were two places where we took boats on and offline, one at the maintenance boathouse just past load and one adjacent to unload. To bring a new boat online the person in tower would select the option to add a boat, then select which boat and where it was coming online at. This would send a signal to enable that particular ride vehicle. Two things would then occur at the switch. A loud industrial buzzer would sound and the lights would glow yellow. Those lights would turn green upon successful completion of the track switch signaling the boat to proceed. The skipper would then press the dispatch button and the boat would go either forward or reverse onto the main track depending on the location. In the event the tower attendant switched the wrong track, the dispatch button wouldn't activate and the boat wouldn't move. This was an important failsafe mechanism intended to keep the boat from going off the track. That's how the ride was supposed to operate.

Apparently a skipper was taking a boat offline at the maintenance boathouse and held the dispatch button too long causing their ride vehicle to ram into the giant boathouse doors. I heard the cost to repair those doors was around $70,000 since they were custom made and quite large. From that time forward only techs were allowed to bring boats on or offline. But the techs didn't do it the normal way. They instead moved the boats around as they did when the ride was closed through a manual button on the back of the vehicle, which bypassed the failsafe.

On the day of the incident, I was in tower and, for whatever reason, I switched the wrong track. The boat was across from unload and I had switched the track over by the maintenance boathouse. Neither myself nor the skipper realized my error. The skipper also failed to acknowledge that the buzzer sounding wasn't for the offline spur or that the track lights weren't glowing. Upon the successful track switch, I gave them the go ahead to bring the boat online. The technician went manually forward and drove it right off the end of the track. The front undercarriage was literally hanging off the track. At this point, the skipper became very upset and the tech yelled some things into the radio that I really shouldn't repeat here. You know in movies how when someone has a dramatic realization the foreground zooms in but the background zooms out, like in Jaws? That happened to me as I realized I had just broken the ride about as bad as a single person possibly could. Here I was a trainer on my way to becoming a lead and I had caused a boat to go off the tracks. I was in tower, so I was the one responsible.

I kept my composure enough to do what I was supposed to in that situation. I called tech base to let them know Jaws was down. Then I called the lead to ask the greeter to close the entrance. Then I had to call someone to relieve me from tower because you shouldn't stay in position when you're the one who broke the ride. Meanwhile, I had to do an overhead spiel to evacuate the queue. I went up to the crow's nest after that and had a good cry thinking I had just ruined my reputation at Universal. They had to bring in tech divers who inflated these giant underwater balloons beneath the boat in order to lift it back onto the track. We were ultimately down about three hours that day.

**That would definitely qualify as a bad day. How did you manage to keep your job?**

I was only suspended for one day. I wrote a report on how the accident happened and how it could be avoided going forward. I detailed how we had been operating the ride outside of how it was designed and that this was a natural result of that. We had systems in place to prevent something like this from happening and we bypassed all of them. So ultimately we failed to prevent something that was quite preventable. I think I sufficiently made my case that I was not the first skipper or even lead to switch the wrong track and not realize it. The only difference was that in my case is that I didn't have the skipper calling to say their boat wouldn't move. I was promoted to lead about a month later.

**Do you remember your last time around the lagoon as a skipper?**

I actually had two last times. The first last time was at the end of my first stint and the second last time was right when I was about to leave the company full time. I remember having this feeling of sadness not knowing if I was ever going to be back there. I imagine it's similar to what fighter pilots feel when they're landing on an aircraft carrier for the last time realizing there's no place in civilian life where they can fly an F-35 again. They'll be relegated to flying commercial aircraft for the rest of their life. It's about realizing you have this skill that you'll never use again. I did leave my shoes in the boathouse after I left the first time. I didn't bother leaving my shoes the second time because tech services had started a policy of going through and removing shoes every few months.

I still daydream sometimes about having the opportunity to do one more show. I'd love to be able to do it for my kids. Occasionally I'll pull up the video on YouTube and perform the spiel for them. They just know it as the shark ride since they've never seen Jaws. They're a little too young for that. But they enjoy the ride video.

Top: The technical console view from the tower posiiton. (Photo courtesy Michael Gray)

Bottom: The operator console on the ride vehicle. (Photo courtesy TomCroom.com)

# MORE THAN ONE WAY
# TO SKIN A SHARK

an interview with

## SETH A. WOLFSON

### Shark Dermatologist
### (aka Skin Repair)

The kill shark awaiting a new skin.

(Photo courtesy Bing Futch)

**How did you come to work for Universal Studios Florida?**

I moved to Orlando looking for work doing special effects makeup in movies. I started out working for Universal in their Makeup Department for about six months or so. I had been bugging the guy who ran the Figure Finish Department for a job. This was the department in charge of all the figure skins, animatronic characters, and scenic stuff on the rides. As soon as there was an opening, I snapped at it and was hired. That's how I got involved with working on the Jaws ride. This was around 1997, I believe. It was a full time position I was hired into. Every night we would have someone go around to inspect all the skins and props throughout the park. With Jaws, we'd have to replace or repair a shark skin every so often.

**What kind of wear and tear were the sharks experiencing on a regular basis?**

Quite a bit. There was wear from the sharks going up and down each day. The fiberglass teeth would break off. The cables on the back end of the shark would sometimes rip through the skins. The latex would rot. We would have to tighten the skins to the sharks. We'd also have to clean them because they would get green mildew and pond scum on them. All of that and more. Someone would definitely be working on Jaws every single night of the week. I would probably go down once or twice a week. King Kong was much more my thing. The Jaws ride was kind of dangerous on account of the water. You always had to work in pairs on that ride in case someone fell into the lagoon.

**Which shark on the ride required the most attention?**

Any of the latex skin sharks. The fin sharks were fiberglass if I remember correctly, so those were fine most of the time. For some reason, the boathouse shark wasn't quite as bad as the other ones.

**Which attraction was more challenging to work on – Jaws or Kongfrontation?**

I don't know what everyone else would say to that, but I was very used to working on Kong and having to go up in those high reaches to take all the fur off. I could do that in my sleep. Personally, Jaws was more of a challenge for me because of the water element. The sharks could be raised up on these huge metal bases. The pond scum in the lagoon made the shark platforms very slippery to walk on. There was one guy who fell and broke his hip. Honestly, Jaws was my least favorite place to go work because it was one of the more dangerous attractions. I don't know if the work on Jaws was any harder but it was definitely came with more risks.

**How did Jaws compare to other attractions in terms of the regular maintenance it needed?**

All rides are different that way. We would replace the shark skins maybe twice a year. Jaws would also shut down a few weeks each year for a major rehab where everything on the ride got extra attention. They would have divers in the water every night working on it. For a while they thought the Jaws repairs could be made entirely underwater thus shortening the downtime, but that didn't work out as expected. I must say that Universal did a really good job making sure the ride ran well and was safe for guests. They really went out of their way to ensure things were working properly. They were a great company to work for.

The kill shark at night, aka "Shark in the Dark." (Photo courtesy Christopher Lord)

**What was the process like for replacing a shark skin?**

It was an all night deal. The lagoon didn't have to be dry for this. We just had to raise the shark out of the water so that we could get onto the platform. It took about four people altogether. First we would remove the jaws, which took about half an hour because you're trying to find the bolts inside the mouth and take them out. Then we would cut the old skin off in chunks and throw it on a forklift. We'd need a crane to lower the new skin onto the shark at just the right angle. After you get the new skin on, the teeth would have to go back in. It was a big production to make this happen in a timely manner.

**Was it ever spooky being in the water at night with these massive mechanical sharks? Surely that's a little scary.**

No, but I'll tell you what was scary – the spiders in the boathouse! There was a walkway above the boat path that you'd have to cross to get to the other side where the shark was. At certain times of the year, this walkway was filled with thousands of spiders and their huge webs. You couldn't get to the other side without walking right through them. I'm terrified of spiders, so that's my scary memory from Jaws. You have to remember that they have black widows down there. And I'm not exaggerating when I say it was thousands and thousands of them. The boathouse was over water and had just enough light that it was a perfect place for them to thrive. I'm sure I wasn't the only one who refused to go through there.

**Do you know who was making these replacement skins that you were installing?**

I don't know who made them originally. Universal eventually opened their own skin shop at a secret location in Orlando, which then made all the skins for Jaws and Jurassic Park. Universal needed to have their own skin shop once the Jurassic Park ride came along. That was right about the time I started working with them. They had this gigantic shark mold for making new skins. They would spray latex all throughout the mold while standing inside of it, just dozens of layers of latex and fabric for reinforcement.

**How did the animated figures on Jurassic Park compare to Jaws?**

They were comparable in the sense that they were both water rides. The Jurassic Park skins were a lot heavier because they were silicone. That also meant that they moved better. The Jurassic animatronics were also a lot more complicated than the Jaws ones, which made them harder to maintain. We would have to either unzip or cut open the dinosaur skins to work on them and then glue them back together when finished. In that sense, Jurassic Park was a more challenging place to work than Jaws. Jurassic Park was the last place I ever wanted to get assigned to work. Making those skins was fun but maintaining the ride was not. Orlando nights still get pretty hot, which made working with the heavy dino skins a lot of work.

**Did the closure of Kong in 2002 and eventually Jaws in 2012 come as a surprise?**

No, they didn't. With Kong, we saw it coming but we were still bummed. That was one of my favorite movies growing up and what got me into makeup effects as a kid. It was a great ride but I could see why they closed it down. It just wasn't as popular as it once was. With Jaws, I can see why they would want to replace it simply because of how much upkeep it took. Jaws was also a great ride. It was one of my favorites, if not my favorite. Jaws and Kong are still what I think of when I think of Universal theme parks.

The fibgerglass dead shark from Scene Five. (Photo courtesy Luke Sawh)

# SPIELING THE JAWS RIDE FROM OHIO TO FLORIDA

*an interview with*

## JOHN BERNARD

**Skipper (2007 - 2010)**
**Jaws Ride Video Archivist**

Skipper John pointing out an item of interest on your port side.

(Photo courtesy John Bernard)

**Which were you a fan of first – Jaws the movie or Jaws the ride?**

The movie. I was entirely too young when I first saw Jaws which was my dad's fault. I watched the film and then rode the ride soon after, so those two experiences happened back to back. I was probably five years old for the movie and six years old for the ride. The biggest thing I remember about my first time on the ride is that I spent most of it with my head in my dad's armpit so I saw almost none of it. I could hear the sounds and feel the boat rocking and the heat from the flames but that was it. I had to have my parents and sister describe the ride to me afterward because I saw so little of it that first time. I grew up in Columbus, Ohio but my dad would always take us to Orlando every other year. We definitely went down whenever a new attraction opened so I kind of grew up with the park.

Fast forwarding a bit, I took a particular interest in the mechanics of the ride years later in high school. I had a lot of questions about how it all worked. I remember the trip we took to Universal when I was about fifteen years old. My parents would ride Jaws and then want to move onto something like Back to the Future and I'd be like, '*You know what? I'm good. You go ahead. I'm gonna hang here.*' And I would chat up the skippers about the ride. They were so nice to sit down with me on their thirty minute breaks and answer all my questions. I really looked up to them. They were my idols in a lot of ways. I ended up reaching out to a network of people who had worked on the ride, guys like Adam Bezark and David Kneupper.

**I saw where you made a great video of that. Speaking of your videos, you have an obvious talent for filmmaking. Millions have viewed your Jaws ride videos on YouTube. When did you start making these short films?**

I went to a public school here in Ohio and my high school was really good about having a strong A/V program. Only when I went to college did I realize that it was world's ahead of other public school programs. So I was exposed to video production and editing very early on. I asked for a camera for my fifteenth birthday and put it to pretty good use. I later went to college as a film major but ended up transferring into business and marketing for my sophomore through senior years.

**One of your earliest Jaws videos appears to be "The Jaws Ride Challenge" in which you see how many times you can ride Jaws in one day. Did you really take twenty-nine tours around the attraction that day?**

We absolutely did and that wasn't even my personal best record at that time. Fortunately, the people working that day were really great to us. After a while they just started letting us use the handicap and side entrances. We would bypass the queue entirely. They fully supported our love for the ride.

**At what point did you want to become a Jaws skipper?**

I always knew I wanted to do it but I figured my geographical handicap of living in Ohio would have gotten in the way. Then after high school I went to Bowling Green State University in northern Ohio, which put even more distance between me and Orlando. There's about a thousand miles between those two places. I figured it was a pipe dream. But one day a member of Universal's Human Resources department reached out to me. They said, '*We've seen your Jaws ride in Ohio and your Jaws ride Challenge videos and we think they're hilarious. Would you have any interest*

"I'm pleased and happy to repeat the news that we have, in fact, caught and killed a large predator that supposedly injured some bathers." (Photo courtesy John Bernard)

*in joining our team?'* You can imagine my surprise. I was absolutely tickled because I had already given up on this dream. I said, *'Thanks, but I'm in college in Ohio. I can't work in Orlando.'* And they said back, *'Well, summer's just around the corner. If you can get down here, we'll hear you out'.*

**That's amazing! You have to be the envy of every Jaws ride fan with that story.**
I didn't share that story much when I started work there in 2007. Only after I stopped working at Jaws in 2010 did I start telling it. My family was pretty funny about it. They honestly thought it was goofy. When summer came, I loaded up my jeep and took a couple friends down to Orlando with me as well. We all interviewed and got jobs at the park. One friend went to work at Mummy and one at the Jurassic Park Visitors Center as a spieler hatching raptors. For my interview, I had to sit in a conference room and yell out all my lines. Next thing I knew I was stepping onto a boat with a name tag and an Amity Boat Tours shirt.

**As someone who idolized the skippers growing up, what was the reality of becoming one?**

Reality is a really good word for it. It's impossible to emphasize the uniqueness of what the skippers go through doing the Jaws ride. The boat moves so much more than you realize. My trainer was Skip the skipper, the guy who gave the very last tour of the ride when it closed. He put me on a boat my very first day of training, which most people don't do until their third day. He knew I had my lines down. I think I was seen as this cocky YouTuber kid from Ohio because a couple other skippers jumped on our boat like, '*Okay, let's see what this kid's got.*' And I completely fell over right in front of them that first time. I had so much trouble getting through my spiel. It was suddenly hard to remember these lines that I'd memorized so well over the years. I was horrible at first. It was also difficult having the kill cord leash connected to the back of your jeans. Being constantly hooked to the console was so unnatural to me and hard to get used to. Skip was very kind and recommended I go home and tie a belt from the back of my trousers to a dresser and practice the show that way. People may not realize it but the kill cord changes the way you move. You definitely don't want to get wrapped up in it or accidentally pull it.

Within a week the spieling coach came over and signed me off. I was so excited to being working there. I was the kid who used my breaks to go hang with the techs. I would go hang out on the island if I had permission from a lead. I actually sustained a pretty nasty spider bite hanging out in the woods by Scene Four. I was trying to capture some slow motion footage of the flame bars and ended up having to go to Emergency Medical because of it. Totally worth it, though. I would meet some of my very best friends at Jaws. I met the best man at my wedding there. I wouldn't have known any of these people if it weren't for the ride. It was magical, honestly.

**Did seeing how everything worked detract from your appreciation of the ride?**

Not at all. The shark still scares me to this day. I know the guests would sometimes laugh at them but what you can't forget is that the sharks are as big as a station wagon. They're huge. They burst out of these deep pits in this oil filled lagoon and then return to the same pits within a matter of seconds. They're actually really dangerous. I remember something one of the dive technicians once told me. These guys were tough as nails mechanic types. They would be working on Jaws at night making repairs where needed. If the repairs couldn't be done above the water then the techs would have to dive down into the lagoon. Again, this is at nighttime. Some of those pits were quite deep. The deepest was in Scene Four where the turntable from the original ride was. That pit was like thirty or forty feet deep. They told me how incredibly scary it was diving down into the murky darkness at night and suddenly coming face to face with this huge frozen great white shark. Even these super tough guys would get scared for a moment. I think it's a testament to why we're all obsessed with Jaws, that primal fear. I still have nightmares about the shark.

**What was the attraction like when it didn't work as intended?**

During my time at Jaws, I came to understand that there was a dark operational and financial underbelly to the ride. I didn't want to see it at first, but after I understood the machine that is Universal I came to understand how it affected the machine that was the Jaws ride. The ride had a rating system for every single effect. The leads of the attraction would have to go around several times a day and make a checklist of these. Each effect had a point value and if the total points of the missing effects got too high, they would close the ride because they deemed it not a quality experience. I saw Universal decrease the threshold for that score over the years, which made the techs have to get really creative as to how they could influence the points to keep Jaws open during park hours. I eventually saw the ride slowly start to deteriorate, which was a tough thing to see. For example, the boathouse shark was out for one of the entire summers I worked there. They lost one of the boats in 2008. Smoke just started pouring out of Ride Vehicle Seven, which got dumped in the graveyard behind Jurassic Park. The final kill shark that bit the wire was intermittent for the last two years of the attraction. Those were hard things to cover for. As someone who loves the ride, you want guests to have the same experience that drew you to Jaws in the first place.

**So where do you draw the line? How many effects should you lose before you shut it down?**

That's a tough question to answer, especially when you encounter guests that came all the way from England or France to see Jaws. That's what got them across the pond, that they could get attacked by Jaws. People would travel a long way for this ride. It broke my heart when they would put us out front in the greeter spot to tell people it was closed for the day. If that was someone's only day at the park, they might never have another chance to ride it ever again. However, Jaws was designed to deliver a certain experience. If it wasn't able to achieve at least a fragment of that because of missing effects, it wasn't really the intended experience. You're no longer riding the Jaws ride if you're missing the sharks, which happened to me on more than one occasion.

**Tell me about how the skippers got along. I've heard there were antics.**

You could spiel that ride fifty times a day, so you had to keep it fresh. We were a group of young adults working hard in the hot summer sun. To make it more fun, we would take certain liberties. One of the games we played happened inside the boathouse when people were distracted by the shark. The shark attacked on the right side of the boathouse. A few of us liked to put things on the left side of the boathouse where there's a little walkway. We'd take items from the unload closet like a sign, a mop, or a grenade launcher and stash them over there. The next skipper that came along would have to replace our item with something else, maybe a water bottle, a net, or a poncho that a guest left behind. It was pretty funny to us that we were doing this game while everyone else was screaming at the shark.

I remember one particular time I was going to leave a wet floor sign on the walkway. I screamed and pointed for people to look at the shark and then ran over to place the sign. I couldn't get it set up right because the boat never stops moving in that scene. Then I see over my shoulder that every single person is looking right at me fumbling with this sign and not the shark! (laughs) They were probably wondering why their skipper was more concerned with wet floors than the killer shark attacking their boat. I started laughing and wound up dropping the wet floor sign in the water. That ultimately caused us to shut down the ride because the sign floated into Scene Four and had it hovered over the mortar tubes it could have flown up and hit a guest. It might also have soared twenty-feet into the sky and landed in the parking lot. So that shut us down. Questions were immediately asked as to how the sign got there but it never got back to me. I remember the lead being like, '*This game has got to stop because we had to shut down because of it today and that's a big deal.*' So I dodged that one.

Another game we played involved the spotlight on the front of the boat. Ordinarily that light came on automatically as the boat went into the boathouse. The skipper had no control over it. The tower position, however, did have control over it. At night we would ask the skippers if they wanted to improvise with the light. If they said yes, a group of us would hang out in the tower and randomly trigger the light throughout the ride. The skipper on boat would then have to run over and incorporate it into their spiel. If it happened in Scene One, maybe they'd shine it on Chief Brody's house to make it seem like part of the show. If it happened in Scene Two, they could pretend to be looking for survivors in the water from Amity Three. In Scene Five they would have to balance holding the light with taking the final shot at the shark. That got to be really funny to watch on the cameras.

**That's pretty funny! It sounds like the skippers really enjoyed what they did, like it wasn't just another job.**
For most people that was true but not everyone loved working on the ride. It was funny some of the personalities that wound up at Jaws. Universal placed some very clear introverts in one of the most extroverted positions in the park. I would actually get energy from the Jaws ride whereas other people were absolutely drained at the end of the day. You could tell right away when someone wasn't a good fit. Those people usually found themselves removed or left on their own. We were all so energetic. I felt the key to happiness on Jaws was remembering that people were there to see the shark foremost. You were not the show. If they wound up liking you and the shark performing together then

Skipper John setting up his camera to capture Scene Two. (Photo courtesy John Bernard)

they would go wild at the end when you put your fist up and yell, '*We're coming home!*' But if you ever tried to upstage the shark, you would get crickets in exchange for your five minutes of energy and screaming. That was incredibly frustrating for some skippers. It took me until my second year to realize that each skipper should adjust the show to complement the energy of the boat. You could use your time at load as a proxy for that. If you got a boat of Jaws fans who knew the entire show, you could throw in a pause and have them yell one of the lines and work in a reaction to that. That would absolutely make their day and it didn't hurt the experience for the rest of the boat. If you had a silent and grumpy boat, you could play it a little more reserved or clumsily and eventually win them onto your side.

**Why were skippers considered ride operators and not entertainers? Because you guys were giving higher energy performances more times a day than other acting positions and earning far less for it.**

I was making $8.75 an hour when I started at Jaws. I had a friend working at Mummy making $8.25 an hour. The extra fifty cents I got was my spiel pay. I had another friend who worked at Poseidon's Fury in the Taylor role earning $15 an hour. Of course, I was doing way, way more shows a day than he was. The operational difference at Universal was that we were pushing the button that started our show whereas the rest of the entertainment actors had their shows happening to them. So if you were John Connor in Terminator or Taylor in Poseidon or a host at Horror Makeup, you weren't in control of the show. The show was happening to you. That's how Universal justified the cost savings. To be honest, people were pretty frustrated with that decision. But Universal could get away with it because people really wanted to be a part of Jaws and would take a pay cut to do it.

**I've heard that spieling improvisation was frowned upon, but that it still happened. How'd you get away with it?**

I didn't always get away with it. I was written up twice for going off script. That was two times out of probably hundreds of times that I did it. We thought it was really funny what we were doing, even though it was wrong. That's why I made that video, "How NOT To Do the Jaws Ride." I think The Office was the number one show on television at the time, so that made us want to show people what really went on at the Jaws ride.

**Tell me a fond memory of working on the attraction.**

I was adamant about playing up the theming around the ride. I would reinforce that we were in Amity Island and not Orlando, even to the extent of asking why so many people on my boat had maps from Universal Studios. This was part of the fun. I had a few opportunities to close the ride during extended park hours. It would be quite late, often around ten at night. That's what we called "Shark in the Dark." Jaws was a totally different experience by night.

One or two of those late night tours would happen during the fireworks show in the main lagoon, the Universal 360 show or whatever was happening at the time. My boat would be half full with people that didn't care about the 360 show. They just wanted to get another ride in before closing while all the other suckers were watching the fireworks. These people were always in a great mood and just slap happy from a full day of fun. They would run through the queue, which had been super long earlier but was now completely empty. They would walk onto the attraction with no wait like they'd won a contest. I loved being out on the water with those guests.

"Uh... try the grenade launcher. Over."
(Photo courtesy John Bernard)

"Wait, you mean these things
are actually loaded!?"
(Photo courtesy John Bernard)

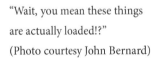

You could play up a couple different things on these nights because in Amity it was supposed to be the 4th of July every single day. And it just so happened that we had actual fireworks going off directly beside the ride. Keeping with that, I would reason that because everyone was off enjoying the fireworks there was no one out here to help us if we had any trouble. Even Chief Brody was ten minutes away. We were all alone and the ride suddenly became that much scarier. We had this beautiful juxtaposition of fireworks bursting in the night sky and absolute terror ripping through the water. We're out here screaming our heads off and no one can hear us because there's this loud patriotic celebration happening. That was next level! Giving tours during fireworks was my favorite thing to do. I also liked giving tours just after it rained because there was this incredible fog about the entire lagoon. It was ominous. The ride felt much darker and grittier, kind of like if Christopher Nolan had directed the Jaws ride.

**What did you hear about the original Jaws ride when you worked there?**
Not much. It was kind of a mystery back then because there weren't any videos of it online. There was one website that had a description of it. Every so often someone would come up and ask, '*Didn't the shark used to blow up at the end?*' So it was strange having guests ask about it and having no idea what they were talking about. All I knew was that the original ride was deemed unsustainable in its original design, I'm glad they decided to change it because that's probably what helped Jaws last as long as it did.

**The early 2000s saw several iconic Universal attractions close. Did you think Jaws would eventually follow suit?**
I always knew it would one day come to an end. Like you said, you could see the pattern of opening day attractions closing one by one. I kept close relationships with the leads and technicians hoping to hear of any rumblings of whether they were going to close Jaws. There were constant rumors about what might replace it. I just accepted it as a reality and tried to enjoy it while it was there. You had to trust that Universal was going to make the right creative decision with its replacement and stay true to what they originally set out to do.

**Do you remember your last time spieling the Jaws ride?**
Yes, I do. It was perfect. Honestly, it was just another lap around the lagoon on a nice sunny but mild day. The crowd was particularly energetic and most all of the effects were working. I was in the groove. By that time, three years in, I could read a boat and match my energy to it. I went out having a good time.

**Did you leave your shoes at the attraction?**
I didn't but I did leave a calculator watch on one of the diver's suits in the boathouse. I was kind of known for wearing these Casio Calculator watches and gifting many skippers their own watches. I even noticed other skippers picking them up after a while. It was actually really handy to be able to calculate the total guests through per hour if you were working Load or in the Tower position. It was more function than fashion. It ended up being a token that some of us had, so I left mine in the boathouse.

Above: "Our first item of interest on your port side is the home of our very own Chief of Police Martin Brody." (Photo courtesy John Bernard)

Right: Several skippers created this tribute to John Bernard in 2011, which was stashed inside the boathouse until the ride's closure. (Photo courtesy John Bernard)

# 5 MUST-SEE VIDEOS BY JOHN BERNARD

Skipper John Bernard has documented the Jaws ride through an incredible series of videos, which have amassed more than sixty-million views. Below are five particularly good vids!

### The Jaws Ride Movie: Death of Gordon

This eight-minute short film explores the events that transpired in Amity just before you set sail with Captain Jake's Amity Boat Tours.

### Jaws Ride: Skippers Off-Script

This hilarious video is full of skippers doing ad-libs and improvs on the ride.

### The Jaws Ride Challenge

Long before he was a skipper, John Bernard sought to ride Jaws thirty-one times in a single day. This video documents his quest to set that record.

### The Jaws Ride: Behind the Scenes Skipper Tribute

This incredible eleven-minute documentary features former skippers discussing the history and legacy of the Jaws ride.

### The Jaws Ride LIVE on stage - feat Skipper Garrett

The Jaws ride roars to life once again as Skipper Garrett guides a live audience through the entire show. Who says you can't still be a skipper?

You can see these videos and more at
**http://YouTube.com/Buzz431**

# CAPTAIN JAKE SENT US

an interview with

## ALEX MORNINGSIDE

### Skipper (2002 - 2008)

"You mean these things are actually loaded!?"

**How did you wind up a skipper at Amity Boat Tours?**

I applied to work at Universal around 2002. I originally wanted to work at The Amazing Adventures of Spider-Man but the girl interviewing me said something along the lines of, '*I think you'd probably do better at Jaws.*' So that's where I went. Kongfrontation was also an option but they were getting ready to close it so she steered me towards Jaws and I resultantly agreed to it. Looking back, I'm glad I went with her suggestion because Jaws turned out to be a great experience. There is truly no other attraction quite like it. I think everyone who worked there felt that way about it.

**What was the best part of being a Jaws skipper?**

Anytime the guests were having a good time with the show. Those are truly my best memories from the attraction. It was always great when your people were really into it. We loved seeing guests come up wearing Jaws shirts either in support of us or the movie. You soon came to realize, if you didn't already know, that both Jaws and the Jaws ride had huge followings all around the world. Some people rode it so much that they came to memorize the spiel and would do it along with you. I know that annoyed some skippers but I always liked when it happened because it meant they were having fun. It also meant less work on my part because I didn't have to spiel as much if they were doing it for me!

I remember one boat tour where the front row was filled with these young Japanese girls. They were so excited to be on the ride but they also talked throughout my entire show. I found out after we got back to unload that they were all skippers on the Jaws ride in Osaka! So we were all technically Jaws skippers. They weren't talking through my show but instead doing the entire spiel along with me in Japanese. I thought that was really cool. I would love to go out there to see their version of the ride but the plane tickets to Japan aren't cheap!

**What was the hardest part of being a Jaws skipper?**

The hardest part of being a skipper, in hind sight, is not having a Jaws ride to work at! (laughs) I'd say the hardest part of working at Jaws was the physical strain it took on your body. It really took a lot out of you to do that ride all day. Performing that show was also really hard on your voice because you're screaming and yelling a lot. New skippers tended to lose their voice after their first day or two. I guess your throat had to build up a certain tolerance to be that loud for that long. Dealing with the weather was also a challenge because this is Florida we're talking about.

**I've been getting different answers from different skippers, so let me ask you – what was the hardest show effect to cover for when it didn't work as expected?**

I would have to say fin number two just before you go into the boathouse. That's the part of the ride where the skipper realizes they have a loaded grenade launcher that they then use to shoot at the shark. I always hated whenever that fin wouldn't pop up because the water explosions still happen regardless of the shark. Without that fin, it looked to guests like you were shooting the grenade launcher at nothing. The cover material for that was also kind of weird. You were supposed to go, 'Oh, look! Let me test out this grenade launcher to see if it actually works!' And then you fire a couple rounds off into the water. It was so awkward.

This wasn't really a malfunction we had to cover for but it was definitely strange. Remember the kill shark at the end? There was a time where he was not biting the power cable for whatever reason. The cable was instead just rubbing against the front of his nose. After about a week of that he got this black mark right above his mouth, which looked exactly like a certain mustache from a certain historical Nazi leader. So we started calling him the "Hitler shark." Fortunately they re-painted him soon after that. Something similar happened one time with the boathouse shark. It had started to take on water which caused the skin to expand in a very noticeable way. That led us to start calling it the "bloathouse shark" until they fixed it. I wish someone had a picture of that. It was weird.

**Speaking of weird, what are some of the more bizarre things you saw go wrong? Everyone knows the sharks were sometimes missing in action, but I've had skippers tell me about rogue ducks complicating their shows.**
I don't know about ducks but I know we had a few issues with squirrels. We actually had to close off the hanging shark out front because of a squirrel one time. I don't know if you ever noticed but there were these tiny wires at the very top of the hanging shark platform intended to keep birds from crapping all over it. They looked almost like needles. One day a squirrel climbed up there and started knocking them down onto guests, which very quickly became a safety concern. We were pretty amused by this rebellious squirrel and his clear taunting of both guests and employees. He came down after an hour or so and we opened the hanging shark back up for photos.

I also had a squirrel jump on my boat one time and stayed on for the entire tour. It got on just after we dispatched and spent the whole show running through people's legs. People weren't too freaked out by it but the squirrel definitely got more attention than the sharks did on that tour.

There was another strange malfunction we had once that did wind up shutting the ride down. All of the non-touring boats around the attraction are either anchored or tied up so that they stay in their designated spots. I remember once coming out of the boathouse and seeing the Layla, which was the red and white boat tied up in that scene, floating out to sea. And by out to sea, I mean it had began to float randomly throughout the ride and eventually onto the path of the boat track, which forced us to shut down until the techs could tie it back up.

**Going off script was forbidden but still happened with hilarious results. Did you ever improvise with your show?**
I was actually one of the few skippers that stayed entirely on script. They had spiel instructors that would hide out on the island to catch people who did veer off script. They would sometimes hide in the bushes or behind a tree or on the catwalk up in the boathouse. One of the supervisors had really bright blonde hair which made it obvious whenever they were hiding out on the island. Whoever spotted her first would get on the radio to tip everyone else off like, 'Head's up, guys. You're being spiel-checked.' And suddenly everyone would get right on script.

There was one girl I remember who went way off script. I was riding as a guest when I noticed what she was doing. It was the part where you come out of the boathouse after the shark appears on the right side. I look over and she's literally hanging upside down on the railing screaming. It was so far off script, not to mention dangerous, but also kind of awesome! I later found out she did that on all her shows. They definitely would've pulled her from boat had they caught her doing that. Getting pulled from boat was a huge disgrace at Jaws. No one wanted that to happen.

Yes, a squirrel once forced the closure of the hanging shark. (Photo courtesy Christopher Lord)

**What are some of your more memorable guest experiences?**

Unfortunately, most of the guest experiences I remember are the really, really weird ones. One thing that got a little annoying after a while were the guests who would always shout that famous line from the movie, '*We're gonna need a bigger boat.*' Usually they would say it right after you find Amity 3 sinking and you radio to base. Sometimes they would keep yelling it until you acknowledged them. In those situations I would often wait until they had said it about five or six times before I finally went, '*Wow, I've never heard that before. Thanks!*'

As a skipper you often had to watch out for people in the front row because they were so close to the part of the boat where you did your show. They would sometimes try to reach up and grab the grenade launcher because it was well within reach for them. You were never supposed to let a guest handle it even though it wasn't an actual weapon. One time I had a really weird experience with a guest on the front row coming out of the boathouse. The doors swing open and this old man leans up and starts tickling me! I was like, '*What the hell man?!*' I didn't say that but I thought it. I just tried to laugh it off and politely said, '*Haha, please don't ever do that again. Ever.*'

I had a guy one time who took his shirt off during the ride. Keep in mind you're not supposed to remove any items of clothing on Jaws be it shirt, shoes or anything else. I kept motioning for him to put his shirt back on and he's going, '*What? What are you asking me to do?*' and so I outright asked him to put it back on. He refused and I wound up stopping my boat in the middle of the ride until he put it back on. Suddenly the entire boat starts yelling at us both. Half the boat is screaming at me to continue the ride and the other half is screaming at him to put his shirt back on. That was one of my worst experiences on boat at Jaws, getting into a power struggle with a guest.

**Did you ever have VIP guests come through the ride?**

Tons of them. One time I had Sinbad the comedian on my boat. He was wearing these sunglasses that he would periodically lower and stare right at me, almost as if to go, '*Hey, you recognize me, right?*' He was really fun to have on the ride. Hulk Hogan came on a few times. He was immediately recognizable. Most celebrities want to keep a low profile but Hulk Hogan wasn't really able to. Same with Mick Foley. I also had Lea Thompson from Back to the Future on my boat once. She was so nice and humble to everyone.

The biggest celebrity I saw come through the ride was former President Jimmy Carter. He rode Jaws surrounded by all of his secret service bodyguards. Everyone working huddled at unload to watch him get off the boat. That was an amazing moment for me personally. He still looked so presidential even though he was dressed like your average tourist. He might have blended in like any other guest were it not for his huge security detail. Most celebrities would ride Jaws along with other guests. They would just sit in the back row out of view with their handlers and tour guide. Jimmy Carter had an entire boat to himself, which totally made sense. No one was going to be watching the shark when there is a former president on boat. After that all the skippers started laying claim to who would get to be on boat if and when former and future presidential figures came on the ride.

I also saw Warwick Davis at the ride, the actor from Star Wars and the Harry Potter films. Years later I saw him at a Star Wars event at Disney and I was like, '*Hey Warwick, what do you think of the new Harry Potter area that they built at Universal?*' and he was like, '*It's pretty good but they never should have taken out Jaws. That was one of my fondest rides ever.*' I couldn't believe that! He told me how much he used to enjoy bringing his family on Jaws.

**Now that the ride is long gone, tell me something top secret that only the skipper knew about.**

Hmm. Did you know about the password for the ride? We had an unofficial password for people who wanted to get on the boat faster. It was pretty simple. They would tell the greeter, '*Captain Jake sent us.*' If you walked up and said that phrase, they would either bring you to the front of the line or let you go through Express depending on how busy it was. We never questioned who used it because they might've been a skipper's family member or a diehard fan of the ride that we had told about it. I don't think they still have passwords at Universal anymore, but that was ours.

**What was it like getting the news that Jaws would be closing in early 2012?**

Terrible. I went to the meeting they had for the skippers over at the Fear Factor stadium. I was one of the last to arrive. They told me right away it would be closing and I didn't really believe it at first. I guess I was kind of jaded by then. You have to understand that we'd nearly closed before and still continued to operate. There were always rumors floating around that we might be replaced with something else. But this time turned out to be real.

I honestly thought Jaws would last forever. I just figured it was Universal's version of It's a Small World and it would always be there. I didn't entirely understand just how much it cost to run the attraction. I now get that it was enormously expensive to keep open. But I considered it a flagship ride for the park. I was kind of happy when I heard that Harry Potter would be taking its spot. At least that was an epic property that could and did bring about some amazing attractions. It would've sucked if they'd just replaced Jaws with another screen-based motion simulator.

**What do you remember about that last month at the Jaws ride?**

I remember us all being so sad that it was coming to an end. People who didn't usually want to work were suddenly fighting to get extra shifts in that month. And everyone wanted to work the last day. I didn't really like to close but I jumped at the opportunity to be there. We all knew that the ride's biggest fans were going to turn up and that these were bound to be some of the best tours ever. We also knew a lot of former skippers from years past would be coming back to ride it again, so that was great as well. I don't usually cry but if I did I would have definitely cried that last day.

And sure enough those were some of the best tours ever. It wasn't just random people going on the ride that day. Everyone who rode Jaws on January 2 knew it was closing and just wanted to experience it one last time. The enthusiasm and energy were incredible. You would typically start to notice that people became increasingly disgruntled as the queue lines became longer on Jaws. Not so on the last day and the lines became quite long, especially right before it closed for the night. The lines were longer than they had been in years but people didn't care. It was a fun atmosphere. Even Universal's CEO came out to support us and the ride. I thought that was pretty special.

**Did you take home anything from the ride to remember it by?**

Universal did gift a lot of items from the ride to the people after it closed. A lot of the skippers got buoys that were used in the theming. That's not actually what most people wanted, though. The most sought after items were the grenade launchers, which I don't think anyone got. After the very last boat came in, they took all the grenade launchers and locked them up probably because they knew people were going to try and steal them.

Misty eyes and warm embraces on the ride's final day of operation. (Photo courtesy Keith Huntington)

# AMITY MEANS FRIENDSHIP BUT SKIPPERS MEAN FAMILY

◆——————————◆◆◆——————————◆

an interview with

## KAYLA RHODUS

### Skipper (2011 - 2012)
### The Final Skipper Hired for Jaws

"Amity Six to Base. Did you copy that transmission? It sounded like Gordon on Amity Three." (Photo courtesy Kayla Rhodus)

**What first made you want to become a Jaws skipper?**

That would have been my first time on the ride when I was sixteen. I went for Rock The Universe, the Christian event they have each year where teenage kids go with their youth groups and they have a giant worship service at some point. My youth group went on Jaws and I can remember thinking, '*This looks pretty easy. I could totally do this!*' The whole ride was awesome. I loved how engaging and entertaining the skipper was. I moved to Orlando two years later when I was eighteen and went onto Universal.com to check for job openings. Sure enough they had an opening for a Jaws skipper, so I applied just for the heck of it. A week later I had an interview where I did a cold read of the script and I got the job! It happened pretty quick. So this was about 2011 that I started at Jaws. I was the very last skipper hired by Universal to work the attraction.

**That distinction is awesome and yet also kind of sad.**

It's sad now that I think about it! I was really happy to have had the experience at Jaws that I did. To prepare for the job, I rented the original movie and watched it three times in one night. I was hooked on it right away. I loved how the ride replicated as much as it could from the movie. It didn't just go for straight terror with the shark attack. The ride made you feel like you were actually walking into Captain Jake's Amity Boat Tours to take a tour of the real Amity Island. The setup for the ride was just so cool.

**Riding Jaws as a guest, you said it looked "pretty easy." How was it once you got there?**

It was hard! It was so very hard, way harder than I expected! Thinking back to when I first rode Jaws, I think my skipper was just so incredible that they made it look effortless. The reality was that it took *a lot* of effort to do that job hour after hour. I feel really stupid for thinking just anybody could do it. I was so, so wrong. (laughs) I was fortunate to have a really good trainer when I started. He was very helpful and encouraged me to make the spiel my own. He explained to me how there are different ways to perform the same lines and that no two spiels were ever the same. He also taught me to make sure I'm having fun with the ride or else the guests won't be.

**What was your favorite scene from the attraction?**

I loved all of them but if I had to pick, it's probably the moment when the skipper realizes that Gordon's boat is sinking and that there are no survivors. This was just before you saw the shark for the first time. It's in that moment that the entire mood of the ride changes. The skipper quickly goes from, '*Oh man, another boat tour like I do every single day of every single summer,*' to '*Oh God, what happened here? I don't know what could've caused this other than a shark!*' Seeing that light bulb click on in the skipper's performance was fun. That was my favorite moment because that's when the excitement and tension really start to build.

**Everyone knows you weren't supposed to go off script but many skippers still did, often with hilarious results. Did you ever add or change your spiel?**

We weren't supposed to but yes, I did. I think most skippers wanted to personalize the spiel to themselves in some way so they would have certain lines they would often throw in. One big one for me was when I first picked up the grenade launcher and realized it was loaded. I was playing a lot of Call of Duty with my brother-in-law at the time, so I would go, '*Oh man! Call of Duty didn't prepare me for this!*'

There was another joke skippers would often make when the gas dock exploded. I can't remember what the exact prices were on the gas pumps, but they were ridiculously out of date. So when the tanks exploded I would go, '*Oh no! The only gas dock in America with $1.50 gas just exploded!*' It would almost always get a laugh from guests since gas was so expensive at the time. Another line I would add into that scene involved the wall of fire. I'd say, '*Okay, you all have to help me blow out these flames! Everyone take a deep breath and pretend the fire is a birthday candle and blow it out!*' And once we'd gotten past the fire I'd turn around and go, '*See there? Who ever said having a boatload of people full of hot air was a bad thing?*' You'd have to gauge each boat to see if they would be receptive to these kinds of jokes or not. It was trial and error.

**You joined up with Amity Boat Tours right at the end when the mechanical sharks were said to be at their most temperamental. What was it like when your finned co-stars didn't appear as expected?**

It was not fun and it would inevitably happen multiple times by the end of each day. A lot of times the kill shark wouldn't come up but all the effects would still happen around it. I'd stare into the water and be like, '*I see him down there! The shark's down there!*' You could still get through that scene because you fire the grenade launcher to trigger some of those sounds and effects. Then you get the dead shark and people figure it's dead because you shot it.

For me the hardest scene to get through when something went wrong was the gas dock explosion. Sometimes the flames wouldn't appear but the sound and music would still play. So you'd be like, '*Oh no! We've got to get out of this area even though nothing is really happening right now!*' And people would hear these explosions but see nothing and look at you like, '*What!?*' The Jaws ride was a lot like live theatre in those moments. You never knew what was going to work and what wasn't. If someone messes up in live theatre, you just keep going . It was the same on Jaws. We wouldn't stop the show just because a shark or effect was missing.

**Did you ever have to hit the dreaded emergency stop button?**

Yes, twice. The first time was on Halloween Horror Nights. I had a boat of very drunken men who were standing up in their seats saying they were about to jump in the water. And they really were about to. So I hit the emergency stop and was like, '*I can't move until everyone is in their seat. Butts in seats!*' And they responded, '*But we wanna go swimming with the shark!*' And I said, '*Yeah and next you'll be swimming with the cops when they pull you out of the water. Plus, there's a twenty foot shark beneath us. You don't really want to be in the water with him, do you? You're also gonna need a tetanus shot if you jump overboard. So sit down and stay that way!*' I really tried hyping it up to scare them anyway I could and fortunately they remained seated from there on.

Skipper Kayla spieling the best scenic tour on the island!

(Photos courtesy Kayla Rhodus)

"We'll be shark bait in ten minutes!" (Photos courtesy Kayla Rhodus)

Another time was when we had Rock the Universe, which was the Christian event where I first rode Jaws a couple of years before. I dreaded that day because I knew the kids would be awful. Here they are running loose throughout the park with little to no adult supervision. I had a boat full of these obnoxious teens that would not stop chanting, '*We love Jesus, yes we do, we love Jesus, how 'bout you?*' Half the boat would sing it and then the other half would sing it back. It was getting louder and louder until it was out of control. So I hit the e-stop and yelled, '*Jesus isn't going to save you here tonight! I am because I'm the one with the grenade launcher! Now do you want to get out of here alive or what?!*' And then they shut up and went along with the ride. Those kids were the worst. I would take a hundred times around the lagoon with drunk people over obnoxious Christian teenagers. Little savages.

**What were the skippers like? I understand it was kind of a sub-culture at Universal.**

We were a family for sure. There's a quote from the movie where Mayor Vaughn says, '*Amity, as you know, means friendship.*' And we would say, '*Amity means friendship but skippers mean family.*' That always held true for me and still does even to this day. I still look at those people as my family. When I started at Jaws I was having a hard time transitioning into my freshman year of college. I didn't really get along with my roommate but I always knew I could go into work and find someone to talk to and make me feel better. I knew I was coming into something that was already established with the Jaws ride. These people had close bonds and had been friends for years and years. I worried that I might not be accepted but that wasn't true at all. They made me feel so welcome from my very first day there. Michael 'Skip' Skipper was like the father of our family. We went to him for everything. He *was* the Jaws ride. When we heard the ride was closing, our first thought was, '*Oh no, what's Skip going to do?*'

**What was it like that morning hearing that Jaws would be closing for good?**

It was so hard. I wasn't at the meeting. I was at home in Venice. One of my friends that did go called me sobbing as soon as they got out saying, '*Kayla, they're closing our home! They're closing the ride!*' Universal told us that no one would be let go, that we could list three preferences for what other attractions in the park we'd like to work at after the closure. That was the hardest part of Jaws closing, knowing that we weren't going to be together anymore. Our family was breaking up in a sense. I guess I was naïve in thinking that they would never, ever close down Jaws. How could they? It was a classic that everyone still seemed to love. I thought it would be there forever.

**What was that last month like?**

Bittersweet. I usually worked four days a week because I was in college but I tried picking up extra shifts that last month. I cherished every single moment of it. We always performed at 100% but that last month everyone gave 110% every time. We hung around after work a little later and hugged each other a little longer. There was this one guy from California, Christopher Lord, who flew out as soon as he heard that the ride would be closing. He was a huge Jaws ride enthusiast. I think he rode it seventeen times that last day he came out. He also recorded one of my last spiels and put it on YouTube. I haven't watched it in a long time because it's actually really hard for me to watch. I did see that it had like five-hundred-thousand views two years ago. Now it's up to 4.2 million views, which is incredible!

**Do you remember your last tour around the lagoon?**

Yes, I do. It was on January 2nd, the very last day the ride was open. There were a lot of last tours happening that evening. Three of my really good friends had just finished their last tours and jumped on my boat. Now it was my turn. I was shaking the entire ride. There were a couple of times where I had to stop because I was crying and my boat would cheer me on. It was such an emotional five minutes of my life. You start to notice and appreciate little parts of the ride that you'd been through a thousand times. You just take in all the little details. Every thing becomes a moment. Of course, the kill shark stopped working that night for the final tours, which was so typical! *Of course!* Of course the shark is gonna break down on the very last night! (laughs) My shift that day didn't start until eleven, so I just wandered the park in my full Jaws skipper uniform. I even had my hat on, so I was all sharked out. I definitely made a point to walk through Hogsmeade before my final shift. And yes, I kept my uniform.

About a month later, Universal got all the skippers together for a little closing ceremony where we each got a piece of the ride. I have a wooden buoy that once hung in the boathouse. It's one of my most valued possessions. I think Skip got the door to the crow's nest because it had a really cool Jaws ride mural on it.

**Did you stay at Universal after Jaws closed?**

Yes, I wound up working at Dragon Challenge at Islands of Adventure. I only lasted a month there. It just wasn't the same for me. Jaws had such an impact on my life that it was really all I wanted to do at Universal. I wanted something theatrical and amazing and engaging like that. Dragon Challenge was none of those things. Dragon Challenge was literally putting my hands in throw up at least once a day. It wasn't what I wanted from working at Universal. I know a lot of Jaws skippers felt the same way. We kind of thought, '*Why would we still work here when our home is gone?*' And so a lot of us left.

**Have you been to Diagon Alley?**

Yeah. I actually went back to work as a server at Margaritaville for a while and would often go into the park but not into where Amity used to be. I would avoid it at all costs. I didn't want to be there if I couldn't hear the faint sound of the gas dock exploding in the distance. I would always go see Bruce hanging up in San Francisco, though. Then about two-and-a-half years ago, I finally went to Diagon Alley and, of course, it was absolutely beautiful. I love how they have little things hidden in there that honor the Jaws ride. They paid homage to what was there before and that was a really important thing in my mind. Harry Potter may be great but it's not classic Universal. Jaws is classic Universal. I think it's important that we never forget them.

"We really roasted him, didn't we?!"

Skipper Kayla calls off the marines! (Photo courtesy Kayla Rhodus)

# JAWS
## THE FINAL VOYAGE
### 1-2-2012

On January 2, 2012, one of Universal's most iconic rides sailed out to sea for the very last time. Skippers commemorated Amity's final fourth of July by giving out red, white, and blue bead necklaces to guests. Wait times steadily increased throughout the final day, peaking at nearly ninety minutes as night fell on Amity. Forty-eight lucky guests were chosen throughout the day to receive tickets to the final public boat tour, which took place just past 9 PM led by Skipper Michael "Skip" Skipper. A large crowd gathered at the unload dock to cheer Amity 6's return with an impromptu sing-a-long of "Show Me the Way To Go Home" from Jaws. After this, Skip gave a private final tour for members of the closing team, who then posed for the photo seen below.

(Photo courtesy Kayla Rhodus)

Although skippers were not officially allowed to keep their uniform, they were given special "Closing Team" t-shirts and lanyards to mark the occassion. In an unusual move, Universal also gifted pieces of the attraction theming to Jaws ride team members.

# ATTRACTIONS THAT HAVE CLOSED SINCE JAWS

# ATTRACTIONS THAT HAVE
# OPENED SINCE JAWS

UNIVERSAL'S CINEMATIC SPECTACULAR

100 YEARS OF MOVIE MEMORIES

TRANSFORMERS
THE RIDE—3D

# CHASING JAWS FROM HOLLYWOOD TO OSAKA

an interview with

## CHRISTOPHER LORD

### Jaws Ride Enthusiast

Christopher brandishing a 40mm grenade launcher while visting the ride in 1998. (Photo courtesy Christopher Lord)

**Were you a fan of Jaws before you experienced the ride?**

It was around 1986 when I first saw Jaws 2 on television. That one was my introduction to the franchise. I was eight-years-old and Jaws 3 came on television not long after that, which I recorded on videotape and re-watched as many times as I possibly could. I eventually caught the original Jaws during a Thanksgiving broadcast and it has since become my all-time favorite film. I find it to be darn near flawless. Soon after that I had a friend of the family take me to Universal Studios Hollywood. This was back when the studio tour had such classic attractions as Battlestar Galactica, King Kong, and, of course, Jaws. They still had the original Orca on the backlot too. I would go back each year to see the Jaws attraction usually on my birthday. I've always had a very high respect for the work that goes into these things, not only in their development but also their operation.

I was later an employee of Universal Studios Hollywood from 1998 until 2003. That offered me a lot of great access to the backlot. Honestly, I considered it a privilege. I won't say I discovered it, but I did find that Tina's Joy from Jaws 2 is still on the backlot by the Jaws attraction. I actually tried to have a few people disprove that it was really Tina's Joy but they only confirmed it for me - it's the real boat from the movie. Unfortunately, it's rotting away and in rough condition. I left Universal Hollywood in 2003 when it overlapped my employment with Jet Blue Airways at Long Beach Airport. Going into the aviation world allowed me to have access to domestic flights at little to no cost, all standby of course. My favorite destination of choice was Orlando.

**Do you remember first hearing that there was a Jaws attraction being built at Universal Studios Florida?**

Oh yeah. I remember seeing lots of commercials for Universal Studios Florida when it first opened. There were several television specials about it that had shots of the Jaws ride. I said to myself, '*I have got to get out there one day and ride that!*' But living on the west coast as an adolescent, you don't really have any easy way to get out to Florida. I was also wholly unaware of the challenges that had been going on behind the scenes at Jaws. There wasn't social media back then so that information didn't reach the public as much as it would today.

I finally flew out to Florida with my dad in 1998. This was my first trip to the park there. They were still building Citywalk and Islands of Adventure at the time. I videotaped every inch of that trip with one of those big over-the-shoulder VHS cameras. Remember those? We went to the park twice that trip. I spent one of those days just hanging around Jaws, which unfortunately broke down late in the afternoon. I stuck around hoping to get another ride in before closing. There was a very gracious skipper named Bart who talked to me about the ride while it was down. He even let me see the control tower at the load dock and explained how each part of the ride worked. It was an incredible memory to go home with. It made my Jaws ride experience that much more unique and personal and inspired me to become a Universal employee.

I thought the Florida ride was such a fun adventure. I loved how they actually took you out on the water unlike in California where you're basically watching the shark from land. The immersion in Florida was so much more grand. You had no idea where the shark was going to pop up. He could have come from any direction at any time. That ride was simply unlike anything I'd ever seen in a theme park. I was fortunate that social media wasn't around back then because I was able to go in with a fresh perspective not knowing what to expect. I felt such awe and glee on that ride. Just being in the Amity section of the park put a smile on my face as a Jaws fan.

**What set Jaws apart from other rides?**

I think the spieling component was a big factor in setting it apart. The boat skipper bridged a connection between Jaws being a ride experience and also a show with an actor. That's where the attraction really excelled. It also had to do with the quality of the story. Consider Kongfrontation, which was a similar kind of attraction. Both Jaws and Kong had someone spieling the story of the attraction, but Jaws was more exciting due to it having a much faster pace. Kong only had three scenes which made for a much smaller journey while Jaws had five scenes. Of course, Kong had the benefit of scale. That show building was *huge* and the animatronics were gigantic. Jaws, however, had the benefit of an open world where you were outside on the water. It also helped that you had a long lead-up to the shark's first reveal. The danger didn't really begin until you turned the corner at the lighthouse, so you had time to get involved in the story the attraction was trying to tell. A lot of people compare Jaws to Disney's Jungle Cruise, but I don't. Jungle Cruise tries for something completely different with its storyline. It's comedic and slapstick whereas Jaws was exciting and even scary.

**How important were the skippers to the attraction?**

In some ways, the skipper was the most important part of the ride because they sold it to you. Each of them had their own unique gift too because they all did it just a little bit differently. If I ever had a dream job for a summer, that would be it. I applied to be a tour guide in California many, many times but never made it. I even got my class A license attempting to become a tram driver so that I could ride through the Jaws attraction multiple times each day, but I didn't get either of those jobs.

**Did you ever come to suspect that Jaws was on the chopping block to eventually be replaced?**

Not at first, no. I never thought that Jaws would go. Maybe that was because I didn't want to believe it could happen. Then one day in 2009, I was getting off the boat and saw park surveyors standing over by the ride exit. I stopped in my tracks and said, '*Oh no.*' I grabbed surveys for everyone in my family and asked them to please give the Jaws ride five-stars. In my opinion, the exit survey is a very important stage in the development of change for a theme park attraction. It shows you what they're thinking about doing next or at least considering. The closure announcement came as a shock, but not a 100% shock.

**How did you react to the closure announcement?**

I found out when I woke up that morning. They had given the thirty-day closure notice on Facebook. I called my wife on my way to work at Jet Blue in California. I know I was nerding out, but I was honestly fighting back tears. I told her, '*I'm going to Orlando tonight after work. If you want to come with me, pack a bag and meet me at the airport.*' And she did. She brought our two-year-old son and her mother as well. I spent that trip just hanging around the Amity area knowing this was the last time I would ever see any of it. And, unfortunately, the attraction was in really

Opposite: Bruce attacks the tram in Hollywood. (Photo courtesy Christopher Lord)

poor shape by then. That's something Universal tends to let happen when they know they're going to be closing an attraction. They'll let it go a little bit because they're not putting any more money into the maintenance. The shark that bites the cable in Scene Five was in especially poor shape. But that didn't stop me from enjoying it. I went on the ride seventeen times that day.

I don't think most people riding with me that day knew it was closing. You could tell the skippers were a little affected by it because they were all talking about it. They were great to me, though. I was on the last boat of the night, which they held so that my wife could come from across the park to join me. They held it so that she had time to ride it with me. I won't lie, the tears were flowing. I had to say goodbye.

**Have you been back since then?**

Yes, many times and yes, I've been to Diagon Alley. Honestly, I've come to respect the whole Harry Potter thing and what it's done for all the Universal parks. Having seen the entire industry struggle throughout the early 2000s, I'm happy to see what a gold mine Universal has had with all the Potter stuff. Was it unfortunate to lose Jaws? Yes, but it was the perfect space to build something new. It took up over seven acres of land in the back of the park. That is incredibly prime real estate. Plus, it's no secret that Jaws was extremely expensive to keep operational. That was a huge strike against the attraction.

I was very pleased that they kept the hanging shark around in San Francisco. That's something people still really enjoy taking selfies with. For whatever reason, Universal Studios Hollywood doesn't seem to value that. They took out their hanging shark when they built Springfield and never brought it back. That always frustrated me because Jaws is still relevant to their audience whether they realize it or not.

**What was it like visiting the Jaws ride in Osaka, Japan?**

It's very weird to visit an attraction you said goodbye to ten months earlier and still have nearly the same level of excitement and fun. I'd already been through the closure of the Jaws ride in Orlando, but here I was getting on a boat again hearing that familiar music in the background. The Osaka ride was ninety-five-percent the exact same as Orlando. I was totally enveloped in it. Of course, I didn't understand a single word the Japanese skipper was saying. They had their own approach to the spiel that was a little different than what I was used to.

In many ways, the Japanese ride was superior to the American one, especially where the environment was concerned. I thought the attraction itself operated stronger, which made sense considering it was a little younger than the Orlando one. The Osaka ride opened in 2001, which meant it was a little healthier. Their Amity section wasn't as large as ours was, but they have a very large Jaws gift shop with a lot of unique items that aren't available anywhere in the states. The Japanese queue entrance is pretty cool. It just has these giant red letters that spell out JAWS. It was strange seeing Neptune's Folly and the Amity Police Boat from Jaws: The Revenge in their queue. Universal Studios Florida long claimed to have had the actual props from the movie, but the park in Japan claims the same thing.

Opposite: The kill shark bites the cable in Osaka. (Photo courtesy Christopher Lord)

**I've seen pics of the Japanese boats, which are laughably fake. They look nothing like their screen counterparts!**
I know, right? It was easy to believe that Universal Studios Florida had the boats from Revenge because the entire park was built only a few years after that sequel came out. Plus, they had additional Revenge props in the Boneyard. They also filmed in the Bahamas on that one, so it would make sense for the boats to still be on the east coast. I believe those were truly screen-used. The ones in Japan? Not at all.

**How similar was the Osaka ride to the Orlando ride?**
Like I said, ninety-five-percent of it is the exact same ride, though there were a few differences. Remember the bridge that separated Scene Five from the unload dock? In Osaka, it's just before the lighthouse in Scene One. This is me nitpicking a little, but their boathouse scene reverses some of the effects with the barrels and the boats falling into the water. The score also starts too early as you leave that scene, which means the action doesn't line up with the music. That then causes the music for Scene Five to be off a little bit, which is kind of jarring if you know how it's supposed to be. But it's also easy to get past when you're in the moment.

Another difference involves the kill shark that bites the cable. In Orlando, he swam up and bit the cable. In Osaka, the cable is permanently in his mouth. I guess that's to make sure he gets it every time. One nitpick that I thought detracted from the experience involved the dead shark at the very end. In Florida, you had a water spray hit when that shark lunged at the boat. That spray was located between the shark and the boat, which meant it blasted water right next to guests. In Osaka, the spray is behind the shark about fifteen feet away. It's not nearly as impactful because you don't have that loud bang happening right next to you. It just doesn't get the same jump from people. But these nitpicks are just that. It's still the same attraction I've loved all these years. It was kind of eerie getting to ride it again after having seen it close in Florida, sort of like reliving your childhood. It was pure nostalgia, same as when I rode Back to the Future there. I tried to beat my record from Orlando of seventeen times on Jaws, but thunderstorms came in and closed down the ride. My last two trips around the attraction were in the pouring rain.

**Tell me your best Jaws ride memory.**
That would have to be one time when I was flying home from Orlando to California. It was dusk when the airline took off to the south and turned right, which allowed me to look down and see both Universal and Islands of Adventure from my window. I could even see the Jaws ride! It was a perfect moment just for me. Scene Four went off at this exact same time. I could see the gas dock flames from the airplane. I just sat there looking down and took it all in for the few seconds it lasted. That's something probably no one else would ever care about, but I did. It was very personal. I'm passionate about theme parks and flying. Both of those things came together for me in that moment. It's a memory etched in my mind that I will never forget.

Top: Christopher in skipper duds outside the Jaws ride in Osaka.

Bottom: The Hollywood shark out of water! (Photos courtesy Christopher Lord)

# COLLECTING JAWS

an interview with
## JIM BELLER
**Jaws Authority / Preservationist**

Jaws super-fan Jim Beller poses with a tiny fraction of his
massive collection. (Photo courtesy JawsCollector.com)

**I have to know – how did you first get into Jaws?**

I was nine-years-old when I first heard about Jaws. It was the last day of school and my third grade teacher had a Time Magazine on her desk, the one that said "Super Shark" on the cover. I was big into monsters back then – Dracula, King Kong, Wolf-man, all of that stuff. I asked what her magazine was about and she told me about this movie coming out about a monster shark that eats people. As soon as she said the words "monster shark," I knew right then I had to see this movie. It was actually opening that night, June 20, and my parents were going to see it in Boston. I asked if they would take me and my mom said, '*No, we're going to see it tonight. I'll take you and your friends to see it next week if it's okay.*' The first words out of my mouth the next morning were to ask whether or not I could see it and she said yes. We had some family who thought it might be a bad idea, but my mom told them, '*If he watches all those Christopher Lee Dracula movies on television then he can certainly see Jaws.*'

So the next week she took me and my friends to see it at the Charles Theater in Boston. It was the first movie I ever saw there being a line for. I still remember the experience quite vividly. The movie was, of course, great. There was one scene my mom told me to cover my eyes for but I still watched on through my fingers. This was when the shark ate Quint and there's blood everywhere. The audience was so into it, too. I remember the whole place went crazy when Ben Gardner's head dropped down.

It seems to me that nine-years-old is just about the age to get hooked on something. I've discussed this with other people too. It seems that if you get into something at that age, it'll be there for the rest of your life. I've had interest before and since that age, but nothing else quite like Jaws. Then I started collecting it. I wanted to get my hands on everything I possibly could related to the film. I think there's probably a reason why I began that. Back then there was no way to watch the movie at home. This was before home video. Adults could go see it in theaters at any point during its theatrical run, but kids didn't really have that option. Collecting all that stuff was sort of my way of holding onto the movie. And I took great care of my Jaws stuff for some weird reason. I still have most of it in mint condition. I practically destroyed my Star Wars figures growing up, but not my Jaws stuff. I kept collecting as I got older and my collection grew. It grew a ton when the internet and eBay came about.

**Were you aware of the Jaws attraction on the Universal Studios Hollywood Tour?**

I was aware and I wanted to go and see it so badly. Unfortunately, we were a middle-class family living out on the east coast. We couldn't afford a cross country trip for something like that, so I didn't get to experience it until I was much older. I distinctly remember seeing footage on the news of the shark with those huge carrot teeth. They were promoting it like crazy. They even had it promoted on the John Denver show.

**How did you first hear about the ride at Universal Studios Florida?**

I read about it in USA Today. They took out a huge four-page ad that included a giant map of the entire park. I immediately realized that this was going to be something different than the California attraction, that it was going to be a much bigger ride. I remember hearing about the troubles they were having with it breaking down so much. I was bummed when it closed shortly after opening and a little concerned that they might not ever re-open it. I was so glad when they did and finally visited the park in 1994 after it had re-opened.

**What was your impression of the Jaws ride when you finally experienced it?**

I loved it. It was so much fun. I knew a little bit about it, but I didn't know what the whole ride entailed. This was before we had internet video, so the ride hadn't been spoiled for me ahead of time. I did know which side of the boat to sit on for the best view. I thought the ride was so brilliant and clever. Seeing that shark fin pop up for the first time was thrilling. My favorite part of the ride was just after you left the boathouse. The shark came up so close to the boat! I actually jumped because I didn't know it was going to happen. Then the big explosion went off ,which was great. We went in November, so the park was kind of dead because school was in session then. None of the rides had a line except for Jaws. There was always a line at Jaws. The theming was also great. I'm from New England and I can vouch that the architecture of all the houses and buildings was very New England-y. The lighthouse and church in particular looked brilliant. Whoever did the art direction really did a fantastic job.

I remember thinking how amazing it must have been to work there. I couldn't imagine doing what the skippers do, though. They do that spiel over and over making each time sound like it was their first. I have no idea how they do that each day.

**I assume you would've hit the merchandise cart pretty hard?**

Absolutely! I saved up a lot of money for that purpose because I knew there would be stuff there. I darted for the merchandise cart as soon as I got off the boat. I bought t-shirts, pins, toys, bumper stickers, license plates, back-packs, all sorts of stuff. I bought two of everything they had on the cart. The woman working there couldn't believe it - she was freaking out. There was something she only had one copy of and I was like, '*What's the deal? You got any more? Do you have extras stashed under the cart?*' I came home with giant bags full of Jaws stuff. We actually had to go to the car immediately after that because I had bought way more stuff than we could possibly carry around the park.

The funny thing is I had already started buying Jaws ride stuff before I even visited the park. Someone had gotten me a direct phone number to their merchandise warehouse. These incredibly nice people that worked there would describe all their Jaws merchandise to me over the phone and allow me to order it direct from them. I would send them a check and they would mail me my purchases. They knew I was a huge fan and were so great about putting stuff aside for me.

A few of the many Jaws t-shirts sold in the park over the years. (Photos courtesy JawsCollector.com)

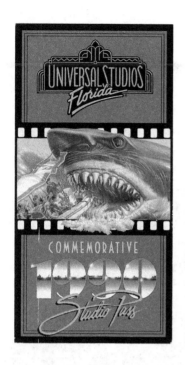

**What are some of your personal favorite Jaws ride-related items?**

The coolest items I've come across are actually authentic items from the ride itself that were sold to me by people who worked there. Things like the "You Will Get Wet" sign and the Jaws directional sign. Those are really rare pieces to own. The funny thing about those is that they were acquired by employees during a time when they were updating parts of the attraction. These are things that ordinarily would have been thrown out but someone decided to grab them and put them on eBay. I got both of them pretty cheap. I only paid a couple of hundred for the "You Will Get Wet" sign. This was before the ride closed, though. Stuff like this goes for much, much more now that the ride is gone and everyone wants a piece of it. I was excited to get them.

**Do you get e-mails from people trying to buy those off you?**

Oh sure, I've gotten offers for them but nothing that's made me say yes yet.

**What was it like learning that the ride would be closing in early 2012?**

It came as a complete surprise to me. From my own perspective, Jaws just seems to get bigger and bigger every year. They're always playing it on television or putting it back into theaters so that new audiences can discover it. People love sharks and always will. We're all fascinated by them and Jaws is *the* shark movie. Nothing else comes close. Plus, it's a classic now right up there with Psycho. I don't think it will ever go away in terms of popularity. So I was baffled when they announced they were putting Harry Potter in where Jaws once was. Harry Potter isn't even a Universal movie! But I guess they want more kids going to the park.

It's just a shame that they had to take a ride out to put something new in. I know Disney does it too, but Disney doesn't go around closing their biggest and most iconic rides. They're not closing Space Mountain when they decide to close something. Could you imagine that? Space Mountain is a big part of Disney. Universal, however, they'll close anything. It doesn't matter to them. I still can't believe they closed King Kong.

**I've noticed you not only collect items from Hollywood and Florida, but also Universal Studios Japan.**

Japan has far better stuff than our parks, to be honest. Better stuff and more of it. It helps that the ride is still going strong there. Some of their items are a little on the strange side. I've got a fork and spoon set from the Japan ride where Bruce the shark is the handle. I've got a bottle of Jaws wine if you can believe it. I've also got a Jaws ride tissue box, which is a plush version of the Orca with the shark jumping onto the back of the boat. The Orca part folds around any regular size tissue box. How clever is that? Universal Studios Florida never tried anything like that. I can't even begin to tell you how much more stuff they have than we do. I'm glad the ride is still operating there, but I'll never see it. Osaka is just too far. I'm also glad Jaws is still going out on the studio tour in Hollywood. Yes, it's a bummer that the Orca is gone and so is Ben Gardner's boat, but Bruce is still there.

Opposite: Jim Beller poses with his collection. (Photos courtesy JawsCollector.com)

(Photos courtesy JawsCollector.com)

**Do you have a personal favorite Jaws ride item in your collection?**

Probably the "You Will Get Wet" and studio directory signs. Beyond those, I have several of the Amity Boat Tours shirts that the actual skippers wore. I also have a tooth from one of the sharks. Remember the Jaws: The Revenge shark they used to have on display in the park? I know a lot of people would reach over the guardrail and steal its teeth, but I never did that. There was a guy who reached over and cut off a piece of his skin and I did buy that years later. I also really like a construction hat that I have from when they were first building the ride in 1989 or 1990. It has stickers of all the different rides on it.

To see what is arguably the largest collection
of Jaws ride merchandise in the world, visit Jim at

# JawsCollector.com

# THE SHARK THAT GOT AWAY

In 2018, Jaws super fan John Ryan stumbled across a one-of-a-kind-collectible. He found a seller on Craigslist claiming to have one of the original sharks from Spielberg's Jaws. Knowing this to be impossible as they were destroyed, John went to see the shark anyway and discovered it was actually one of the fin sharks used in Scene Two of the Jaws ride! He immediately bought the thirteen-foot-long fish and loaded it onto a trailer for the journey home.

One question remained . . . how did a Jaws ride shark travel over nine-hundred miles north from Orlando, Florida to Frederick, Maryland? That the shark's appearance in Maryland pre-dated the ride's closure only deepend the mystery. Several clues soon emerged. The 1993 ride sharks were made by Maryland-based engineering firm Eastport/Oceaneering. And the property on which the fin shark was found? It was previously owned by Eastport project manager and current Universal park executive Michael Hightower. I guess this is what happens when you take your work home with you!

(All photos courtesy John Ryan)
(Thanks to the Titans, Terrors, & Toys Blog for
doing the detective work on this fish tale!)

| If you're standing HERE in | Then you're HERE from |
|:---:|:---:|
| # Diagon Alley | # Amity Village |
| The Brick Wall Entrance | The Midway Grill |
| London Brick Apartment Facade | The Hanging Shark |
| Sugarplum's Sweet Shop | Jaws Ride Load Platform |
| Knockturn Alley | Jaws Ride Unload Platform |
| Hogwarts Express Tunnel | Scene Five of the Jaws Ride |
| Gringott's Dragon | Bridewell's Gas Dock |
| Gringott's Ride Entrance | Chief Brody's House |

We're going to need a bigger wand.

# BY SEA AND STORM

## Ocean and Rain Art by Tom Ryan

Florida-based artist Tom Ryan has been painting the sea and the sky and all the weird and wonderful things in between... including Jaws and the Jaws Ride! He paints using either seawater or rainwater, meaning there's a little bit of Martha's Vineyard in each of his Jaws-inspired works.

For prints and originals, visit
BySeaAndStorm.com

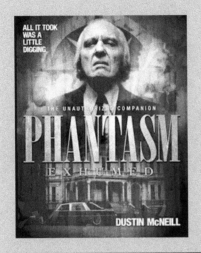

By: Carly age 8

To: The Reader

# Acknowledgements

Very Special Thanks to
Bob Ward, James-Michael Roddy, Tom Reidenbach

Proofreading thanks to
Stephanie Marshall

Special Thanks to
James E. Adamson, Peter Alexander, Alan J. Arena, Jim Beller, John Bernard, Adam Bezark, Steve Brown, Jeff Clay, Tom Croom, Tom Donahue, Bruce Farber, Bing Futch, LisaMarie Gabriele, Dan Gurwitz, Jeremy Homan, Nathan Key, Frank Kincaid, David Kneupper, Christopher Lord, Mark Messersmith, Tom Mitchell, Bill Moore, Alex Morningside, Colin Peterson, Marc Plogstedt, Kayla Rhodus, Dan Robles, John Ryan, Tom Ryan, Luke Sawh, Diane Stapleton, Justin Stone, Levi Tinker, John Wiser, Scott Weller, Seth A. Wolfson

Thanks to JawsRide.net and the
"Kongfrontation Facebook Group for the 8th Wonder & Lost Universal Attractions"

Thanks to my parents, David and Karen, for taking me to Universal Studios Florida so much growing up. And thanks to my sister, Andrea, for never complaining about getting back in line for Jaws again and again.

Love and thanks to Lindsay Squires McNeill and Carly Ryan Roberts
for their boundless support, endless patience, and continued encouragement.

Farewell and adieu to you, fair Spanish ladies.

Farewell and adieu, you ladies of Spain.

For we've received orders for to sail back to Boston.

And so nevermore shall we see you again.

CPSIA information can be obtained
at www.ICGtesting.com
Printed in the USA
LVHW10s1342310818
588793LV00004B/255/P